STAR WARS
BATTLEFRONT
EA

INTRODUCTION

WELCOME TO
STAR WARS BATTLEFRONT

Welcome to Star Wars Battlefront. As you are reading this, I am guessing you have just sat down, dimmed the lights, and are getting ready to play.

It is my hope that when playing Star Wars Battlefront, you will have an amazing Star Wars experience that will transport you to a galaxy far, far away.

I also hope you will have the same feelings of awe and wonder that I had when experiencing Star Wars for the first time all those years ago.

A feeling I got the opportunity to feel once more when visiting Lucasfilm and learning that I would become a part in making this game for you.

It is time to grab your blasters, hop into your X-wings, and make your way to Battlefront. May the Force be with you, always!

— Niklas Fegraeus, Design Director

GETTING STARTED

What kind of gamer are you? Are you new to shooters? Maybe you're a *Star Wars* fan, and you want to get into Battlefront to get the full *Star Wars* experience. Either way, there's nothing to worry about because this official strategy guide will help you through both the basics and the advanced tactics of *Star Wars* Battlefront. Get a feel for the game by playing through the training missions, and you will have a grasp on the mechanics in no time.

This guide teaches you everything from how to navigate the menus to how to use your weapons and special characters in ways that will give you the advantage over other players. Live the full experience that is *Star Wars* Battlefront, and look through these tactics and strategies to gain the upper hand and the opportunity to learn each piece of this game efficiently and effectively. Whether you're a brand-new player to first-person or third-person shooters or practically an expert, this guide will show you some things you might never have known. Read carefully, don't be afraid to practice some of these tactics in trial runs, and most of all, remember to have fun. May the Force be with you!

INTERFACE

Game Screen—On Foot

Game Information

The top area of the screen in reserved for relevant game information, such as scores, time, or remaining lives, depending on your current game mode.

Reticle

The reticle in the center of the screen indicates where you are aiming. Its appearance changes depending on the type of weapon you have equipped.

Heat Gauge

As you fire your blaster, a Heat Gauge appears under the reticle. As you continue firing, the gauge grows and turns red in color. Ceasing fire for a short period of time automatically reduces the heat. Fire for too long, and your blaster overheats, preventing you from firing until it cools back down. If your weapon overheats, an active yellow sequence is triggered. Press the button indicated on the screen when the falling dot reaches the yellow area of the gauge to cool down your weapon. Should you succeed, this sequence increases in difficulty for each consecutive overheat. However if you fail, your blaster will fill with extreme heat and render the weapon completely useless for an even longer period of time.

Hand

This shows your current hand of Star Cards. The background of a Star Card empties when used and gradually fills as the cool-down time of the Star Card passes. Some cards require charges before you can use them; you can find Charge pick-ups in various levels.

Health

As you take damage from enemy attacks, your health decreases. It regenerates if you avoid taking damage for a short time.

Scanner

The scanner shows the locations of both enemies and allies. Blue objects are allies, a yellow dot indicates your partner, and red objects are enemy forces. Sections of the scanner flash red to indicate an adversary in that direction. As the foe gets closer to your location, these red flashes move toward the center of the scanner. Objectives appear on the scanner as white dots when neutral or as blue or red, depending on which team controls it.

Game Screen—In Vehicles

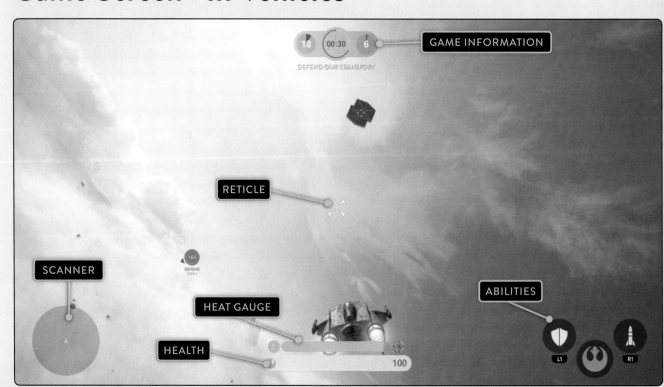

Abilities

These icons represent your vehicle's unique offensive and defensive abilities. Press the left button to activate the left ability, press the right button to activate the right ability, and press the top button to activate the middle ability. Each ability requires a brief cool-down time before you can use it again.

Throttle (Air Vehicles Only)

This indicates your current speed. Move the throttle stick or keys up or down to increase or decrease your speed.

Note that increasing the throttle channels power from the weapon systems to the engines, reducing the damage your weapons can inflict. Inversely, decreasing the throttle channels power from the engines to the weapon systems and increases the damage of your weapons.

Health

Your health decreases as you take damage from enemy attacks. To refill your health during Fighter Squadron and Mission game modes, find and collect a Vehicle Repair pick-up.

Scanner

The scanner shows the locations of both enemies and allies. A yellow object is your partner, blue objects are allies, and red objects are enemy forces. Sections of the scanner flash red to indicate enemy infantry, while enemy heroes and vehicles are displayed as red dots. Your allies appear as blue circles, regardless of distance.

Note that in Fighter Squadron, enemy ships appear only as red directional flashes on the scanner.

Collectibles (Missions Only)

In single-player game modes, these icons indicate the total number of collectibles hidden in a mission and how many you have collected.

Evasive Cool-down (Air Vehicles Only)

You can perform Evasive Maneuvers in certain air vehicles, such as X-wings or TIE fighters, by pressing the left directional or function button, the up directional or function button, or the right directional or function button. This icon represents the cool-down time until you can perform another Evasive Maneuver.

STAR CARDS

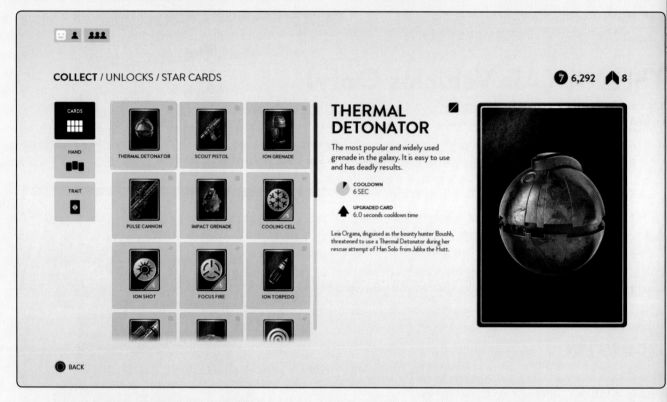

Star Cards assembled into a hand represent different weapons and equipment you can take into battle. A hand consists of two Star Cards and one Charged Star Card.

To view your Star Card collection or purchase new Star Cards, enter the COLLECT menu, select UNLOCKS, and then select STAR CARDS. Highlight a card to view its effects, unlock cost, and upgrade cost (if available).

You can use the left and right Star Cards repeatedly during a battle, as they are limited only by their cool-down time.

The center Star Card slot is reserved for powerful cards that require you to find a Charge token on the battlefield before you can use them.

Unlocking Star Cards

Each Star Card requires a certain amount number of credits to unlock.

Upgrades

Certain Star Cards can be upgraded. Upgrading a Star Card increases the benefits in some way, such as decreasing its cool-down time, increasing the time it is active, or increasing its damage potential.

Creating Hands

Select HAND from the Star Cards menu, and then select a slot to assign any unlocked Star Cards to your hand. You can create two sets of cards to bring into battle. If you have a partner, you also have the option of selecting his or her chosen hand and potentially trying out Star Cards you have yet to unlock.

FORMING A PARTY

Select the three-person icon in the upper-left corner of the menu screen to bring up a list of your friends currently online, and then select their names to invite them to your party. A party can contain up to eight players.

Partners

You can set one of your party members as your partner by selecting the single-person icon in the upper-left corner of the screen, located immediately to the right of your player icon.

If a player dies, his or her character can spawn near their partner if the partner is alive and not in an immediate firefight. Partners also share their first hands with one another, potentially allowing access to Star Cards you have yet to unlock.

COMPANION

Whether you're in a galaxy far, far away or somewhere closer to home, get ready for battle with the official *Star Wars* Battlefront Companion.

Featuring the tactical card-based game, the Companion lets you earn in-game credits that unlock Star Cards, weapons, and more in *Star Wars* Battlefront.

In addition to Base Command, the Companion also lets Rebels and Imperials alike check game stats and progression, customize load-outs and appearance, connect with friends, and get notified when they're playing *Star Wars* Battlefront—as well as gather intel on your friends' stats and progression so you can see how you match up!

Get the Companion app in the iOS App Store and Google Play for Android, or use the Companion on the web at www.starwarsbattlefront.com.

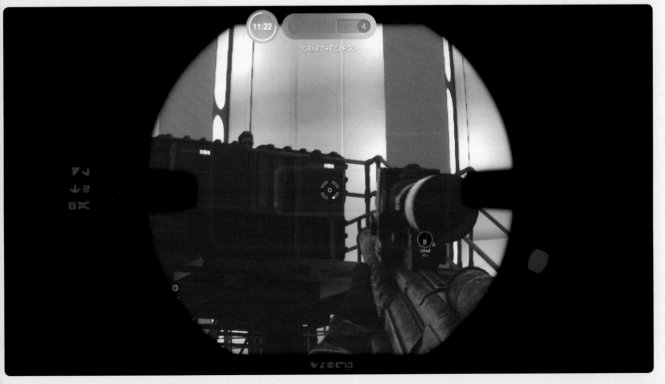

MUTIPLAYER TACTICS

Tactics are some of the most important things you can practice in Star Wars Battlefront. Your shots must be accurate and they should land if you are going to be successful in a gunfight, however being able to shoot your enemy isn't enough to keep you alive for an extended amount of time. Good tactics combine both your skill with a blaster and your wit on the battlefield to score the most points for your team, as you defend the Empire or fight for the Rebellion.

Pack for the Occasion

The most frustrating thing that happens in any first-person shooter game, let alone what happens in specific modes here in *Star Wars* Battlefront, is being dropped into a match without the right tools for the job. Taking a "shotgun" to a Blaster Rifle fight may lead to your demise more than you might think. However, a "shotgun" like the CA-87 in a game mode like Blast, and on a map like the Rebel Base on Hoth could put you on the top of the leaderboards because of how effective this weapon is in this situation.

Generally, game modes such as Supremacy, Walker Assault, and Droid Run are going to be the modes that call for the utmost range for weaponry. Blast, Cargo, and Drop Zone are game modes that play at a more mid-range to close range engagement, but Hero Hunt and Heroes Vs. Villains are special circumstances due to the differences in playstyle of the *Star Wars* heroes.

Pick Your Battles

Picking your battles carefully can lead you to the most success. See an enemy equipped with a mid to long-ranged blaster in the distance? Try to avoid them and take an alternate route in your immediate area to close the gap with this foe to reduce their advantage.

Distance is a very important factor in the gameplay of *Star Wars* Battlefront, especially in some of the larger game modes like Supremacy and Walker Assault. Equpping both a blaster for close to mid-ranged firefights and a Cycler Rifle or Pulse Cannon will keep you ready for most situations. However, it is still important to stay keen about the types of enemies you are fighting against.

Cover

Use everything in your vicinity as cover and protect yourself with a Squad Shield or Personal Shield to protect yourself when there just isn't any cover. Because of the regeneration aspect in the game, cover is sometimes the only way you can regain health without being killed first. The *Star Wars* universe is extreme in the sense of terrain and ground cover. If there isn't a piece of ship wreckage nearby, a cargo container or structure, there is more than likely a cliff, some bushes, a couple of trees, or at least some giant rocks to hide behind either for stealth or for protection while you regenerate health.

As it was stated before, there are several uses for both natural cover and manufactured. For the most part, it does not matter which mode you are playing because there is always a need for cover. The best way to use cover is to always stay behind something no matter the situation. If there is a wall you can see over, try crouching and popping up to shoot your enemies. Keep the lower half of your body covered by the object to make yourself a much more difficult target to hit. When you are up against an object that covers your entire body while standing, don't completely jump out of cover to engage an enemy. The best way to go about engaging the enemy is to quickly peek out and attempt to aquire your target. If no one is there, and the coast is clear, move forward and find another piece of cover, or slip back behind the object and wait for your opportunity to strike another target.

Vehicle Combat

There are a plethora of vehicles in *Star Wars* Battlefront, both ground and air vehicles. It is important to know when to use these vehicles and determine if it is a better idea keep your boots on the ground and take an objective on foot. Because of the overwhelming firepower that comes from the Empire, Imperial forces have a much greater number in vehicles, but that does not ultimately make them more powerful. Between the AT-AT, AT-ST, Speederbike, and each of the starfighters there is always a counter to these vehicles, or some way to avoid them.

GROUND VEHICLES

In modes like Walker Assault and Supremacy, AT-ST walkers can be extremely dangerous when they are being used to hold down specific locations. This is where Star Cards like Ion Grenade, Ion Torpedo, and Ion Shot come into play. A well placed Ion Grenade can destroy an AT-ST if it has taken a bit of damage. The problem with this is you must sacrifice a Star Card slot in order to carry one of these items with you. This is the time where you and your partner must maintain coordination to remain as a well balanced duo. It is a good idea to designate one partner to focus on vehicle watch, while the other is equipped for full trooper battle. Obviously there will always be more troopers on the battlefield than vehicles, but having the tools to deal with a walker is incredibly more safe than not having the tools when you really need them.

As the Empire, using walkers and Speederbikes to control the battlefield is extremely advantageous. Block choke points with heavy blaster fire for a short amount of time. This slows down any enemies attempting to escape an area or infiltrate one of your objectives. Keep your enemy busy and move on. The longer you sit in one location, the longer the Rebel forces have to set up an anti-vehicle ambush or counter-attack. Remember to attack or block, then move on to the next location. It is a good idea to move from one location, to the next, and then back again. Be sure to alternate and don't stay in one position for too long.

AIR VEHICLES

Starfighters and speeders work on power distribution. The amount of energy you are using matters and it affects your actions. The more power you have cycling to your engines affects your speed and increases your thrust, causing your vehicle to travel faster. However, when you cycle your power to your engines, you take that power away from your blasters and make them weaker. Slowing down and conserving thruster power affects the strength of your blasters, so they are much stronger when you lower your speed. When dog fighting in big game modes, but especially in Fighter Squadron, there are several reasons to pay attention to your thruster gauge. Speed up to chase down enemies, but slow down to splash them with damage quickly.

Take your skills into battle and maneuver through the terrain to take advantage of your air superiority. Blaster fire from air vehicles will not take out enemy forces on the ground at an extreme rate, but they will do damage to both vehicles and infantry. More importantly, being able to attack from the sky and and fly away at extreme speeds leaves you with the advantage to attack without real fear of retaliation. Assist your teammates on the ground while the air space is yours. Use the blaster fire from air vehicles to support your troops. Keep an eye on your radar to stay keen to your surroundings, but try not to fly around aimlessly. Your team needs you to take advantage of your powerful weaponry at all times.

BATTLE BEYOND

Something very unique to Star Wars Battlefront is the action happening in both the background and the foreground that composes the Star Wars environment. There are many diverse aspects to Battle Beyond, but they all complete the Star Wars experience.

What is Battle Beyond? Battle Beyond is the reason you see the flying Rebel Cruiser or crashing Imperial Star Destroyer in the backgrounds of Outpost Beta on Hoth or in the skies of Tatooine around the Jundland Wastes. It is also why you see iconic characters from all over the Star Wars universe on the battlefield with you. While you can interact with most of the objects and pieces that are considered part of the Battle Beyond system, some are purely for atmosphere. This section discusses each one to give you a little insight on how they affect your gameplay experience.

ENVIRONMENTAL OBJECTS/CHARACTERS

Object/Character	Location	Detail 1	Detail 2
Y-wings	All Walker Assault maps	Fire on AT-ATs when called in	Players can destroy them
Power generator	Walker Assault only	Blows up during cutscene at EoR for Empire win	—
GR-75 Medium Transport	Walker Assault only	Blows up during cutscene at EoR for Empire win	—
Jawas	Only on Tatooine	Run from players when nearby or shot at	—
Ewoks	Only on Endor	Run from players when nearby or shot at	—
MC80 Liberty Type Star Cruiser	Jundland Wastes, Survival on Tatooine and Sullust, and the Overpower Training Mission	Triggered by Rebel map progression	Interacts with Imperial Star Destroyer that can appear
CR90 Corellian Corvette	Hoth and Tatooine	Accompanies Star Cruiser	—
II-class Star Destroyer	Outpost Beta, Jundland Wastes, SoroSuub Centroplex, Sulphur Fields, Survival on Hoth and Tatooine, and Overpower Training	Triggered by Imperial map progression	Interacts with Rebel ships that can appear
Executor-class Super Star Destroyer	Outpost Beta, Jundland Wastes, SoroSuub Centroplex, Sulphur Fields, Survival on Hoth and Tatooine, and Overpower Training	Triggered by Imperial map progression	Background only
Nebulon-B Escort Frigate	—	Triggered by Rebel map progression	Imperial Laser Turrets fire at it
Ion cannon	Outpost Beta	Triggered by Rebel map progression; fires at Star Destroyers	Destroyed by Star Destroyer during Empire progression
Dogfighting	Jawa Refuge and Sulphur Fields	Amount of fighters varies per map and mode	Number can further be affected by which side is winning
AT-AT	Jawa Refuge and Survival on Hoth	Walk a set path	—
Smoke plumes	Survival on Hoth	Triggered on quick kills in succession	Can happen on either Rebel or Imperial side, depending on who is getting killed
Banthas	On Tatooine only	Walk a set path	—

HEROES

PLAYABLE CHARACTERS

DARTH VADER

Darth Vader, Dark Lord of the Sith, is notorious around the galaxy as the right hand of the Emperor and one of the most powerful beings in existence. Born as a slave and later trained to be a Jedi Knight, Darth Vader is extremely skilled with a lightsaber and a master of the Dark Side. He serves the Empire, leading an elite Imperial task force in the hunt for Rebels across the galaxy. Lord Vader works under the notion that it is better to be feared than loved, constantly reminding his inferiors of this belief.

Darth Vader is an extremely powerful melee character, hindered only by his movement speed. Vader cannot run, but he can make large jumps using his Force abilities to compensate for his poor agility. With his ability to deflect incoming blaster bolts and his high amount of hit points, anyone attempting to attack him head-on will more than likely be struck down. Like all playable heroes and villains, Darth Vader has three unique abilities that all have specific uses. When these abilities are used properly, Vader can become nearly unstoppable.

Ability	Description	Situation
Force Choke	Using his Force power, Darth Vader can render enemies defenseless by picking them up and choking the life out of them.	Enemies not affected by the choke can interrupt this ability, so make sure that Vader is in the clear before picking up your target. If you're successful, this ability is a guaranteed kill against Rebel troopers.
Saber Throw	Darth Vader throws his lightsaber forward and hits everything within the throw range. The lightsaber is then instantly returned via Vader's Force ability.	Throwing his lightsaber is not Darth Vader's most powerful ability, but it is his only ability with a long reach. Use it whenever your target is at mid range.
Heavy Strike	Darth Vader spins in a full 360-degree turn, using his full strength to take out anyone within reach.	This ability is meant for that moment when Vader is surrounded by Rebel troopers and must get rid of them efficiently. Using this ability kills all foes in Vader's immediate vicinity.

LUKE SKYWALKER

Luke Skywalker, born on Tatooine and son of the legendary Jedi Knight Anakin Skywalker, is one of the most powerful Jedi to exist in the time of the Galactic Empire. Having a large part in the Rebellion against the Empire, Skywalker is full of passion and skilled with a lightsaber. Control this hero on the battlefield throughout *Star Wars* Battlefront to take down entire groups of stormtroopers and help the Rebellion.

Luke Skywalker has many strengths and just a few weaknesses that you should know about before controlling him on the battlefield. The Jedi is primarily a melee character whose strength lies in face-to-face combat, but he can create distance between himself and his foes if necessary by using his Force Push. With his 20 percent faster running speed, he can close the gap on a single enemy, thus controlling the battle however he chooses. With that said, Luke has three abilities, all with very different tactical advantages. Keep these effects in mind when controlling Luke Skywalker—using them properly makes you as effective as possible.

Ability	Description	Situation
Force Push	Using his Force power, Luke can send a wave of energy toward his target, dealing heavy damage and pushing the foe back some distance.	Use this ability when you must quickly kill an enemy at a short distance or when you become overwhelmed.
Saber Rush	Luke lunges forward using Force energy and takes a wide slash at whomever is at the end of his lunge.	Use Saber Rush when you need to quickly close a distance gap where foes are keeping Luke at range. This ability can inflict a great deal of damage if you judge the distance correctly.
Heavy Strike	Luke spins in a full 360-degree turn, using his full strength to take out anyone within reach.	This ability is meant for that moment when Luke is surrounded by stormtroopers and must get rid of them efficiently. Using this ability kills all enemies in Luke's immediate vicinity.

BOBA FETT

Boba Fett, the bounty hunter in Mandolorian Armor, is a battle-hardened warrior who only works when the money is right. Fett is one of the most respected bounty hunters in the galaxy and was trained as a young child after leaving his home of Kamino. Because of this, Boba Fett does not work for cheap, although some special circumstances may be possible for targets like the smuggler Han Solo.

Fett is primarily a ranged character and should always be treated as such. Because of his jetpack, the bounty hunter can traverse almost any terrain and normally escape from a bad situation whenever appropriate. Avoid getting close to any enemy attackers. Even though Boba Fett is a tough, experienced warrior who can brush off a few hits, he is still vulnerable to short-range combat and should avoid those situations at all costs.

Ability	Description	Situation
Wrist Rocket	Boba Fett has a highly explosive wrist-fired dart that has a wide explosive range and can be fired from any location.	The Wrist Rocket is great for taking out multiple opponents at once or firing at enemy heroes who can reflect blaster bolts (like Luke Skywalker).
Flame Thrower	Fett's wrist-fired flamethrower launches a stream of short-range fire, useful for affecting multiple enemies within range.	Flame Thrower is designed to use when Boba Fett is stuck in a situation that he may not want to be in. You can also use it tactically as a touch-and-go move. For the greatest efficiency, land from flying through the air, catch a few foes on fire, and take off.
Jetpack	The jetpack attached to Boba Fett's back allows him to jump and reach most heights or fly over the battlefield eying his prey.	The jetpack is one of the most important abilities that Boba Fett has. Use it to get anywhere quickly and to escape death by going where most characters cannot.

HAN SOLO

This human smuggler from Corellia has a bad attitude and loves getting paid, so much so that he has gained the skills and has the instinct to get him out of any situation. Han Solo is known for aiding the Rebellion and assisting Luke Skywalker and Leia Organa in their efforts to crumble the Empire.

Han Solo is another primarily ranged character who has a problem with enemies directly in his face (albeit no fear of them). Han's blaster is one of the most powerful blasters in the game and should be treated as such, but it is a single-shot weapon that requires precise accuracy. The smuggler has a few abilities that make his blaster pistol even more powerful. If they are combined in a specific order, they can take down even the most powerful characters in a matter of seconds.

Ability	Description	Situation
Rapid Fire	Han Solo can rapidly hip-fire his blaster pistol without it overheating.	The ability to fire the already powerful blaster pistol as quickly as you can pull the trigger gives you a great advantage when Han must attack a large number of enemy troopers.
Lucky Shot	This incredibly powerful blaster shot deals an area-of-effect explosive damage, effective against both opponents and vehicles.	Lucky Shot is essentially your tool in every situation. Using this ability each time its cool-down wears off aids you significantly.
Shoulder Charge	Solo brutally charges shoulder first straight forward, taking down everything in his path.	Use this ability to get Han out of tight situations, or if you see a group of stormtroopers that is just too close together. The Shoulder Charge runs over everyone in Han's path for a short burst.

LEIA ORGANA

Leia Organa, Luke Skywalker's twin, was adopted by Senator Bail Organa directly after birth in order to split the twins and hide them from their father, Darth Vader. Because of her adopted parents, she was named Princess Leia and later became one of the heads of the Rebellion. Leading her Rebel troops into battle, she has become highly respected amongst her new people after her home planet was destroyed by the Death Star.

Princess Leia is fully a support character and uses her leadership on the battlefield to heavily assist her fellow troopers. She is slightly more powerful than the average trooper and an ace with a blaster rifle. Use her abilities to support your team and lead them to victory.

If Leia Organa is on the battlefield, there is a chance that two friendly players can spawn in as the Rebel Honor Guard. Armed with the A280, these special characters are harder to kill because they have an added health pool and they can deal more damage. More importantly, if you or your teammates are spawned in as one of these characters, stay close to Leia and protect her as these characters will also earn more points to your score and sticking together will keep them alive longer. In addition to these bonuses, each Aldreraan Honor Guard character is equipped with a fixed set or Star Cards; both the Smart Rocket and Homing shot are in your arsenal granting you the ability to deal with both vehicles and infantry creating a somewhat unstoppable force.

Ability	Description	Situation
Supply Drop	Leia drops a Power-up Star Card for the friendly troopers.	The Power-up Star Cards are some of the most powerful abilities in *Star Wars* Battlefront, and they are available to all troopers. Use this ability whenever friendly troopers are nearby because they can protect Leia and attack their target with greater ease.
Enhanced Squad Shield	Leia deploys a Squad Shield even more powerful and protective than an average Squad Shield.	Drop this Enhanced Squad Shield when Leia and her squad are stuck in a highly defensive position and need extra protection. Another use for this ability is to dictate your own battlefield, creating a zone that you determine.
Trooper Bane	Leia fires highly powerful shots that take down troopers in one shot and can also fire straight through shields.	Use this ability when there is a large group of troopers in front of Leia or if you must shoot through Leia's shield to attack anyone on the outside of it.

EMPEROR PALPATINE

Emperor Palpatine, also known as Darth Sidious, is the Dark Lord who became the first emperor of the Galactic Empire and took Darth Vader as his apprentice. An extremely powerful Force user, Emperor Palpatine is known by most in the galaxy and highly feared.

The Emperor is primarily a support character who specializes in helping his fellow villains. Because of his mobility and charging abilities, Palpatine can get to his teammates rather quickly. He should normally travel with troopers as bodyguards.

If Emperor Palpatine summons himself to the battlefield, you know things must be serious. When he is in play, it is possible that two friendly players will spawn in as shock troopers. The Emperor's shock troopers are equipped with the E11, and two Star Cards, the Smart Rocket and Homing Shot granting you the ability to deal with anything the Rebel scum can throw at you. These special characters are more difficult to kill than normal troopers as they have an added bonus to their health pool and they can deal more damage. More importantly, if you and your teammates are spawned in as one of these characters, stay close to Emperor Palpatine and protect him as these characters will also earn more points for your score and sticking together will keep them alive longer.

Ability	Description	Situation
Imperial Resources	Palpatine drops a power-up for his team to pick up.	The Power-up Star Cards are some of the most powerful abilities in *Star Wars* Battlefront, and they are available to all troopers. Use this ability whenever friendly troopers are nearby because they can protect Palpatine and attack their target with greater ease.
Chain Lightning	This sends a charge of Force Lighting that attaches to one target and is spread through any other nearby targets with one blast.	Use this ability primarily for groups of troopers standing close to each other. It weakens all of them, making them easier targets for your team.
Force Dash	Emperor Palpatine launches forward extremely rapidly.	To make up for Palpatine's slow movement speed, he can use Force Dash to launch himself forward, getting to any location quickly. Use this whenever you need to be somewhere, as the cool-down returns relatively quickly so you can use it again.

NON-PLAYABLE CHARACTERS

ACKBAR

R2-D2

C-3PO

PATROL LEADER (SCOUT TROOPER)

PLAYABLE APPEARANCES

 Human male (Rebel)

 Twi'Lek (Rebel)

 Human female (Rebel)

 Rodian (Rebel)

 Stormtrooper (Empire)

 Duros (Rebel)

 Scout Trooper (Empire)

 Zabrak (Rebel)

 Shadowtrooper (Empire)

 Ishi Tib (Rebel)

 Sullustian (Rebel)

 Quarren (Rebel)

MISSIONS

You can play *Star Wars* Battlefront in solo or two-player modes by selecting Missions from the Play menu. Three modes offer a variety of gameplay.

▶ Training: Introduces players to various facets of the game in solo or cooperative play.

▶ Battle: Two-player versus mode that allows players to fight as the Rebels or Imperials in the role of infantry or hero.

▶ Survival: Pits one or two Rebel soldiers against 15 increasingly challenging waves of Imperial forces.

NEW RECRUIT

TROPHY: BRONZE **GAMER SCORE: 15**

Simply complete one of the Training, Battle, or Survival missions to earn this award.

TOGETHER WE CAN RULE THE GALAXY

TROPHY: BRONZE **GAMER SCORE: 15**

Complete any mission with a friend. Grab a partner, either online or in local splitscreen, and complete any mission.

YOUR JOURNEY HAS ONLY STARTED

TROPHY: BRONZE **GAMER SCORE: 15**

Complete all 17 missions, including five Training, four Battle, four Hero Battle, and four Survival.

SCRAP COLLECTOR

TROPHY: SILVER **GAMER SCORE: 40**

A star is available on each Battle, Hero Battle, and Survival map, requiring you to find all five collectibles and complete the mission. To attain this Achievement/Trophy, earn one of these stars. Note that you must play Battle missions against AI to complete this requirement.

MASTER

TROPHY: GOLD **GAMER SCORE: 55**

Earn all mission stars on Master difficulty. Achieve all 75 stars in missions to get this one.

PRECISION SHOT

TROPHY: BRONZE **GAMER SCORE: 15**

Get 10 headshots with the Tusken Cycler rifle. The Hunter Star Card Hand in Battle on Hoth and Marksman in Survival on Sullust both contain the Cycler Rifle Star Card. However, once you have obtained all five stars in a mission, you can use the rifle in a customized hand for that mission. Any Imperial or Rebel infantry killed with a headshot from the Cycler rifle in either Battle or Survival count toward this award. Whenever this ability is available in Survival mode, pick off charging stormtroopers from afar with a quick shot to the noggin.

TUTORIAL: PROBE DROIDS

LOCATION: HOTH

WEAPON: A280C BLASTER RIFLE

OPPONENTS: PROBE DROIDS

DIFFICULTY: VERY EASY

MISSION BRIEF

Our scanners have picked up possible Imperial signals around the base. Move out and investigate. Eliminate any potential threats before they can alert the Empire to our presence. We cannot afford to be found out.

A tutorial is available if you press the Use button at the main menu. This short mission runs you through the basics of *Star Wars Battlefront*. You receive an Achievement/Trophy for finishing the tutorial, so it is worth completing even if you feel comfortable with the controls. Note that this is outside of the Missions tab and does not count toward any of the missions-specific Achievements.

Make your way to the designated location. Use the left stick to move to the marker ahead. Points of interest within range are pointed out on the scanner, located in the lower-left corner of the HUD. Enemies show up in red.

Investigate the gorge ahead. Run down the hill into the gorge, and jump the rocks as you proceed up the other side.

FIRST OR THIRD PERSON

When playing as infantry or inside an air vehicle, hold down on the d-pad to switch between first- and third-person perspectives. Check them both out and see which you prefer. As a soldier, tap the button to switch your stance and look over the opposite shoulder.

Investigate unidentified object. Sprint up the hill to the next marker, and crouch behind the boulders. Just ahead, an Imperial Probe Droid scouts the area.

Destroy the Imperial Probe Droid. Aim down the sights by holding the Zoom button, and fire at the droid until it explodes in defeat. It is perfectly okay to hip fire at the enemy, but you do lose a little accuracy.

OVERHEATING THE BLASTER

All blasters are susceptible to overheating if fired for too long. As you discharge the weapon, a curved meter appears below your reticle, building outward until it turns red. This indicates that the weapon is heating up. If the meter fills up, the gun stops working, and you must complete a short, active cooling mini-game to regain control. A new meter appears with a small yellow section on each side. As two dots move from the outside toward the vertex, press the Use button when they are lined up with the yellow. With a perfectly timed cooling flush, the gun is immediately ready to fire again. Fail, and you become vulnerable, since it takes longer to cool off. You can choose to ignore this mini-game to recover once the dots reach the bottom. Cooling your weapon becomes progressively tougher the more times you succeed.

Make your way to the designated location. Once you've taken care of the droid, continue on to the next objective marker. Another Probe Droid patrols in the distance. Again, hold the Zoom button down and destroy the machine. Note that your weapon has some kick to it, so fire in bursts to take your target down. Another marker appears in the distance. Traverse the rocky terrain until you reach the spot.

Destroy the Imperial Probe Droid. You are given the Ion Grenade Star Card, and it is equipped in the Left Ability slot. Turn to another Probe Droid that appears nearby, and press the Left Card button to toss the anti-vehicle explosive in its direction. As long as the grenade detonates close enough, the droid is taken out.

STAR CARD COOL DOWN

After you use a Star Card, such as the Ion Grenade, the ability must cool down before it can be used again. This is represented by the loss of color in the card.

Get the power-up. A new marker shows up just ahead. Run over to it, and grab the power-up that lies on the ground. A Smart Rocket shows up just below your hand in the lower-right corner of the HUD. Pressing the Left and Right Card buttons at the same time activates this new Power Ability.

Destroy the Imperial Probe Droid. Spot a fourth Probe Droid in the distance, and equip the rocket launcher. Aim through the scope, and blow the droid out of the air.

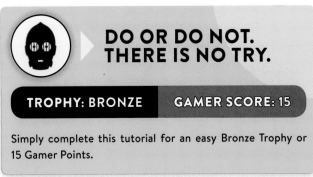

DO OR DO NOT. THERE IS NO TRY.

TROPHY: BRONZE	GAMER SCORE: 15

Simply complete this tutorial for an easy Bronze Trophy or 15 Gamer Points.

TRAINING

NUMBER OF PLAYERS: SOLO PLAY, ONLINE PARTNER CO-OP, LOCAL SPLITSCREEN CO-OP

OBJECTIVE: LEARN THE WAYS OF THE FORCE, AND THEN PILOT X-WINGS, AIRSPEEDERS, AT-STS, AND SPEEDER BIKES

Training missions introduce you to the X-wing fighter, Speeder Bike, AT-ST, heroes, and the Rebel Snowspeeder, with objectives tailored to each. These missions are well worth your time, as they teach the nuances of each vehicle and grant you several Achievements/Trophies.

Three stars are available for each mission. Completing a mission in a set time while fulfilling a specified condition nets them all. Refer to the tables at the beginning of each mission for requirements.

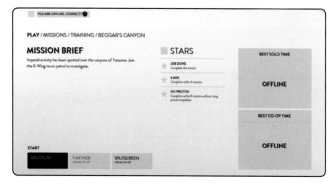

ALL RIGHT, I'LL GIVE IT A TRY

| TROPHY: BRONZE | GAMER SCORE: 15 |

Earn at least one star on all training missions. Complete the five training missions to collect this one.

BEGGAR'S CANYON

TATOOINE CANYON

TIE FIGHTERS
ENTER

START

VEHICLE REPAIR

LOCATION: TATOOINE CANYON	**OPPONENTS:** TIE FIGHTERS, TIE INTERCEPTORS
VEHICLE: X-WING	**DIFFICULTY:** MEDIUM

MISSION BRIEF

Imperial activity has been spotted over the canyons of Tatooine. Join the X-wing recon patrol to investigate.

HOW TO GET STARS

Name	Condition
Job Done	Complete the mission.
6 Min	Complete within six minutes.
No Proton	Complete within six minutes without using Proton Torpedoes.

Follow patrol leader. The mission starts as two other X-wing pilots flying toward a Tatooine canyon join you in search of TIE fighters that have been spotted in the area. Follow the patrol leader through the winding path until you encounter two TIE fighters.

A TIGHT RAVINE

There is no need to navigate deep inside the narrow, tight turns of the canyon. Skim across the tops of the bluffs for least resistance. If a timer starts counting down with the message "STAY INSIDE THE CANYON," just lower the vehicle until it goes away.

Destroy all enemy fighters. Immediately draw a bead on one of the starfighters and take it out with a Proton Torpedo. Chase down the second one, and light it up with your laser cannons. In the meantime, four more Imperial ships fly head-on into the dogfight. Team up with your patrol to take them all down.

PILOTING THE X-WING

Control	Xbox One	PlayStation 4
Energy Distribution (Throttle)	Left Thumbstick	Left Stick
Aim	Right Thumbstick	Right Stick
Fire	RT	R2
Soft Lock (Hold)	LT	L2
Shield	LB	L1
Homing Missile (Proton Torpedo)	RB	R1
Evasive Maneuvers	Left/Up/Right on D-Pad	Left/Up/Right on D-Pad
1st/3rd Person (Hold)	Down on D-Pad	Down on D-Pad

Flying the air vehicles in *Star Wars* Battlefront takes some adjustment, but once you get it, piloting the starfighters is a blast. The right stick aims the aircraft; point the aiming reticle in the direction you want to fly, and the ship follows suit.

The left stick acts as a throttle, but it is more than that. A meter just above the fighter's health indicates your energy distribution. Push up, and energy is shifted to your engines, speeding you up. Push down, and power is sent to your weapon systems, making the X-wing a more powerful force against the TIE fighters. Use the throttle to make quick turns and get behind your opponent, and try matching their speed as you light them up.

Hold the Soft Lock button to lock on to an enemy, which is indicated by a red circle. Your crosshairs move toward your target. Once they rest on top of the ship, press the Right Card button to release a homing missile and cause serious damage, which is often a one-hit kill with the TIE fighters. Watch the movement of your opponent carefully. Your shot can be evaded up to the last second, wasting precious time as your ability recharges.

Laser cannons act just like your blaster on the ground. Press the Fire button to shoot at enemy fighters. You may need to shoot ahead of your target for a successful hit. And, just like the blasters, the cannons overheat with overuse, though there is no active cooling mini-game. Simply let it cool down to continue use.

The X-wing's Left Card Ability is a shield. Activate it when an opponent is targeting you. An alternative means to take an adversary down is slamming into the other fighter. Use your shield to absorb the damage this causes.

The X-wing has three evasive maneuvers that you activate by pressing left, up, or right on the d-pad. These buttons cause the ship to barrel roll left, turn 180 degrees with an Immelmann turn, and barrel roll right, respectively. A red icon appears next to the scanner, which indicates a cool down for your maneuvers.

Once you have destroyed the first six Imperial fighters, another squad enters, including three TIE interceptors and another four TIE fighters. These new ships need to be shot down in the same manner. Eliminate the group, taking advantage of your abilities and health pick-ups whenever possible.

VEHICLE REPAIR PICK-UPS

Watch out for pick-ups that appear around the canyon village. When needed, seek one out and fly through it to repair the ship.

EXTRA LIVES

Four lives are available for this training mission. If you die, you can restart at the last checkpoint by spending one of them.

EARNING THREE STARS

The third star requires completing the mission within six minutes without using Proton Torpedoes. Your blasters take several well-placed shots to destroy a TIE fighter, whereas Proton Torpedoes are typically deadly with one shot. You must find your next target immediately once you defeat a starfighter.

Regroup with the patrol. Simply descend back into the canyon to rejoin the others and complete the mission.

BEST STAR-PILOT IN THE GALAXY

TROPHY: BRONZE	GAMER SCORE: 15

Destroy 10 TIE fighters within two minutes on the Beggar's Canyon Trial. Use homing missiles whenever possible and quickly find your next target. You must limit your down time to achieve this one.

ENDOR CHASE

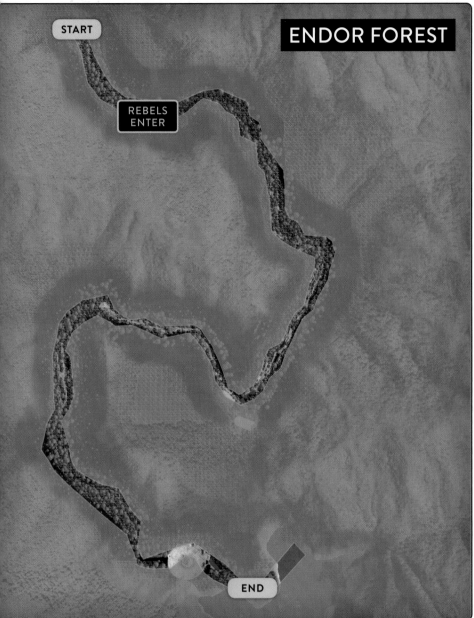

ENDOR FOREST

START

REBELS
ENTER

END

LOCATION: ENDOR FOREST

VEHICLE: SPEEDER BIKE

OPPONENTS: REBEL SCOUTS ON SPEEDER BIKES

DIFFICULTY: EASY

MISSION BRIEF

Rebel forces are reported to be moving to an extraction point in your patrol vicinity. Flush out all Rebels and hunt them down. They must not be allowed to escape.

HOW TO GET STARS

Name	Condition
Normal	Complete the mission.
2.5 Min	Complete within 2 minutes and 30 seconds.
Kill 5	Complete and kill five Rebels.

This training mission serves as another tutorial for vehicle control. You are an Imperial scout trooper piloting a Speeder Bike in a thick forest of Endor. Rebel infantry, mounted on bikes themselves, flee to an extraction point. You must find and pursue them all the way the final destination to complete the mission.

PILOTING A SPEEDER BIKE

Control	Xbox One	PlayStation 4
Throttle Increase/Decrease	Left Thumbstick Up/Down	Left Stick Up/Down
Strafe Left/Right	Left Thumbstick Left/Right	Left Stick Left/Right
Elevation Increase/Decrease	Right Thumbstick Up/Down	Right Stick Up/Down
Aim	Right Thumbstick Left/Right	Right Stick Left/Right
Fire	RT	R2
Soft Lock (Hold)	LT	L2
Speed Boost	LB	L1
1st/3rd Person (Hold)	Down on D-Pad	Down on D-Pad

The Speeder Bike controls very similarly to the X-wing, except for two things: the throttle doesn't serve as energy distribution (it simply accelerates and brakes) and the right stick operates slightly differently. Left and right still aims your reticle, while up and down increase and decrease elevation, respectively. This is very useful when dealing with obstacles placed in your path, such as downed trees. You can also use the left stick to strafe from side to side, which is invaluable in this location.

The only weapon is your blaster and your only ability is a speed boost, which is mapped to the Left Card slot. This thing is very fast and Endor's forests are extremely dense, so work that throttle carefully while navigating your way through the thicket.

Regroup with patrol. Start out by following the narrow path ahead as you drive toward the first objective marker.

Intercept the Rebels. At a sweeping left turn, a group of Rebels on Imperial Speeder Bikes crosses just ahead. Accelerate directly behind them, being careful to steer under the toppled tree.

SPEND A LIFE

You are given four lives that can be spent after dying to return to the mission. Checkpoints along the route dictate the area where you restart.

VEHICLE REPAIR PICK-UPS

It is possible to glance off a tree and not destroy your bike. Vehicle repair pick-ups are scattered throughout the forest; watch out for them if your Speeder Bike has taken damage.

Use your blaster to take out the Rebels whenever one is in your sights. Hold the Soft Lock button to target one, and shoot with the Fire button. To get the third star, you must dispatch at least five Rebels.

Friendly AT-STs have been deployed in the middle of your route. Strafe left and right to avoid running into them as you remain in the Rebels' trail. As you proceed through the level, more obstacles are continually thrown your way. Keep an eye ahead while continuing to pick off the enemy. Save your speed boosts for the clearings.

Eventually, AT-ATs block part of the path. Carefully navigate around them to avoid a friendly takedown. Tight turns, narrow sections, and logs continue slowing you down. Keep your speed up, even after you receive word that the extraction point has been neutralized. Eventually, you reach your destination, and the mission ends.

DON'T LET THOSE REBELS ESCAPE

If you trail too far behind, a message appears on-screen that says the Rebels are escaping, along with a 30-second timer. Speed up to get back within acceptable range. Fail to do so, and you may have to spend a life to continue the mission.

SAFETY AIN'T THE POINT OF A JOYRIDE

TROPHY: BRONZE	GAMER SCORE: 15

Take no damage in the Endor Chase mission. The Speeder Bike is very quick at full throttle. Keep your eyes on the path ahead, using both sticks to navigate around the many obstacles in the Endor Forest. Save speed boosts for clearings so that you don't inadvertently go headfirst into a tree.

OVERPOWER

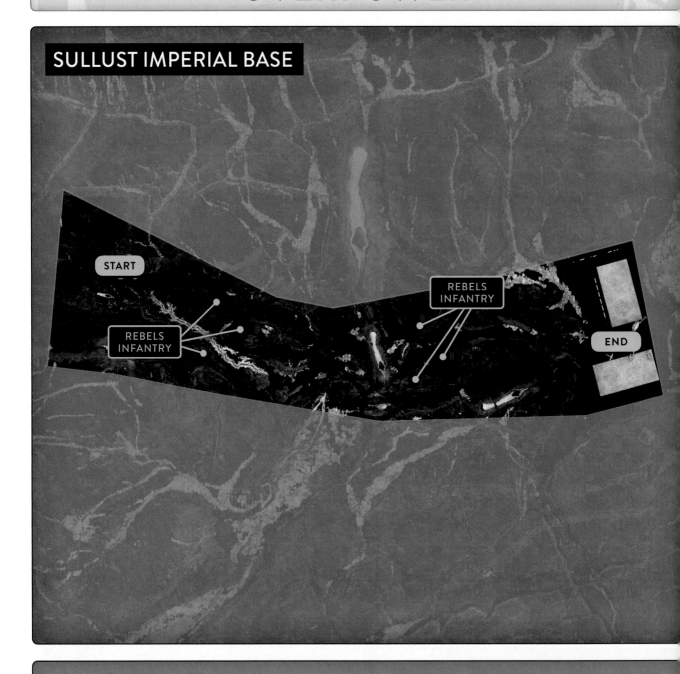

SULLUST IMPERIAL BASE

START

REBELS INFANTRY

REBELS INFANTRY

END

LOCATION: SULLUST IMPERIAL BASE

VEHICLE: AT-ST

OPPONENTS: A-WINGS, X-WINGS, REBEL INFANTRY

DIFFICULTY: MEDIUM

MISSION BRIEF

Lord Vader is on approach to Sullust and expects the Imperial base to be cleared of Rebels before his arrival. Escort the mighty AT-AT walker, and wipe them out.

HOW TO GET STARS

Name	Condition
Job Done	Complete the mission.
6 Min	Complete within six minutes.
A-wings	Complete and take out eight A-wings.

Regroup with the AT-AT. You take control of an AT-ST, who must escort and assist an AT-AT as it wipes out any Rebels who occupy the Sullust Imperial base. This mission runs you through all of the nuances of the AT-ST, teaching how to best utilize its powerful weaponry. Control of the scout walker should be familiar because it handles just like a soldier. Move out of the hangar to get the mission started.

CONTROLLING AN AT-ST

Control	Xbox One	PlayStation 4
Move	Left Thumbstick	Left Stick
Aim	Right Thumbstick Left/Right	Right Stick Left/Right
Fire	RT	R2
Zoom (Aim Assist)	LT	L2
Concussion Grenade Launcher	LB	L1
Homing Missiles	RB	R1
Sprint	Left Thumbstick (Click)	L3 (Click)
Abandon Vehicle	X	Square

An AT-ST controls very similarly to normal soldiers, as they move, aim, and even sprint in the same way. They are equipped with three weapons: a grenade launcher, concussion missiles, and a blaster. The grenades are ideal for groups of infantry, while the missiles are great for homing in on targets.

Escort the AT-AT. Take your position ahead of the transport, and lead it down the path toward the Rebel forces. Sprinting too far awa[y] results in a warning to return to your post, so keep close to the big guy.

Engage the Rebel ground forces. Small groups of Rebel infantry show up on the three ridges ahead, giving you a great opportunity t[o] test out the AT-ST's main guns. Sweep from one side to the other, and wipe them all out.

FOUR LIVES

If the Rebels take you down, spend one of your four extra lives to return to the action at the last checkpoint reached.

Destroy the A-wings. Continue down the path, where A-wings attack from the skies above. Fortunately, the bipedal is equipped with homing missiles, which easily rips them to shreds—assuming it has enough time to home in on the invader. Keep progressing toward your destination as you pick off fighters with your rockets. Be ready with your next shot once the weapon cools down.

Watch the flight patterns of the A-wings to note the best opportunities to take them down. Your homing missiles require a little time to lock on to their targets. The moment a starfighter appears in the distance is a great time to launch the explosive, giving it plenty of time to do its job.

Engage the Rebel ground forces. With the starfighter threat out of the way, continue ahead until three more groups of Rebels appear in a setup similar to before. Use your Concussion Grenades (mapped to the Left Card slot) to wipe them out with ease. Combine this with your main cannon to make quick work of the opposition.

Take down the X-wings. Farther down the road, look to the skies again, as X-wing starfighters make strafing runs at the AT-AT. Whenever possible, use your homing missiles in conjunction with your cannon to knock them out of the air.

Escort the AT-AT. Keep marching toward the landing pads ahead, maintaining gunfire on the remaining Rebels who hopelessly continue to fight from the ground and walkway above. Once it is safe to do so, the Imperial shuttle approaches for landing, making the mission a success.

EARNING THREE STARS

To earn all three stars, you must complete the mission in six minutes while taking down at least eight A-wings. As long as you stay on the move as you wipe out the Rebel forces, the time isn't too much trouble. Use all of your weaponry at each encounter to speed things up. Taking out the target number of starfighters is a bigger feat. As soon as they appear in the distance, fire a missile in their direction. Maintain plenty of space between the AT-ST and the A-wing, or else the homing missile won't have enough time to get a bead on its target. As soon as it cools down, be ready to fire the next projectile.

THE DARK SIDE

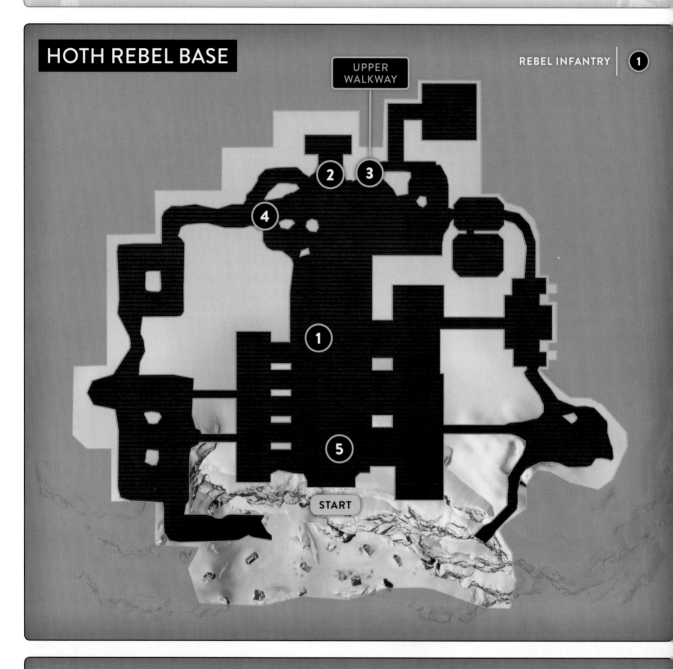

HOTH REBEL BASE

UPPER WALKWAY

REBEL INFANTRY | 1

START

LOCATION: HOTH REBEL BASE

HERO: DARTH VADER OR EMPEROR PALPATINE

OPPONENTS: REBEL INFANTRY

DIFFICULTY: EASY

MISSION BRIEF

The Rebel forces are scrambling to maintain control of their base as dark Lords of the Sith invade. Embrace the dark side, and wipe them out.

HOW TO GET STARS

Name	Condition
Job Done	Complete the mission.
3 Min	Complete within three minutes.
Efficient	Complete with 75 percent or more health left.

Eliminate the Rebels and take control of the base. The Lords of the Sith enter the Rebel base with a small squad of snowtroopers. Before starting your massacre of the helpless Rebels, you must choose between Darth Vader and Emperor Palpatine. The two options offer differing play styles, but they both provide devastating power. As you move into the structure, Rebel forces appear farther inside. Reinforcements appear in waves as you defeat each group.

PLAYING THE HERO

DARTH VADER ABILITIES

Ability Name	Button	Description
Force Choke	Left Card Ability	Choke current target for an instant kill.
Heavy Strike	Top Card Ability	Perform a strong charging group saber attack. Use this against small packs to wipe them out with one swing of your weapon.
Saber Throw	Right Card Ability	Throw your lightsaber at distant enemies. You can take out multiple foes with a well-placed toss.
Saber Defense	Zoom (Hold)	Use the saber to deflect blaster bolts back at the target. Keep defense up between attacks whenever shots are incoming.
Saber Strike	Fire	Strike with the lightsaber.
Lock on to Target	Melee Attack	Lock on to the target.

EMPEROR PALPATINE ABILITIES

Ability Name	Button	Description
Chain Lightning	Left Card Ability	This powerful, long-range lightning attack chains between nearby enemies. It is highly effective against groups of Rebels.
Imperial Resources	Top Card Ability	Spawn a hero health pick-up just in front of Palpatine. Grab one immediately if your health is down, or save it for later.
Force Dash	Right Card Ability	Perform a quick, twisting leap to escape cornering or close ground on a target in a hurry.
Block	Zoom (Hold)	Use your hands to block blaster shots, greatly reducing damage taken.
Force Lightning	Fire	Perform a short-range lightning strike. Hold to continually stream lightning from fingertips. The white meter drains until the ability must recharge.
Lock on to Target	Melee Attack	Lock on to the target.

Besides their overwhelming power, there are not too many differences between controlling the way a hero is played compared to a normal soldier. Heroes do not use Star Cards and instead are equipped with three abilities, which also require a cool-down period after each use. Those without blasters have another ability mapped to the Zoom button. In these cases, clicking the Melee Attack button locks on to a target. For the two Imperial heroes selectable in this mission, you must be relatively close to your opponent to use the regular attack.

Five waves of Rebel infantry attempt to rid their base of the Imperial trespassers.

1 **Just inside hangar** — Six Rebels with blaster pistols and blaster rifles

2 **Enter through back blast doors** — Five Rebels with blaster rifles and heavy blasters

3 **Second-floor walkway** — Four Rebels with blaster rifles

4 **From main hangar doors** — Four Rebels with blaster rifles and heavy blasters

5 **Final group from main hangar doors** — 11 Rebels with blaster rifles and heavy blasters, including some with shields and Jump Packs

The Rebel soldiers are not much of a match for Darth Vader or Emperor Palpatine, so defeating them is not a huge challenge. However, the final group of 11 soldiers can easily surround you if allowed to do so, and this is where you receive the most damage. Methodically pick off the Rebel scum to complete your hero training.

FORCE LIGHTNING, HEALTH, AND BASE CONTROL METERS

When you play as Palpatine, three meters are utilized on the HUD, while Darth Vader only uses two. At the top of the screen, Base Control shows your mission progress. It slowly fills until you finish off the last group of Rebels. At the bottom, your health is shown as a yellow bar. When playing as Palpatine, a white bar appears above your health that represents his Force Lightning. Once the white is drained completely, this ability must be recharged.

EARNING THREE STARS

To earn all three stars in a run, you must complete the mission within three minutes and with at least 75 percent health remaining at the end. The final wave of Rebels is fairly large, so you should stick to the outside to keep your health up. Of course, Palpatine can simply deploy a hero health pick-up for a small recovery.

INVASION

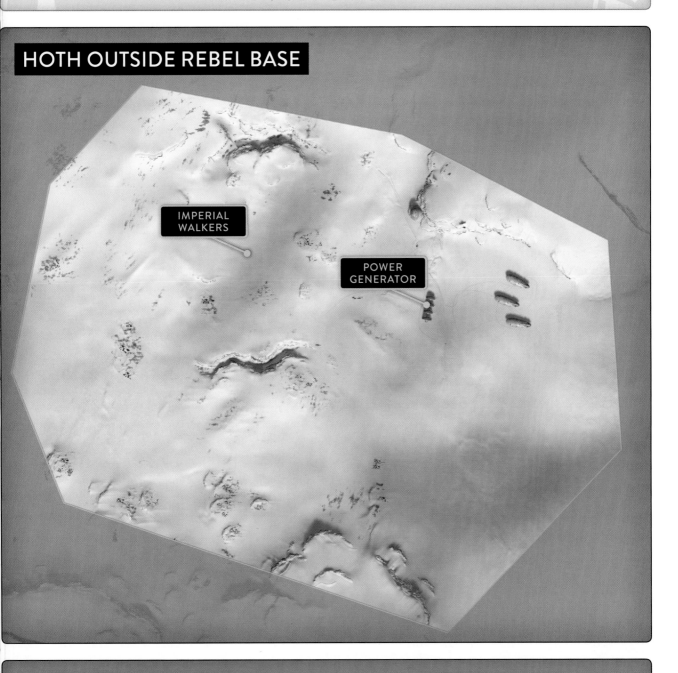

HOTH OUTSIDE REBEL BASE

IMPERIAL
WALKERS

POWER
GENERATOR

LOCATION: HOTH OUTSIDE REBEL BASE

VEHICLE: SNOWSPEEDER

OPPONENTS: AT-STS, AT-ATS

DIFFICULTY: MEDIUM

MISSION BRIEF

The Empire **has** *discovered a Rebel base, and it must be defended until all transports are away. Protect the power generator at all costs!*

HOW TO GET STARS

Name	Condition
Job Done	Complete the mission.
8 Min	Complete within eight minutes.
Takedown	Complete without failing a TOW-cable takedown.

At the Hoth Rebel base, Imperial scout walkers march toward the power generator. An evacuation has been ordered, but it takes time to get the three Rebel transports loaded and off the ground. The generator must be protected or the shields will fail, giving the Empire access to the fleeing vessels. The mission is divided into three segments—one for each transport ship.

Destroy the AT-STs. Three pairs of AT-STs move toward the generator. Check your scanner, find the two closest to the machine, and head their way. Hit the speed boost to get there quickly, and take them down with your laser cannons. Throughout your strafing runs, jam on the Fire button to cause maximum damage. Use the same tactics to eliminate the other four to continue the mission. Note that a light touch to a badly injured walker may be enough to take it down, but be careful that you don't commit suicide in the process.

If the Imperial walkers are allowed to get within range of the power generator, they begin attacking. A power generator meter at the top of the HUD shows their progress. If the meter fully depletes, the mission is over.

PILOTING THE T-47 AIRSPEEDER/SNOWSPEEDER

Control	Xbox One	PlayStation 4
Throttle	Left Thumbstick	Left Stick
Aim	Right Thumbstick	Right Stick
Fire	RT	R2
Soft Lock (Hold)	LT	L2
Speed Boost	LB	L1
Sensor Jammer	RB	R1
TOW-Cable	LB + RB	L1 + R1
Evasive Maneuvers	Left/Up/Right on D-Pad	Left/Up/Right on D-Pad
1st/3rd Person (Hold)	Down on D-Pad	Down on D-Pad

The Snowspeeder is flown in the same manner as the starfighters, except there is no energy distribution. The left stick only acts as the throttle. Going full throttle does not fill the yellow meter all the way; this extra speed is saved for your speed boost ability.

Much like the starfighters, the Snowspeeder has three evasive maneuvers, which you activate by pressing left, up, and right on the d-pad. Left and right cause the ship to bank in those directions, making a really tight 180-degree turn. When you push up, the ship rapidly ascends to a higher altitude before settling back down.

Laser cannons provide the only weaponry for the aircraft, though its TOW-cable can be lethal against an AT-AT. A sensor jammer is available, though it is not necessary in this mission.

Destroy the AT-AT. Next, a lone AT-AT moves in to attack. This provides an opportunity to teach the basics of taking the walker down with a TOW-cable. Follow the given instructions, and drop it to its knees.

DESTROYING AN AT-AT WITH THE TOW-CABLE

The long, unstable legs of the All Terrain Armored Transport provide a quicker way to defeat this behemoth as opposed to firing at its weakened belly. Wrap a long cable around its legs until it falls to the ground.

Fly your ship near the AT-AT, and activate the TOW-cable when prompted to do so. This brings up a vertical bar with an Airspeeder icon inside. Press up and down on the right stick to keep the icon inside the bar. As long as the icon remains white, you are fine. It turns red when you are in danger of losing the TOW-cable's hold, though you do have a little time to recover before it is completely lost.

Four dots appear to the left, which turn blue each time you successfully complete a lap. Whenever one changes color, the vertical bar shrinks until your icon barely fits inside. Make very light adjustments to the stick to keep it in the middle. After the fourth dot, you receive confirmation of your success, and the walker is taken down. Be ready to quickly pull back to avoid flying into the ground.

Taking damage can cause the cable to break and make you fail the procedure. At the very least, it can knock you off course, sending you into danger. Quickly bring the icon back into the safe range. Note that weapon fire from any walker can cause this effect. Also, watch out when a walker is located close to a wall or cliff. This makes it extremely tough to fly around it without losing contact. In this location, though, you have no worries because of the open environment.

Destroy the enemy walkers. At this point, two more AT-ATs show up. Take them down in the same manner as before. After you successfully destroy the walkers, the second transport lifts off.

LIVES TO SPEND

Crash the Snowspeeder, and you must spend one of your four lives to resume the mission. This restarts you at the start of the last checkpoint reached.

Destroy the enemy walkers. For the final objective, several AT-STs accompany three more AT-ATs. You can destroy these vehicles in any order. Use the laser cannons on the scout walkers, and destroy the transports using your TOW-cable. With this group eliminated, the third and final transport ship escapes.

EARNING THREE STARS

To earn all three stars in a run, you must destroy the final group of Imperial walkers before the timer reaches eight minutes, without failing a TOW-cable takedown. Use your speed boost when traveling between walkers, and quickly switch targets as you defeat AT-STs. Avoid taking too much damage when you perform the TOW-cable maneuvers.

BATTLES

PLAYERS: SOLO PLAY, ONLINE VERSUS AGAINST PARTNER, LOCAL VERSUS IN SPLITSCREEN

OBJECTIVE: ELIMINATE OPPONENTS AND COLLECT THEIR DROPPED TOKENS TO SCORE IN A ONE-ON-ONE BATTLE AGAINST FRIENDS OR AI—FIRST TO 100 POINTS WINS.

HOW TO GET STARS

Name	Condition
Normal	Win on Normal difficulty against AI.
Hard	Win on Hard difficulty against AI.
Master	Win on Master difficulty against AI.
Collectibles	Win on any difficulty against AI and find all collectibles.
Unstoppable	Win on Master difficulty against AI with the enemy scoring less than 40 points.

Battle mode gives you a chance to go one-on-one against your friends or the computer. Select your faction (either Rebel Alliance or Galactic Empire), and then get ready to slaughter the opposing side. To score points, pick up the tokens that downed opponents drop.

At the same time, collect tokens from your own team to deny points for the enemy. Infantry troops are added to each side to assist, though you can disable this by turning off Friendly AI Soldiers at the Faction Selection screen—making it a true head-to-head match. The first team to reach 100 points wins the game.

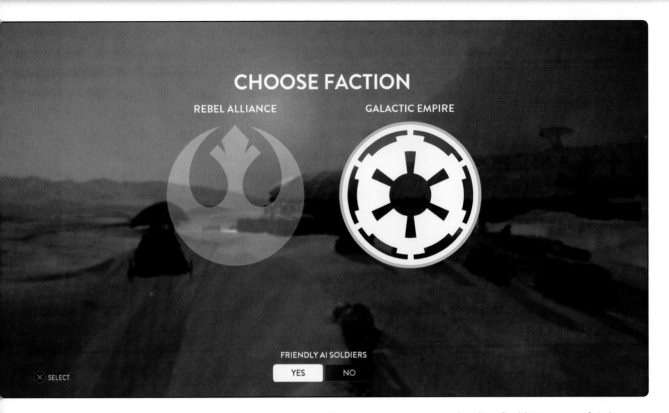

Regular battles pit Rebel infantry against Imperial troopers. Hero Battles allow you to massacre hordes of soldiers as one of six heroes: Luke Skywalker, Han Solo, Princess Leia, Darth Vader, Emperor Palpatine, or Boba Fett.

HERO BATTLES

Hero Battles are played in the same manner as regular battles, except that any human players choose a hero to use. The first side to 100 points wins the match. Just like regular battles, you can choose to enable or disable Friendly AI Soldiers. All computer bots, whether friend or foe, are played by the same selection of infantry as in normal battle mode. There are no power-ups or Charge pick-ups in Hero Battles. Instead, hero health pick-ups appear at specific locations, allowing you to heal when injured. Remember that heroes cannot use turrets.

DIFFICULTY

Select between three difficulties when beginning a Battle game: Normal, Hard, and Master. As the difficulty increases, opponents become tougher to take down, inflict more damage, and are quicker to react. Enemy composition is slightly different on Normal than higher settings. Refer to the charts in the AI Opposition section later in this chapter for information about when enemies are introduced to the game.

WEAPON SELECTION

When you are selecting between the 11 blasters, consider the type of environment where the fighting will take place. If longer lines of sight are available against the incoming forces, pick a long-range rifle. If you are fighting inside narrow corridors, then go with a higher rate of fire or damage. Just keep in mind that you cannot score without collecting the dropped tokens, and there is no one else on your team to do it for you. Sniping can be an effective means of taking down your opponents, but it can be difficult to reach the tokens in time. Note that when you die in a Battle mission, you are not given a chance to change weapons; choose wisely at the start. The following table allows you to quickly compare the stats of each blaster.

WEAPON STATS

Weapon	Image	Damage	Rate of Fire	Range	Cooling Power
A280C					
CA-87					
DH-17					
DL-44					
DLT-19					
E-11					
EE-3					
RT-97C					
SE-14C					
T-21					
T-21B					

STAR CARD HAND SELECTION

Before starting a Battle mission, you are given the chance to select your Star Card Hand. Each mission presents two unique presets that have been put together exclusively for that map. This allows you to play with Star Cards that you may not have unlocked to that point. If preferred, you may also use your customized Multiplayer Hand. Note that when you die in a Battle mission, you are not given a chance to change Star Card Hands, so choose wisely at the start. The following table briefly describes each Star Card offered in the presets.

STAR CARD PRESETS

Star Card	Image	Description
Barrage		Fires three explosive grenades that explode on impact. Great against groups of infantry.
Bowcaster		Charge-up bolt launcher that fires up to five explosive shots in a horizontal arc.
Cooling Cell		Immediately resets Heat on your weapon, allowing for extended use.
Cycler Rifle		The bullet from this rifle penetrates shields and can kill in one shot. Unlike the blasters, this gun suffers from bullet drop, so consider that when firing from distance. Take out jumptroopers immediately with this high-powered weapon.
Explosive Shot		Shots temporarily explode on contact.
Focus Fire		Activate this ability to greatly increase accuracy.
Homing Shot		Shot that homes in on its target from afar.
Impact Grenade		This high-powered explosive detonates on impact, so be sure there is distance between you and your target. Use against tougher foes or a small group.
Jump Pack		Very useful equipment for most locations. It is required to reach many of the collectibles and offers access to otherwise inaccessible locations. It also comes in handy when you must quickly flee a dangerous spot.
Personal Shield		Protects you from blaster fire for a short period. Use when overwhelmed or when firing a weapon that requires more time.
Pulse Cannon		Charge up your shots with this rifle for a powerful attack.
Scan Pulse		Scans all around you, detecting enemy locations even if they are behind cover. This is an incredibly beneficial Star Card to have in any situation.
Thermal Detonator		A high-damage timed grenade that is extremely effective against groups of infantry. Useless against vehicles.

HUD

The area around the outside of the HUD displays important information on your current progress. A damage indicator pops up whenever you are hit. Power-ups and pick-ups are shown as they come into range. The score for each side is given at the top of the screen, on each side of the elapsed time. Note that tokens are indicated on the scanner as white dots.

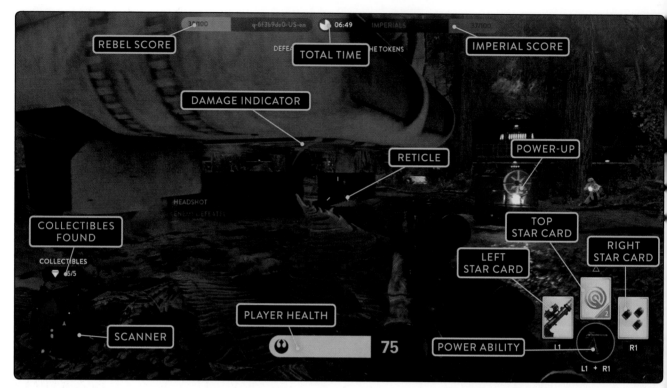

REBEL SCORE

TOTAL TIME

IMPERIAL SCORE

DAMAGE INDICATOR

RETICLE

POWER-UP

COLLECTIBLES FOUND

TOP STAR CARD

RIGHT STAR CARD

LEFT STAR CARD

PLAYER HEALTH

SCANNER

POWER ABILITY

AI OPPOSITION

Each team is filled with AI infantry, though you can disable this by turning off Friendly AI Soldiers when selecting your faction. As your score increases, the types of enemies introduced become more challenging. The following tables show how many of each type make up your opposition as your points increase. jumptroopers and heavytroopers are both worth five points, while all other AI gives two points. A human player is worth five points in a normal battle with Friendly AI enabled or 20 points otherwise.

Score	0	10+	25+	50+	70+	80+
AI agents with blaster rifle	2	3	2	6	6	8
AI agents with blaster pistol	2	1	1	0	2	2
AI agents with sniper rifle	1	2	2	0	2	0
AI agents with rocket launcher	0	2	2	2	0	0
AI agents with heavy blaster rifle	0	0	1	1	2	0
AI agents with Jump Pack	0	0	0	1	0	2

ENEMY COMPOSITION BASED ON PLAYER'S SCORE ON HARD OR MASTER DIFFICULTY

Score	0	10+	25+	50+	70+	80+
AI agents with blaster rifle	2	5	3	2	2	10
AI agents with blaster pistol	2	1	1	0	4	0
AI agents with sniper rifle	1	2	2	2	4	0
AI agents with rocket launcher	0	2	2	4	0	0
AI agents with heavy blaster rifle	0	0	2	2	4	0
AI agents with Jump Pack	0	0	0	2	0	4

THE HEROES

Heroes are extremely powerful, with the ability to obliterate squads of infantry with ease. Some excel at going on the offensive, while others may be better served in a supporting role. Try out all six to find your favorite.

ZOOM (AIM ASSIST)/LOCK ON TO YOUR TARGET

Some heroes have an extra ability attached to the Zoom button, such as Boba Fett's jetpack and Darth Vader's Saber Defense. In these instances, use the Melee Attack button to zoom in or lock on to a target.

LUKE SKYWALKER ABILITIES

Ability Name	Button	Description
Force Push	Left Card Ability	Push enemies away, causing damage to those knocked down.
Heavy Strike	Top Card Ability	Deal a Heavy Strike that is ideal against groups.
Saber Rush	Right Card Ability	Leap forward with a strong attack.
Saber Defense	Zoom (Hold)	Use the lightsaber to deflect blaster bolts back at the target. Keep your defense up between attacks whenever shots are incoming.
Saber Strike	Fire	Strike with the lightsaber.

HAN SOLO ABILITIES

Ability Name	Button	Description
Shoulder Charge	Left Card Ability	Put shoulder down for a dash melee attack.
Rapid Fire	Top Card Ability	Quickly pull the trigger while rapid fire is active.
Lucky Shot	Right Card Ability	Charge up for a strong area of efect attack. This is great against vehicles but doesn't really help here.
Aim	Zoom (Hold)	Use the zoom ability, just like regular soldiers.
Modified DL44	Fire	Fire the blaster pistol.

PRINCESS LEIA ABILITIES

Ability Name	Button	Description
Trooper Bane	Left Card Ability	Perform one-hit kills for a short time.
Enhanced Squad Shield	Top Card Ability	Use a stronger squad shield.
Supply Drop	Right Card Ability	Spawn a power-up just in front of Leia. This is not much use without other players to take advantage of the item.
Aim	Zoom (Hold)	Use the zoom ability, just like regular soldiers.
E11 Blaster Rifle	Fire	Fire the blaster rifle.

DARTH VADER ABILITIES

Ability Name	Button	Description
Force Choke	Left Card Ability	Choke current target for an instant kill.
Heavy Strike	Top Card Ability	Perform a strong charging group lightsaber attack. Use this against small packs to wipe them out with one swing of your weapon.
Saber Throw	Right Card Ability	Throw your lightsaber at distant enemies. You can take out multiple foes with a well-placed toss. Click the Melee Attack button to lock on to your target.
Saber Defense	Zoom (Hold)	Use the lightsaber to deflect blaster bolts back at the target. Keep defense up between attacks whenever shots are incoming.
Saber Strike	Fire	Strike with the lightsaber.

EMPEROR PALPATINE ABILITIES

Ability Name	Button	Description
Chain Lightning	Left Card Ability	This powerful, long-range lightning attack chains between nearby enemies. It is highly effective against groups of Rebels.
Imperial Resources	Top Card Ability	Spawns a hero health pick-up just in front of Palpatine. Grab one immediately if your health is down, or save it for later.
Force Dash	Right Card Ability	Perform a quick, twisting leap to escape cornering or close ground on a target in a hurry.
Block	Zoom (Hold)	Use your hands to block blaster shots, greatly reducing damage taken.
Force Lightning	Fire	Perform a short-range lightning strike. Hold to continually stream lightning from fingertips. The white meter drains until the ability must recharge.

BOBA FETT ABILITIES

Ability Name	Button	Description
Wrist Rocket	Left Card Ability	Launch a rocket at your foes. Take to the skies, and rain explosives down on unsuspecting soldiers.
Flame Thrower	Right Card Ability	Shoot a powerful burst of flame that scorches anyone within range.
Jetpack	Zoom	Use a jetpack to ascend into the air. Hold to remain in flight, where you can use all weapons. A meter above the health bar represents remaining fuel. If it gets completely depleted, descend to the ground and allow it to recharge.
EE3 Blaster Rifle	Fire	Fire the blaster rifle. Click the Melee Attack button to lock on to your target.

E-WEB BLASTERS

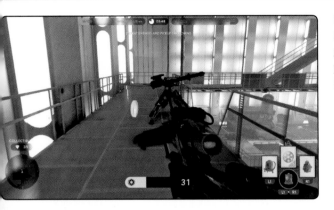

E-Web blasters are found throughout the various locations in Battle mode. These stationary weapons are effective against groups of soldiers, though you are vulnerable to flanking when you use them. Note that these are unusable in Hero Battles because heroes cannot man them.

COLLECTING TOKENS

POINT VALUE FOR TOKENS

Enemy Type	Points
Human player (normal battle without AI/Hero Battle with or without AI)	20
Human player (normal battle with AI)	5
Jumptroopers and Heavytroopers	5
All other AI soldiers	2

When a soldier or hero is killed, a token is dropped from the body. In order to score points, you must collect this item before it disappears or another player gets it. Grabbing a friendly token keeps your opponent from scoring. Rebels drop yellow circles, while the Imperial fighters release squares. A token slowly shrinks until it disappears. On Normal difficulty, this takes 20 seconds; Hard or Master only gives you 10 seconds until it is gone.

Note that AI players do not actually pick up tokens. Instead, they only score if you are unable to get the token before it disappears. Tokens are shown on the scanner as white dots.

You cannot score if you do not go after the tokens, but sometimes it is wise to stay back and avoid moving into a slaughter. Remember that the closer you take down enemies, the quicker you can pick up the tokens. Keep this in mind when deciding where to take on the opposition.

POWER-UPS

Regular battles offer power-ups, randomly located at specific areas around the four maps. These items respawn after a set amount of time, so it is worth learning these locations well. The following table lists the possible power-ups, along with a brief description.

Power-up	Image	Description
Blaster Cannon		Stationary blaster that can be placed anywhere there is space. Operates just like the E-Web blasters.
Infantry Turret		Automated defense that targets infantry. It remains active until destroyed.
Orbital Strike		An artillery barrage that rains destruction on a chosen outdoor location. Aim your shot until the blue reticle lines up with the desired target, and then fire. An aware enemy has time to move out of the way, though. Great against a mob of soldiers.
Proximity Bomb		Detonates when anyone gets too close. A beeping sound alerts you when one is approached.
Smart Rocket		This powerful rocket/missile hybrid locks on to vehicles but can also be quick fired against infantry.
Squad Shield		Activate this shield to put up a small circular shield for 90 seconds. Anyone inside cannot shoot out, but it does block blasters, explosions, grenades, and Cycler rifles. Friend or foe can destroy the transmitter that projects the shield.
Thermal Imploder		An extremely high-damage grenade with a big area of effect. Be careful that you don't end up in the explosion yourself.

CHARGE AND HERO HEALTH PICK-UPS

In regular battles, Charge pick-ups offer an additional use of your Charged Star Card. Hero health pick-ups spawn around the battlefield in Hero Battles; collect them to recover a small amount of health. These items respawn after a set amount of time, so learn the locations well, as they may become a necessity.

COLLECTIBLES

ach battle mission contains five collectibles hidden around the environment. They can e floating against the bright sky, deep in a cave, against a cliff, and even outside map oundaries. Many are located too high for a conventional hop, requiring a Jump Pack r Boba Fett's jetpack to reach them. Boba Fett is invaluable when you are collectible unting because he can ascend into the air and get a great aerial view at almost any me. If you plan to spend some time looking for these items, it is best to turn off the riendly AI option. Otherwise, your opponent may build a decent lead before you are eady to fight. Refer to the following Map sections for all 40 collectible locations.

STARS

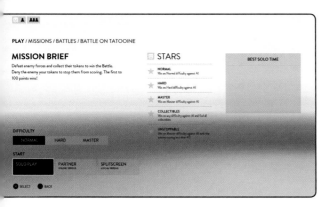

In Battle mode, 20 stars are up for grabs: five for each of the four maps in both regular and Hero Battles. Winning on Master difficulty against AI, collecting all five collectibles, and limiting your opponent to fewer than 40 points earns all five stars at once. Note that completing a battle on Hard or Master difficulty earns the easier stars, as well.

OFF TO A GOOD START

| TROPHY: BRONZE | GAMER SCORE: 15 |

Win any battle mission on Normal difficulty CPU. Play a solo game of Battle on Normal difficulty and win.

IMPRESSIVE. MOST IMPRESSIVE

| TROPHY: BRONZE | GAMER SCORE: 15 |

Earn a total of five stars from battle missions. Any five of the 20 stars works toward this goal. Completing a map on a higher difficulty earns the stars for the lower difficulties.

BATTLE ON HOTH

MISSION BRIEF

Defeat enemy forces and collect their tokens to win the battle. Deny the enemy your tokens to stop them from scoring.
The first to 100 points wins!

Star Card Presets

HUNTER

Charged Star Card
Focus Fire

Star Card 1
Jump Pack

Star Card 2
Cycler Rifle

DEMOLITIONS

Charged Star Card
Personal Shield

Star Card 1
Thermal Detonator

Star Card 2
Barrage

HOTH

COLLECTIBLES ①

BELOW ▽

Collectibles

① From the start point, turn left and climb to the top of the cliff. A collectible rests on the left side of the plateau.

2 Find the high hilltop that sits above the big cave. Climb to the peak to find a collectible.

3 Look for the narrow entrance to the main cave, located not too far away from the tall tank. Just before you reach the cavern, find a collectible tucked into the side of the tunnel.

4 Find the tall tank connected to an Imperial shuttle above. Another collectible is hiding behind some nearby boulders.

5 A big hole in the middle of the map leads down into the big cavern. Move to the high side of the opening, and search between the rocks for a collectible.

Hoth's snowy, rocky environment offers very long sightlines with high vantage points. A good marksman can have a field day from the high cliffs around the map. Be ready to quickly run down the tokens after picking soldiers off from afar, especially on Hard or Master.

The two Star Card Hand options offer two greatly differing play styles. Hunter includes a Jump Pack, which allows you to reach higher locations quickly and escape danger in a pinch. Settle into one of the great vantage points of Hoth, activate Focus Fire, and dispatch enemies from afar with the Cycler rifle and long-range blaster. Don't forget that you must collect points from the downed soldiers in order to score. Demolitions is more about total destruction. Direct your Thermal Detonator and Barrage at groups of infantry to quickly rack up a high kill count. Equip a high-rate of fire, high-damage blaster, activate the Personal Shield, and clear out any remaining foes as you collect the tokens.

HERO BATTLE ON HOTH

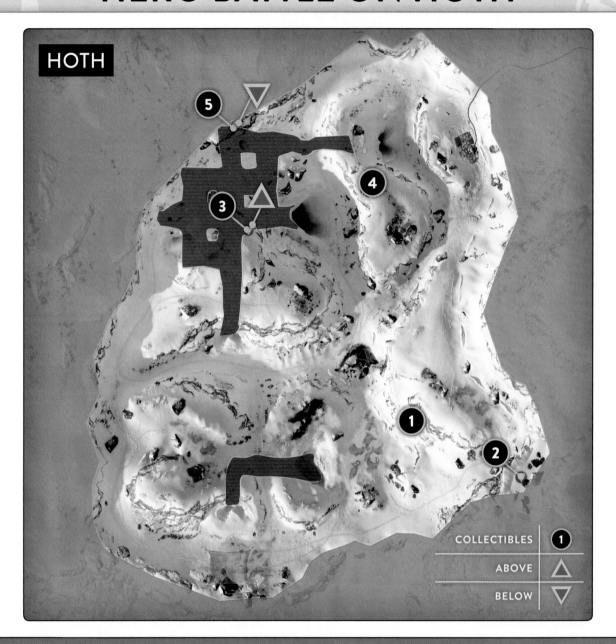

HOTH

COLLECTIBLES	1
ABOVE	△
BELOW	▽

LOCATION: HOTH

MISSION BRIEF

Defeat enemy forces and collect their tokens to win the battle. Deny the enemy your tokens to stop them from scoring.
The first to 100 points wins!

Collectibles

1 From the start of the mission, run straight ahead and spot the TIE fighter wreckage on the left. Scale the cliff to the right of the debris to find a collectible resting on the side of the mountain.

2 From the start of the mission, climb to the very top of the cliff ahead. A collectible lies just inside the map boundary.

3 Fly up to the high peak in the middle of the map to find a collectible sitting out in the open.

4 An E-Web stationary blaster sits on a plateau between a big hole in the ground and the tall tank. Climb up one ledge to find this collectible hiding behind a big rock.

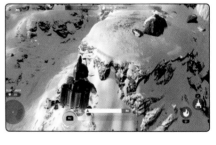

With his jetpack and Wrist Rockets, Boba Fett excels at the vast, mountainous terrain of Hoth, flying up and down the hilly terrain with ease. Take him into the caves, and his Flame Thrower scorches anyone inside. Han Solo and Princess Leia can also enjoy some good target practice on this map, especially combined with the Rapid Fire and Trooper Bane abilities, respectively.

5 Descend into the big cavern and search behind a large stalagmite. You can find this collectible between the two E-Web blasters.

BATTLE ON TATOOINE

MISSION BRIEF

Defeat enemy forces and collect their tokens to win the battle. Deny the enemy your tokens to stop them from scoring.
The first to 100 points wins!

Star Card Presets

GRENADIER

Star Card 1
Bowcaster

Charged Star Card
Explosive Shot

Star Card 2
Impact Grenade

ESCAPIST

Star Card 1
Jump Pack

Charged Star Card
Personal Shield

Star Card 2
Barrage

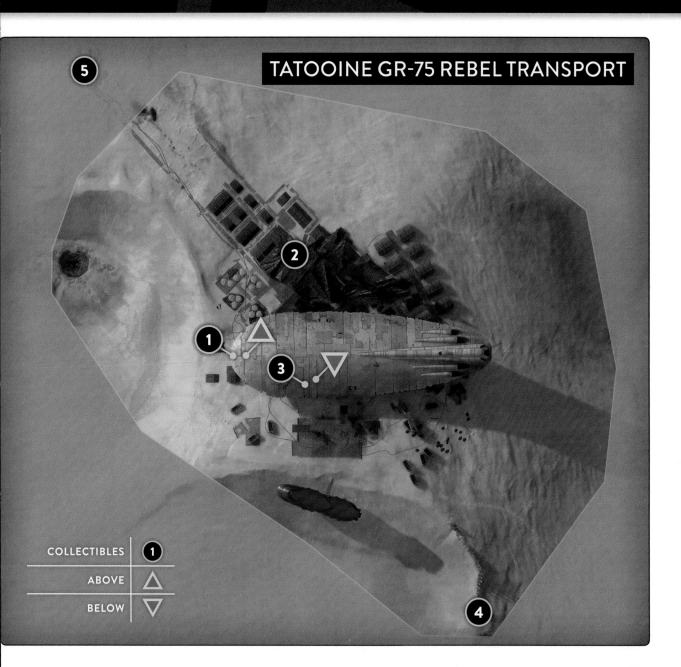

TATOOINE GR-75 REBEL TRANSPORT

COLLECTIBLES	1
ABOVE	△
BELOW	▽

Collectibles

1 From the start, take the steps ahead to the metal walkway, and then boost onto the GR-75 Rebel transport. Resting at the front of the ship is a collectible, unobtainable without a Jump Pack.

2 From the first collectible, hop off the other side of the ship onto the green tarp. Drop down to the lower level to snag another one.

3 Underneath the transport, another collectible is tucked into a narrow gap behind the computers.

4 Off one side of the map, near the sail barge, rests a skull and spine of a krayt dragon. Find a collectible lying next to the bones.

5 From the sail barge, head to the opposite side of the map. This collectible is found just out of bounds. Quickly grab it, and then get back in play before the timer counts all the way down.

A GR-75 medium transport, ready for loading, dominates the map in Battle on Tatooine. Equipment litters the central area, providing all kinds of cover with multiple distinct lanes that offer decent lines of sight. Open desert terrain surrounds the outside of the map. AI opponents do not chase too far, so you can do some sniping from the map boundaries. With a Jump Pack equipped, you can get on top of the transport and pick off foes from a nice vantage point. Don't expect it to last too long, though, as they start hiding beneath the ship.

The Escapist and Grenadier Star Card Hands offer options without much in common. The former is all about blowing things up. If you like destruction, this is the hand for you. Obliterate incoming infantry with three deadly weapons to choose from. The latter choice provides a Jump Pack for quick exits, which is great when things get a little overwhelming. Throw down a barrage of grenades and activate the shield for a clean getaway. This hand is essential when you are pursuing the collectibles, as one sits high on the top of the transport.

HERO BATTLE ON TATOOINE

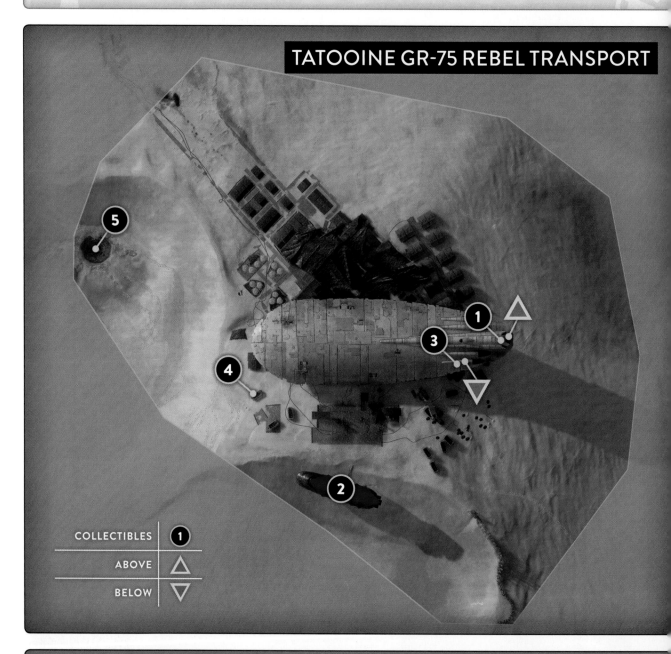

TATOOINE GR-75 REBEL TRANSPORT

COLLECTIBLES	1
ABOVE	△
BELOW	▽

LOCATION: TATOOINE GR-75 REBEL TRANSPORT

MISSION BRIEF

Defeat enemy forces and collect their tokens to win the battle. Deny the enemy your tokens to stop them from scoring.
The first to 100 points wins!

Collectibles

1 Fly onto the transport ship, and head all the way to the back to find the collectible sitting behind the command pod.

2 A sail barge is parked at one end of the map, near the krayt dragon bones. Underneath the vessel sits a collectible; run around the ship to snag it.

3 Directly underneath the tail of the transport ship, look inside a small carrier for the collectible hiding inside.

4 Under the rear of the transport sits a pile of small carriers. A collectible sits inside one, hiding out of sight from anyone without a jetpack.

5 From the rear of the transport, turn out to the desert, and then look down the hill to the right to spot the Great Pit of Carkoon. Another collectible floats above the hole. Use Boba Fett's jetpack to collect the prize. Don't worry: the sarlacc will not emerge from its home.

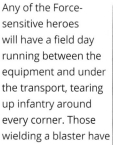

Any of the Force-sensitive heroes will have a field day running between the equipment and under the transport, tearing up infantry around every corner. Those wielding a blaster have plenty of cover, with decent sightlines to infantry spawn points. Boba Fett is essential when hunting for collectibles—one floats above a sarlacc pit, and another sits high on the back of the transport.

BATTLE ON ENDOR

LOCATION: ENDOR EMPIRE BASE

MISSION BRIEF

Defeat enemy forces and collect their tokens to win the battle. Deny the enemy your tokens to stop them from scoring.
The first to 100 points wins!

Star Card Presets

SCOUT

Charged Star Card
Scan Pulse

Star Card 1
Homing Shot

Star Card 2
Barrage

WOOKIEE

Charged Star Card
Personal Shield

Star Card 1
Bowcaster

Star Card 2
Impact Grenade

ENDOR EMPIRE BASE

COLLECTIBLES | 1

Collectibles

1. From the start, search between the computers on the right to find the first collectible.

2 From the start, exit the base and head right. Follow the trail around to the right until you reach a fork in the path. A collectible rests in the grass nearby.

3 From the previous collectible, cut under or over the landing pad and find the hollowed-out log. A collectible sits behind a tree on the other side.

4 Head to the second floor of the base, on the opposite side from where the mission starts. Enter the rightmost hallway to find a collectible.

5 Find the tank that sits behind the Imperial shuttles. A collectible rests between it and the wall.

two-story, U-shaped base surrounds an Imperial shuttle landing pad, and dense Endor forest adds variety to one end of the map. he base hallways make for some exciting gunfights, while the second-floor balconies offer nice lines of sight against infantry as they ove from one side of the map to the other. Remember, though, that you are just as vulnerable when you go after their tokens.

he Scout and Wookiee Star Card Hands both offer some serious firepower in the Star Cards, combined with an extremely useful harged Star Card. Scan Pulse comes in handy when you are not sure what may be around the next corner, while Personal Shield is reat in combination with Bowcaster as you try to line up the perfect shot. The Jump Pack is not available on this map with either hand reset; fortunately, you don't need it to get any of the collectibles.

HERO BATTLE ON ENDOR

ENDOR EMPIRE BASE

COLLECTIBLES | 1

LOCATION: ENDOR EMPIRE BASE

MISSION BRIEF

Defeat enemy forces and collect their tokens to win the battle. Deny the enemy your tokens to stop them from scoring.
The first to 100 points wins!

Collectibles

1 From the spawn point, move up to the second floor and go out the far left door. A collectible floats above the ledge on the left.

2 From the starting point, exit the base and head right. Just beyond the last door, a collectible rests on a rock ledge high above. Use Boba Fett's jetpack to nab it.

3 Move over to the front Imperial shuttle, and fly onto the left side to gain another collectible that sits just inside the folded wing.

4 From the third collectible, head to the forest area, left of the landing pad. A collectible sits atop the hollowed-out log.

5 Enter the base, opposite from where you started. Head upstairs and find the back room, where the Empire has set up some kind of power generator. A collectible rests on the fourth pylon on the right. Extremely narrow ledges run around each one, so you can hop from one pylon to the next until you reach the item. You can also grab it with the jetpack, but you do take damage when you drop to the floor, so fly carefully.

Boba Fett can fly between the base second floor and the courtyard with ease, and his jetpack is required to reach a few of the collectibles. The open outdoor area is ideal for Han Solo's long-distance fighting, while Darth Vader's and Luke Skywalker's lightsaber prowess makes quick work of infantry as they pour down the narrow hallways.

BATTLE ON SULLUST

LOCATION: SULLUST EMPIRE AT-AT HANGAR

MISSION BRIEF

*Defeat enemy forces and collect their tokens to win the battle. Deny the enemy your tokens to stop them from scoring.
The first to 100 points wins!*

Star Card Presets

ELITE

Charged Star Card
Focus Fire

Star Card 1
Jump Pack

Star Card 2
Pulse Cannon

MERCENARY

Charged Star Card
Cooling Cell

Star Card 1
Jump Pack

Star Card 2
Impact Grenade

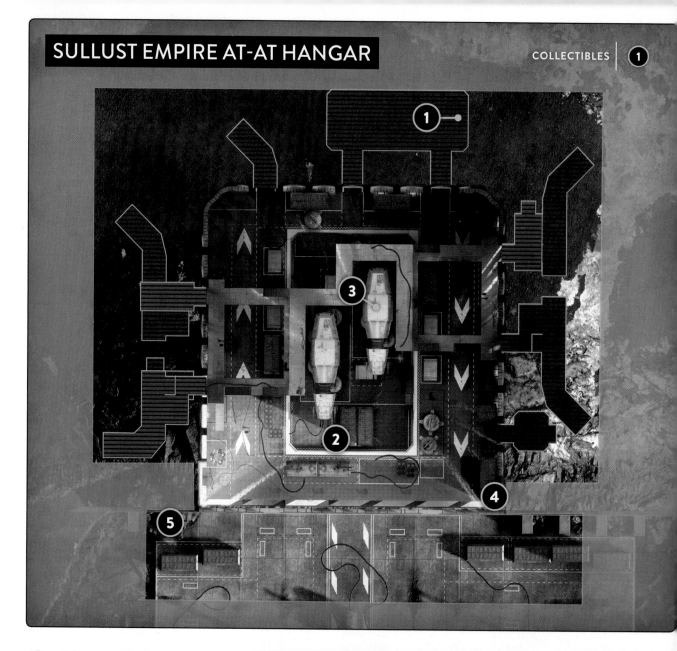

Collectibles

1 Enter the right doorway behind the AT-ATs, and grab the collectible that sits between the computers on the right.

2 Hop down into the AT-AT pit and search around the boxes in front of the left walker to find a collectible.

3 Climb to the top walkway and jump onto the back of the right AT-AT (from the perspective of someone looking into the hangar).

4 Just inside the hangar on the right as you look inside, a collectible hides in the shadow of a cargo container.

5 Exit the hangar and make a right. Boost onto the upper container and turn toward the building, where a collectible rests on the right pillar. Activate the Jump Pack to reach it.

A huge, four-story AT-AT hangar delivers some exciting vertical battles around the two walkers parked inside. Metal walkways surround the machines at every level, which means that attacks can come from anywhere; stay alert. Doors branch off the first three floors in nearly every direction, creating numerous locations to hide out in. Good marksmen have numerous sniper locations to choose from, with long sight lines.

Both Star Card options include the Jump Pack, which is good because this vertical map is ideal for vertical movement. Plus, you need the ability to get all of the collectibles. Elite is a sniper's hand, with the Pulse Cannon and the increased accuracy of Focus Fire. Mercenary offers the explosive power of the Impact Grenade with Cooling Cell, which gives you extended use of your blaster without fear of overheating.

HERO BATTLE ON SULLUST

SULLUST EMPIRE AT-AT HANGAR

COLLECTIBLES | 1

LOCATION: SULLUST EMPIRE AT-AT HANGAR

MISSION BRIEF

Defeat enemy forces and collect their tokens to win the battle. Deny the enemy your tokens to stop them from scoring.
The first to 100 points wins!

Collectibles

1 The first collectible is visible in the mission intro. At the start, immediately turn around and grab the item.

2 A collectible rests on the head of the left AT-AT (from the perspective of someone looking into the hangar). To get it, hop from the upper walkway or fly up there with Boba Fett's jetpack.

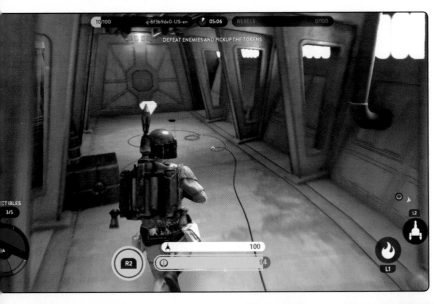

3 Enter the left door at the back of the hangar, and follow the corridor back to find a collectible.

4 Two containers are stacked against the back wall behind the left AT-AT. Boost to the top to grab a collectible.

5 Exit the hangar and make an immediate left. Fly up to the second pillar to grab the final collectible.

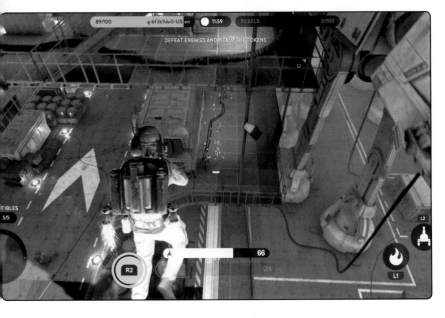

Boba Fett's ability to fly between the walkways makes him invaluable when fighting in the hangar. Furthermore, you need his jetpack to get all of the collectibles. The surrounding hallways are great for melee heroes, but most of the battles seem to take place inside the garage. Deadeyes can take position on an AT-AT as Princess Leia or Han Solo and pick off infantry as they climb their way up.

SURVIVAL

NUMBER OF PLAYERS: SOLO PLAY, ONLINE PARTNER CO-OP, LOCAL SPLITSCREEN CO-OP

OBJECTIVE: DEFEAT 15 WAVES OF INCREASINGLY MORE DIFFICULT IMPERIAL FORCES.

HOW TO GET STARS

Name	Condition
Normal	Complete on Normal difficulty.
Hard	Complete on Hard difficulty.
Master	Complete on Master difficulty.
No Deaths	Complete on Master difficulty without spending a life.
Collectibles	Complete on any difficulty and find all collectibles.

ITEM DROPS

Item	Available after waves...
Drop Pod	2, 5, 8, 11, 14
Life Pick-up	3, 6, 9, 12
Charge Pick-up	1, 4, 7, 10, 13

Survival mode pits one or two players against waves of Imperial troopers, Probe Droids, and AT-STs. To complete the mission, you must defeat 15 increasingly challenging waves of enemies. The action takes place across four maps, one for each planet.

Your objective is to simply survive while eliminating all Imperial forces. After a wave is complete, a timer counts down to another set of enemies, which gradually becomes tougher as the mission goes on. This gives you time to collect items and set up for the next onslaught.

DIFFICULTY

There are three difficulties in Survival: Normal, Hard, and Master. As the difficulty increases, enemies become stronger and tougher to take down. Normal has a separate enemy composition than Hard and Master. Adversaries are introduced gradually, and the easier the difficulty is, the more time you have to react to the incoming threats.

WEAPON SELECTION

When selecting between the 11 blasters, consider the type of environment where the fighting will take place. If longer lines of sight are available against the incoming forces, pick a long-range rifle. If taking the action inside the narrow corridors, then go with a higher rate of fire or damage. The following table allows you to quickly compare the stats of each blaster.

WEAPON STATS

Weapon	Image	Damage	Rate of Fire	Range	Cooling Power
A280C					
CA-87					
DH-17					
DL-44					
DLT-19					
E-11					
EE-3					
RT-97C					
SE-14C					
T-21					
T-21B					

STAR CARD HAND SELECTION

Before starting a Survival mission, you are allowed to select between two preset Star Card Hands. These hands, made up of the usual two Star Cards and a Charged Star Card, offer up two alternate ways to load out your character. Earn all five stars for a mission to unlock your customized Multiplayer Hand for that mission. This allows you to use any Star Cards that you have unlocked through Multiplayer. The following table briefly describes each Star Card offered in the presets.

STAR CARD PRESETS

Star Card	Image	Description
Barrage		Fires three explosive grenades that explode on impact. Great against groups of infantry.
Bowcaster		Charge-up bolt launcher that fires up to five explosive shots in a horizontal arc. Use against Imperial forces as they charge your location, especially if they are lined up side-by-side.
Cooling Cell		Immediately resets Heat on your weapon, allowing for extended use.
Cycler Rifle		The bullet from this rifle penetrates shields and can kill in one shot. Unlike the blasters, this gun suffers from bullet drop, so consider that when firing from distance. Take out jumptroopers immediately with this high-powered weapon.
Focus Fire		Activate this ability to greatly increase accuracy.
Impact Grenade		This high-powered explosive detonates on impact, so be sure there is distance between you and your target. Use against tougher foes or a small group.
Ion Grenade		Explosive that offers an Ion, anti-vehicle detonation. Aim carefully against AT-STs and Probe Droids for maximum damage.
Ion Shot		Activate this Charged Star Card for a few seconds of Ion shots, which is great for machinery like the AT-ST.
Ion Torpedo		Locks on to Probe Droids and vehicles. This is the best option against the TIE fighters of Sullust since they can be locked on.
Jump Pack		Very useful equipment for most locations. It is required to reach many of the collectibles and offers access to otherwise inaccessible locations. It also comes in handy when you must quickly flee a dangerous spot.
Personal Shield		Protects you from blaster fire for a short period. Use when overwhelmed or when firing a weapon that requires more time.
Thermal Detonator		A high-damage timed grenade that is extremely effective against groups of infantry. Useless against vehicles.

HUD

The area around the outside of your HUD displays important information on your current progress. A damage indicator pops up whenever you are hit. Drop pods and available power-ups are shown as they come into range. This image points out the most important aspects of your HUD in a Survival mission.

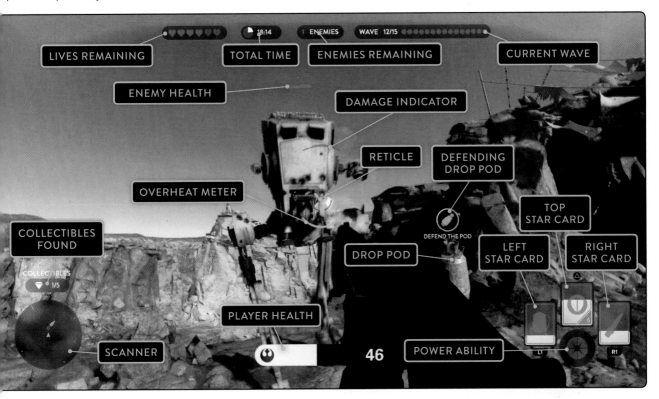

LIVES REMAINING · TOTAL TIME · ENEMIES REMAINING · CURRENT WAVE · ENEMY HEALTH · DAMAGE INDICATOR · RETICLE · DEFENDING DROP POD · OVERHEAT METER · TOP STAR CARD · COLLECTIBLES FOUND · DROP POD · LEFT STAR CARD · RIGHT STAR CARD · PLAYER HEALTH · POWER ABILITY · SCANNER

LIVES

You begin a Survival mission with two lives, as represented by the hearts at the top of the HUD. When you die, you must spend a life to return to the action at the point where you were taken out. Before resuming the mission, you can select a new weapon and hand (if desired). Life pick-ups become available at certain points during a mission, with the ability to have a maximum of six lives in reserve. Note that one star requires you to complete Master difficulty without spending a life. Also, be aware that the lives are shared when you play Co-op or Splitscreen.

ADMIRAL ACKBAR

WAVE 15 DONE

Pay to attention to the ramblings of Admiral Ackbar. He warns when enemies are nearby, when a drop pod is incoming, and when new Imperial forces are added. Use his information to plan ahead. Certain situations may require you to move to an alternate location or go after a power-up that has been left behind.

IMPERIAL FORCES

No matter the scenario, Imperial forces move toward your location for 15 waves of intense action. As you progress through the mission, tougher enemies are introduced in bigger numbers, making the rounds increasingly more challenging. Once a wave is complete, a timer counts down toward the next, and the wave indicator moves up one. The number of enemies remaining in a wave is shown in the top-center of your heads-up display. It is indicated as 10+ when there are 10 foes or more, and 5+ when five to nine opponents remain. Otherwise, the exact number of enemies is given. There are nine types of adversaries in all, each with its own unique weaponry and tactics. The enemies you face at each wave changes depending on the locale and difficulty chosen.

Troopers

There are six types of troopers who attack during a Survival mission. From stormtroopers and snowtrooopers to shadowtrooopers and scout troopers, the full gamut of ground forces tests your mettle. The following table lists these enemy types, along with the equipment they carry and a short note for each.

Enemy Type	Weapon(s)/Ability	Note
Stormtroopers / Snowtroopers	E-11 Blaster Rifle	Easily taken out with one shot. Not much of a threat, except in high numbers.
Stormtroopers with Smart Rockets	Smart Rocket	Just like stormtroopers but carry Smart Rockets, which means they fight from a distance.
Shocktroopers	DLT-19 Heavy Blaster	With a powerful weapon and tough armor, they require serious firepower to take down. As Imperial forces approach your position, focus fire on these troops. Use cover to minimize damage from their Heavy Blasters.
Jumptroopers	RT-97C Heavy Blaster, Personal Shield, Jet Pack	Cannot use Personal Shield and jet pack at the same time. Wait for one to rise into the air, and quickly take them out. They can become a nuisance if not dispatched quickly.
Shadowtrooper	T-21 Heavy Blaster and Flash Grenade	Not quite as tough as shocktroopers, but they still hold their ground. Their powerful heavy blaster can take you down quickly. Kill them before they get within range or from behind cover. Watch out for the Flash Grenade, which disorients you and makes you vulnerable.
Scout Trooper (Sniper)	A280C Heavy Blaster and Smoke Grenade (Blaster pistol at close range)	They fight from distance and frequently sidestep your shots. They use a Smoke Grenade to obscure your vision, switching to a blaster pistol when approached.

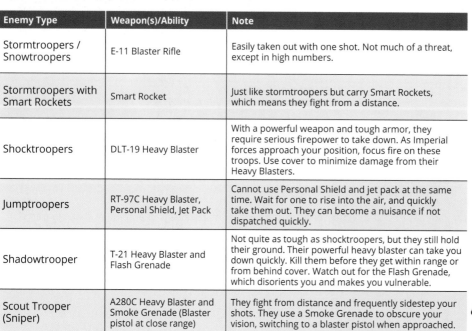

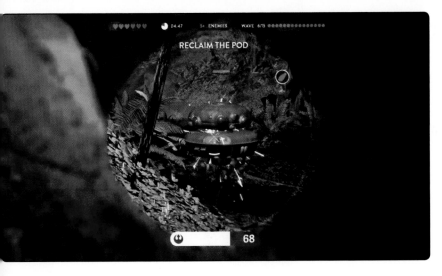

Probe Droids

The Viper Probe Droids are usually introduced in the early waves of a Survival mission. The recon droid gets fairly close and fires a weak blaster at the Rebels. These droids are extremely susceptible to Ion damage and explode when defeated. The resulting detonation can eliminate nearby enemies. Ion grenades are great for taking out a duo of droids. Blasters are relatively weak against these foes, but they eventually go down.

AT-STs

Keep an eye and ear out for incoming AT-STs. Admiral Ackbar always makes it a point to announce their arrival in your area. They are extremely tough to defeat and can take you out with ease. However, the bipedal machines cannot enter many areas, such as the tight corridors of Hoth or treetop villages of Endor. Use this to your advantage, and weed out the foot soldiers first. Then, you can concentrate your firepower on the big targets. Ion weapons, such as the Ion Grenade, Ion Shot, Ion Torpedo, and Vehicle Turret, are especially effective against them.

AT-STs typically make a solo appearance at first, but later waves may introduce two or three at a time. Never try to directly take on more than one, and be ready to flee the scene if you begin taking too much damage. The Jump Pack is great for putting quick distance between you and the enemy.

On Sullust, two turbolasers sit just outside of the hangar. These turrets fire powerful energy bursts that are extremely effective against AT-STs, but you must get them when they are within range of the turret. The guns have limited movement and have trouble reaching foes in certain areas.

TIE Fighters

In Survival on Sullust, TIE fighters are introduced to the fray. Ion weapons are most effective against these vehicles. Equip the Ion Torpedo Star Card to gain the ability to lock on to the flying machines. Turbolasers also work very well against them.

E-WEB BLASTERS AND TURBOLASERS

There are plenty of items to help the Rebels out, including turrets that have been placed in various positions around the four maps. The most popular is the E-Web stationary blaster, which is very effective against a big group of troopers. Watch your flank when operating the weapon, as you are vulnerable from the sides and rear. Although the turret has a shield, it does not stand up too long against enemy weapon fire.

In Survival on Sullust, two turbolaser turrets sit just outside the hangar. These are heavy, anti-vehicle laser cannons that work very well against AT-STs and TIE fighters. Fire ahead of the flying vehicles to take them down. Waiting until they fly straight out or toward your locations makes shooting them down much easier.

DROP PODS

Five times throughout each mission, Admiral Ackbar sends over some help for the Rebels. These escape pods turned treasure chests are dropped after waves 2, 5, 8, 11, and 14. Appearing on the map as soon as they crash down, the drop pods are vital to survival. There are five possible locations on each map, but you don't know in what order they will appear. Each pod contains three random power-ups, but you must first claim it, which takes some time to achieve.

To claim a drop pod, walk up to it and hold down the Use button until the pod icon turns blue. Now the circle outline around the icon turns blue, acting as a timer. After 40 uninterrupted seconds, the pod is claimed, and three power-ups pop out from the open door. An enemy may attempt to claim the pod during the 40-second timer. If he is successful, the icon turns red, and the timer resets. If you do not return to the pod and reclaim it before the red circle is complete, it is destroyed.

Things to note about the drop pods:

- An enemy will not claim a drop pod until you have started the process of claiming it yourself. Therefore, it is sometimes best to save it for later when fewer enemies can get between you and the loot.

- Once a pod has been successfully claimed, the power-ups pop out and remain there until you have collected them or the mission ends. This means that you can save the power-ups for the later, tougher waves. When playing a two-player game, communicate with your partner whenever you decide to go after a power-up.

- Only troopers can claim a pod, so if Probe Droids or AT-STs are all that remain, there is no threat to your resources.

Power-Ups

Most power-ups available in other modes of *Star Wars* Battlefront can appear from inside the drop pod. The following table lists the possible power-ups, along with a brief description.

Power-up	Description
Blaster Cannon	Stationary blaster that can be placed anywhere there is space. Operates just like the E-Web blasters.
Infantry Turret	Automated defense that targets infantry. It remains active until destroyed.
Orbital Strike	An artillery barrage that rains destruction on a chosen outdoor location. Aim your shot until the blue reticule lines up with the desired target, and then fire. An aware enemy has time to move out of the way, though. Great against a mob of soldiers.
Proximity Bomb	Drop the bomb near objectives or any location you want protected. It detonates when an enemy gets too close. A beeping sound alerts you when one is approached.
Smart Rocket	This powerful rocket/missile hybrid locks on to vehicles but can also be quickly fired against infantry.
Squad Shield	Activate this shield to put up a small circular shield for 90 seconds. Anyone inside cannot shoot out, but it does block blasters, explosions, and grenades. Friend or foe can destroy the transmitter that projects the shield.
Thermal Imploder	An extremely high-damage grenade with a big area of effect. Be careful that you don't end up in the explosion yourself.
Vehicle Turret	An automated defense that targets vehicles with Ion shots. It remains active until destroyed.

LIFE AND CHARGE PICK-UPS

To even the odds a bit, Life and Charge pick-ups drop at various times during your mission. Lives appear after waves 3, 6, 9, and 12. Charge pick-ups appear after waves 1, 4, 7, 10, and 13. A Life pick-up adds an extra life to your reserves, indicated at the top of the HUD. You can carry a maximum of six lives at one time. A Charge pick-up adds a charge to your Charge Star Card, giving you another use of the ability. No worries about collecting all of the Charges, as there is no limit. Once these pick-ups appear on the map, they remain until they are gathered or the mission ends.

GENERAL TIPS AND STRATEGIES

You can employ numerous strategies to defeat the 15 waves of Imperial forces, but success really comes down to the following: execute quick and accurate attacks, flee the action when health starts to get low, and avoid being surrounded. Here are a few more tips that can help in any Survival mission.

Go on the offensive. Check the radar often to get a good idea of where the Imperial forces are coming from. Use this information to go on the offensive, and try to flank their position. With two players, try surrounding their location and bombarding them with weapon fire.

Keep an eye on the radar, and avoid being surrounded. Glance at the radar often to get a good idea of where the Imperial forces are coming from. Avoid getting pinned against a wall with multiple access points for the enemy, as it becomes tougher to escape when surrounded on all sides. Corridors offer up a way to line up incoming adversaries and mow them down, but foes often split up and enter both sides of the hallway.

Location, location, location. When holding your ground against an enemy onslaught, pick your location wisely. Minimize their access points, and use turrets and explosives to assist in your defense. Keep an eye on the number of enemies remaining and the radar so you can continually reassess the situation.

Take advantage of all power-ups, pick-ups, Star Cards, and turrets. Claim drop pods when the opportunity arises to strengthen your arsenal. Use everything at your disposal to defeat the hordes of Imperial forces. Use your blaster on the weaker foes, such as the standard stormtroopers and snowtroopers, while saving your stronger weaponry for the well-armored soldiers, such as the shocktroopers and shadowtroopers. When you have reduced the opposition down to just AT-STs, use the provided cover to avoid direct hits while unloading Ion damage on the vehicle.

COLLECTIBLES

Each Survival mission contains five well-hidden collectibles. These white, diamond-shaped icons can be found anywhere around the environment; they can be floating against the bright sky, deep in a cave, against a cliff, and even outside map boundaries. Many float high in the air and require a Jump Pack to collect them, so keep that in mind when selecting your loadout. Refer to the following Map sections for all 20 locations.

STARS

The five stars listed in the table at the start of this chapter are available for each of the four maps. Completing the mission on Master difficulty without spending a life while picking up all five collectibles earns all five at once. Once five stars have been received, your customized Multiplayer Hand becomes available for that mission.

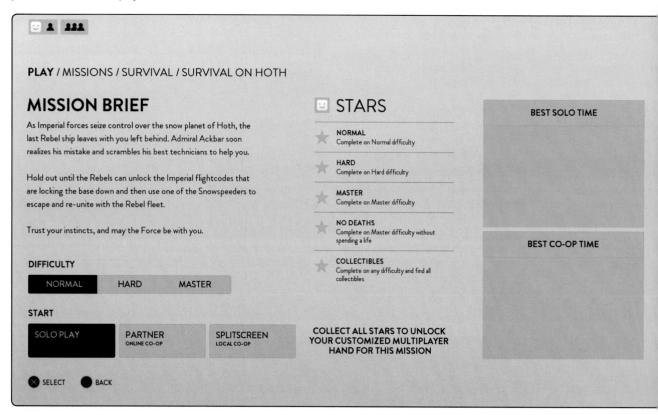

PLAY / MISSIONS / SURVIVAL / SURVIVAL ON HOTH

MISSION BRIEF

As Imperial forces seize control over the snow planet of Hoth, the last Rebel ship leaves with you left behind. Admiral Ackbar soon realizes his mistake and scrambles his best technicians to help you.

Hold out until the Rebels can unlock the Imperial flightcodes that are locking the base down and then use one of the Snowspeeders to escape and re-unite with the Rebel fleet.

Trust your instincts, and may the Force be with you.

DIFFICULTY

NORMAL | HARD | MASTER

START

SOLO PLAY | PARTNER ONLINE CO-OP | SPLITSCREEN LOCAL CO-OP

STARS

★ NORMAL
Complete on Normal difficulty

★ HARD
Complete on Hard difficulty

★ MASTER
Complete on Master difficulty

★ NO DEATHS
Complete on Master difficulty without spending a life

★ COLLECTIBLES
Complete on any difficulty and find all collectibles

COLLECT ALL STARS TO UNLOCK YOUR CUSTOMIZED MULTIPLAYER HAND FOR THIS MISSION

BEST SOLO TIME

BEST CO-OP TIME

✕ SELECT　⬤ BACK

SURVIVOR

TROPHY: BRONZE | **GAMER SCORE: 15**

Earn a total of five stars from Survival missions. Any five of the 20 stars works toward this goal. Completing a map on a higher difficulty earns the stars for the lower difficulties, as well.

ON THE BALL

TROPHY: BRONZE | **GAMER SCORE: 15**

Complete any Survival mission on Master difficulty within 25 minutes. Grab a partner and aggressively pursue the Imperial forces to complete the mission within this time limit.

ACKBAR'S ELITE

TROPHY: SILVER | **GAMER SCORE: 40**

Complete any Survival mission on Master difficulty without dying. Cranking the difficulty to Master is hard enough, but completing a mission without spending a life is quite tough. Get a partner, flank the Imperial forces' position, and do not get surrounded. Avoid going head-to-head with an AT-ST, especially if other enemies are nearby. Each level offers safer locations to fight, such as the Hoth corridors or Endor treetops. Use these areas, and be careful that your opponents do not flank your position.

SURVIVAL ON TATOOINE

After a daring escape from an Imperial attack, you find yourself stranded in a desolate canyon on Tatooine.

Admiral Ackbar has ordered a rescue operation, but the Imperial forces are rapidly closing in on your position. You must fight until help arrives.

May the Force be with you.

LOCATION: TATOOINE CANYON

ENEMY TYPES: STORMTROOPERS, SHOCKTROOPERS, AT-STS, JUMPTROOPERS, SCOUT TROOPERS, STORMTROOPERS WITH SMART ROCKET, SHADOWTROOPERS

Star Card Presets

RAIDER

Star Card 1
Barrage

Charged Star Card
Ion Shot

Star Card 2
Jump Pack

ANNIHILATOR

Star Card 1
Ion Torpedo

Charged Star Card
Personal Shield

Star Card 2
Jump Pack

TATOOINE CANYON

COLLECTIBLES	1
DROP POD	

Collectibles

1 The first collectible hangs in the air, high above the huts where the mission begins. Get onto the second level of the cliffs on the left, and turn around. Boost off the rock, using the Jump Pack to reach it.

75

2 You can see the second collectible from the beginning of the mission. High up in the air, it floats near the rock formation straight ahead from the starting point. To reach it, climb or jump onto the upper cliff on the other side of the collectible, and then use the Jump Pack to nab it.

3 Look for the tower with lines connected to the top. Hovering just above is the third collectible. Use your Jump Pack from the nearby cliff to score the item.

4 Find the high point on the far side of the map from the mission start, where tattered pieces of fabric hang from long lines of rope. Floating high above the low area between this point and the map boundary is another collectible. Fire the Jump Pack off the cliff toward the item to get it. Be careful that you do not fly off the map, or else you must wait for your Jump Pack to recharge so that you can get back up.

5 Head toward the Imperial shuttle, but instead of climbing up toward it, follow the middle path into a shallow cave. The final collectible is tucked tightly into the right corner.

After crash-landing in the rocky terrain of Tatooine, there isn't much time to get your bearings, because Imperial forces are hot on the trail of the Rebels. A rescue operation is incoming, but you must hold off the enemy until help arrives. You start out near an abandoned camp at the bottom of a deep canyon, surrounded by high cliffs.

Both Star Card preset options contain the Jump Pack, which is very useful when traversing the steep cliffs of Tatooine. It is also essential when you're hunting collectibles, since four of the five items float high in the air. Annihilator is best against vehicles. The Ion Torpedo allows for locking on to an AT-ST across the long distances of the canyon floor, and the Personal Shield keeps you safe from blaster fire while using the Ion weapon. Raider also gives an anti-vehicle option with the Ion Shot, pairing it up with Barrage, which is powerful against groups of infantry. Choosing your loadout comes down to preference.

There are a few semi-protected spots around the map. A shallow cave located below the parked Imperial shuttle offers fortification most of the way around, but escaping trouble is tough. A camp located at the far end from the mission start gives a nice vantage point with relative security. The canyon floor is extremely vulnerable from the cliffs above, so move quickly when this is your path of choice. Use this to your advantage when Imperial forces are located down below.

When moving around the high cliffs, be aware of the big drop-offs around the map boundary. If you end up falling off the side, it can be tough to get out, though the Jump Pack does make this possible. You have 10 seconds to get back into play. Stay calm, step back from the wall, and boost yourself back up with the Jump Pack. However, if you fall too far down, you must wait to be brought back, using one of your precious lives to do so.

Enemies equipped with long-range weapons, such as the scout troopers and stormtroopers with rockets, can be dangerous with the long sight lines in the canyon. Stay aware of your adversaries' locations, and quickly duck around a wall to avoid taking unnecessary damage. You can also use the cliff sides as cover, but be careful of flanking foes.

SURVIVAL ON SULLUST

A group of Rebels is sent into the heart of the Empire war machine, the lava planet of Sullust, in order to secure plans pivotal to the rebellion.

After successfully retrieving the documents, the group is compromised, with resulting heavy casualties. You must now hold out until help can arrive.

Good luck, and may the Force be with you.

LOCATION: SULLUST EMPIRE HANGAR

ENEMY TYPES: STORMTROOPERS, PROBE DROIDS, SHOCKTROOPERS, TIE FIGHTERS, AT-STS, SCOUT TROOPERS, JUMPTROOPERS, STORMTROOPERS WITH SMART ROCKET, SHADOWTROOPERS

Star Card Presets

MARKSMAN

Star Card 1
Cycler Rifle

Charged Star Card
Ion Shot

Star Card 2
Jump Pack

SOLDIER

Star Card 1
Ion Torpedo

Charged Star Card
Focus Fire

Star Card 2
Jump Pack

COLLECTIBLES   1

DROP POD

Collectibles

1   Inside the hangar, get on top of the Imperial shuttle, either by using a Jump Pack or the nearby steps. Just inside the right wing is a collectible.

2 As you look at the hangar, move to the far left side. A collectible rests against the uppermost cliff, on the same level as the hangar.

3 As you look at the hangar doorway, go right past a big tank, and search on the far side of the last concrete pillar.

4 Find a collectible resting on the rock plateau near the metal pedestrian bridge.

5 You must use a Jump Pack to reach this one, floating high above a lava pit to the right of the vehicle bridges. Aim your jump well so that you do not end up in the lava.

The planet of Sullust is comprised of sheets of lava rock, separated by narrow valleys and streams of hot lava. The map is made up of various levels that lead up to a big hangar containing an Imperial shuttle. Bridges and steps connect many of the tiers.

The Sullust Star Card options both include the Jump Pack, which is required to reach one of the collectibles. This also allows for easier movement around the planet's multi-leveled, rocky surface. Picking a preset comes down to preference. The Cycler Rifle gives you an occasional one-hit kill, shield-penetrating shot, while Focus Fire gives you improved accuracy—great when fighting distant foes from the upper cliff. The Ion Torpedo is the best option for dealing with the TIE fighters and can also be devastating against the AT-STs.

Much of the map sits below the hangar level, so the upper cliff has a nice vantage point. Find cover and pick off enemies as they stream in across the vehicle bridges. Troopers can hide from your sights by moving behind the rocky cliffs. When traversing the rocky terrain below, scan the area carefully; much of the location is extremely vulnerable to enemy fire.

A river of lava flows around the side and bottom of the map. If you fall in, the red-hot lava quickly eats away at your health. Immediately use your Jump Pack to boost out of there, or get ready to spend a life to return to the game.

An E-Web blaster sits at the back of the hangar and is relatively safe from vehicles. This gives you a nice location from which to mow down any infantry members that enter the building. However, be aware that you are fairly vulnerable from the sides. Scan the radar occasionally to spot incoming foes.

Unique to Sullust, TIE fighters patrol the skies above. Their familiar sound warns of incoming strafing runs. Any Ion weapon can damage the flying vehicle, but it can be tough to hit, unless you use the Ion Torpedo with the ability to lock on to its target.

Two turbolasers sit just outside the Imperial hangar. These anti-vehicle turrets work extremely well against AT-STs and TIE fighters. Aim just ahead of the speedy star fighter to hit it as it soars across the sky. This is a much easier target because it flies directly away from or toward the turret. The high-powered laser cannon does overheat, so watch the meter just below the reticle. While it can take quite a bit of abuse, it can also be destroyed. Take control of one, and its health bar displays in place of your own.

SURVIVAL ON ENDOR

Admiral Ackbar has ordered a series of dawn raids on the forest moon of Endor. As charges detonate, their rumbling sound marks the successful completion of your mission.

However, the noise also alerts Imperial forces that are now moving into position to intercept. You must now hold out against the Imperial troops and survive at all costs before Admiral Ackbar and the Rebel fleet can come to your rescue.

May the Force be with you.

LOCATION: ENDOR EWOK VILLAGE

ENEMY TYPES: STORMTROOPERS, SHOCKTROOPERS, PROBE DROIDS, SCOUT TROOPERS, JUMPTROOPERS, AT-STS, STORMTROOPERS WITH SMART ROCKET, SHADOWTROOPERS

Star Card Presets

STALKER

Charged Star Card
Personal Shield

Star Card 1
Bowcaster

Star Card 2
Ion Torpedo

SCOUNDREL

Charged Star Card
Ion Shot

Star Card 1
Ion Grenade

Star Card 2
Jump Pack

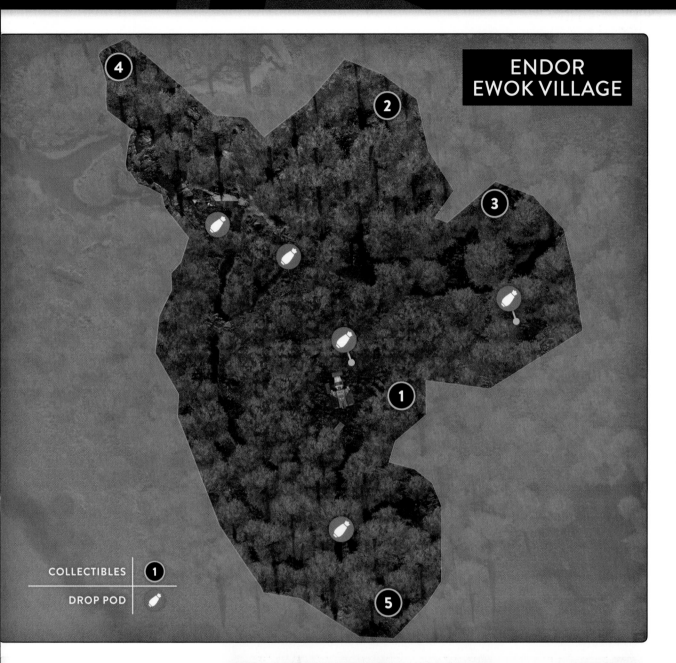

ENDOR EWOK VILLAGE

COLLECTIBLES | 1
DROP POD | 🔫

Collectibles

1 From the start, turn around and move up the hill past the sabotaged Imperial base and shuttle. Search behind the tree just beyond the tanks to find the first collectible.

2 Turn right from the start of the mission, and move under the Ewok village. Continue to the cliffs ahead to find a collectible sitting in a small clearing.

3 Turn right from the start of the mission, and move underneath the Ewok village. Head right to the cliff boundary, where another collectible sits in a clearing next to the outside of the map.

4 A destroyed AT-AT has come to rest toward one end of the Endor map. Starting from the Ewok village, run past the Imperial vehicle until you reach a narrowing of the map boundaries. Grab the collectible that floats above a puddle.

5 From the start of the mission, turn left and run to the far end of the map. Near the left cliffs rests another collectible, sitting out in the open. If you hug the perimeter of the map, you will run into it.

Set on the Forest Moon of Endor, much of this survival map is fairly wide open, despite the thicket of trees. You can usually use a tree or two to escape a foe's gunfire, but you are not safe for long.

The two Star Card Hands play quite differently, but they both offer up vehicle-ready firepower. Stalker's Ion Torpedo allows you to lock on to AT-STs at a distance. The Bowcaster works well in the wider openings of the forest against a line of approaching troopers, and the Personal Shield is great for protection as you charge the bolt launcher. Scoundrel provides two Ion weapons for use against the AT-STs and Probe Droids. You don't need the Jump Pack to get the collectibles, but it does allow access to the higher platforms in the Ewok village.

Putting your back against the boundary offers some protection from flanking Imperial forces, but most areas still offer wide openings to your location. Look for a narrow strip beyond the annihilated AT-AT. Its small opening is easy to defend, but if things get overwhelming, it can be difficult to escape. Watch for hollowed-out logs scattered around the forest. They provide a short respite from enemy fire, but they are few and far between.

The forest canopy above offers great vantage points. Use the provided ramps to reach the walkways and huts among the trees. Foot soldiers climb to this first level, but you can use a Jump Pack to reach even higher platforms. Imperial forces won't join you there, but there are many locations where they can hide from your gunfire. Weed out what you can, but you may have to drop down to finish the enemy off. If the AT-STs are too much for you, flee to the safety of the Ewok' village overhead, and bombard them with Ion Grenades.

The collectibles in Survival on Endor are all located around the outside of the map. Hug the entire perimeter, and you should find all five. Each one lies on the ground, so no Jump Pack is required. Adding to the ambiance of the map, Ewoks are active throughout the village. They run when approached or shot at, and they even drop rocks from above.

NOT BAD FOR A LITTLE FURBALL

TROPHY: BRONZE	GAMER SCORE: 15

Get hit in the head by a rock from an Ewok on Endor. Spend enough time underneath the Ewok village, and an Ewok eventually hits you.

SURVIVAL ON HOTH

As Imperial forces seize control over the snow planet of Hoth, the last Rebel ship leaves, with you left behind. Admiral Ackbar soon realizes his mistake and scrambles his best technicians to help you.

Hold out until the Rebels can unlock the Imperial flight codes that are locking the base down, and then use one of the Snowspeeders to escape and reunite with the Rebel fleet.

Trust your instincts, and may the Force be with you.

LOCATION: HOTH REBEL BASE

ENEMY TYPES: SNOWTROOPERS, PROBE DROIDS, SHOCKTROOPERS, JUMPTROOPERS, AT-STS, SHADOWTROOPERS, SCOUT TROOPERS

Star Card Presets

SURVIVOR

Star Card 1
Bowcaster

Charged Star Card
Ion Shot

Star Card 2
Impact Grenade

ROGUE

Star Card 1
Barrage

Charged Star Card
Cooling Cell

Star Card 2
Thermal Detonator

HOTH REBEL BASE

COLLECTIBLES ①
DROP POD 🔋

Collectibles

① From the start of the mission, turn around and enter the doorway in the back corner of the hangar. Follow the corridor back to a dead end to find the first collectible.

2 Enter the hangar through the main doorway, and run past the X-wing. Turn right between the big hexagonal storage containers and the computer. Make a quick left, and search behind the boxes for another collectible.

3 Inside the hangar, move behind the Snowspeeder and search inside the small personnel transport. The next collectible sits inside.

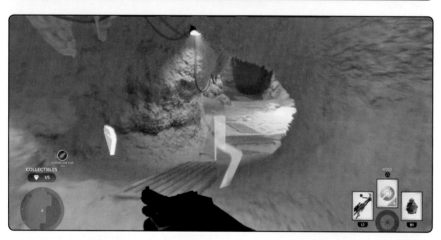

4 Enter the corridors on the left side of the hangar. This collectible rests inside the far hallway that runs parallel with the hangar.

5 From inside the hangar, head upstairs and enter the right door. Continue into the laboratory on the right to find a collectible.

recently confiscated Rebel base is the setting for Survival on Hoth. A hangar provides long sight lines to the blast doors, along with ght, narrow corridors on each side. These tunnels connect to the main area through multiple doorways and a second-floor laboratory. ake any Orbital Strike power-ups out front, where a small area provides the only outdoor theater.

urvivor and Rogue are the two preset Star Card Hands offered p at the start of the mission. Both give formidable firepower ith their Star Cards. Survivor includes the Ion Shot Charged Star ard, which is a great help when dealing with the AT-STs. Rogue's ooling Cell allows for extended blaster use, but the second adout definitely has a disadvantage against vehicles.

raised walkway at the back of the hangar gives the best vantage oint as troops enter the structure. Watch out for flanking naneuvers, though, as you are vulnerable from both sides. When ou have reduced the opposition to just one or more AT-STs, use his location's natural cover to pick away at each vehicle's health. Quickly duck out of sight before one can get a lock on you.

he hangar offers some long sight lines, but otherwise, the base s fairly tight. Choose a high rate-of-fire and damage weapon o win the gun battles inside the narrow snow tunnels. As the mperial forces pour into these death traps, they line up for easy rey. However, it isn't always that simple: they often split up and ttempt to surround your location. AT-STs cannot follow you into hese hallways, so take advantage of them when only vehicles emain. This is also a great time to pick up collectibles and other kems that lie around.

Vith the relatively small map, the five drop pod locations are asily accessible from the central hangar. The escape pods are lropped at two locations outside, in the back of the hangar, and n clearings situated in the middle of the right and left corridors. ust after defeating waves 2, 5, 8, 11, and 14, move toward the niddle in anticipation of the pod and its internal goodies.

MULTIPLAYER GAME MODES

There are nine game modes in Star Wars Battlefront, and they all have different features and requirements for victory. You can occupy the many places in the Star Wars galaxy via Supremacy, Walker Assault, Blast, Drop Zone, Droid Run, Cargo, Hero Hunt, Heroes Vs. Villains, and Fighter Squadron. Use the strategies, tips, and specific methodology outlined below to overthrow the Empire or crush the Rebel scum.

SUPREMACY

Experience intense frontline combat over control points.

Rebels and stormtroopers fight to capture and hold strategic locations on the planet. The frontline moves back and forth as these control points shift hands. To win, one side must claim all enemy control points.

MULTIPLAYER GAME MODES

OBJECTIVES

Capture the enemy control point to push them back.

▶ Defend your own control point from being captured.

▶ Capture all control points to win the game.

OVERVIEW

In Supremacy, the name says it all: the goal of this game mode is to show which team can dominate the other by pushing opponents all the way back to their own ship. Each match begins with a single neutral control point in the centermost position of each map that is completely up for grabs. The first challenge for each team is to take this control point. Once the center control point is taken, the opposing team is pushed back, and the next control point becomes available for capture. At this point, the game is similar to tug-of-war because there can only be one available control point for each team. Once you capture a forward control point from your adversary, a friendly control point becomes locked. After a team captures a control point, there is a short "push forward" period that gives each team a chance to move to the next area of the map and capture the next point. During this time, all the pick-ups disappear, only to reappear in the new area. To claim your victory, push the enemy back to their own ship and control every point on the battlefield.

SUPREMACY TACTICS

▶ Because Supremacy only takes place on the larger sections of each planet, use the blasters with mid- to long-range capabilities, such as the T-21. Being able to defend your team's control point from a distance gives you a better scope of the rest of the battlefield while you can remain out of sight.

▶ Equipping the Jump Pack Star Card grants you incredible mobility and allows you to return to your active control point before your opponent has the chance to fully take it. The Jump Pack also gives you the ability to immediately get back in the fight, preventing the opposing team from moving in on your territory if you are killed across enemy lines.

▶ Drop Infantry Turrets on your friendly control point to slow the enemy's advance on your territory, giving you and your squad a chance to get back and save the point. Don't rely on the Infantry Turret to protect the control point completely, as it is very limited. Instead, use it as an aid for buying you a little more time.

▶ Communicate with your teammates to let them know when either point is being taken. This can mean the difference between the movement of the battle zone. If your team calls out any enemies near your control point, but you happen to be located near your foes' point, do everything you can to get inside. If adversaries are capturing your control point, it will not matter if you capture theirs first.

WALKER ASSAULT

Battle over the massive AT-ATs in this mobile attack and defend game.

The Empire has deployed formidable AT-ATs to wipe out the Rebel resistance once and for all. To combat this powerful threat, the Rebels have hidden away multiple uplinks that must be defended at all costs. These uplinks can call in Y-wings from the galaxy to bomb the AT-ATs. It is only during the bombing raid that the AT-ATs can be damaged.

If one or more AT-ATs reach their destination, the Empire wins. If all AT-ATs are destroyed, victory belongs to the Rebels.

OBJECTIVES

▶ Empire: Keep uplinks offline to stop the Rebel bombing raids.

▶ Rebels: Keep uplinks active to add more Y-wings to the bombing raid.

▶ Empire: Defend the AT-ATs from Rebel attacks during bombing raids.

▶ Rebels: Attack the AT-ATs during the raid to destroy them.

▶ Empire: If the AT-ATs survive, you win.

▶ Rebels: Destroy all AT-ATs to win.

OVERVIEW

The concept of Walker Assault is simple: the Empire must safely protect the AT-AT walkers traveling past the three uplink checkpoints, or the Rebel forces must destroy all walkers present on the planet. The way that each side accomplishes its goal is the complex piece that requires both teamwork and a little bit of situational luck. Walker Assault takes place in the largest sections of each planet, which means that there is plenty of room to roam and a lot of area to cover. Work side by side with your partner and in coordination with the rest of your team to cover as much land as possible. There are only two stages in Walker Assault, but these two stages cycle through three whole sections of each map. The first stage is the uplink stage. The Rebels must attempt to activate one or both of the uplinks for the longest possible time, while the Imperial stormtroopers work to prevent the uplinks from being activated. The longer the uplinks are activated, the more Y-wings are called in during the walker stage. During the walker stage, Y-wings enter the battlefield and fire disabling bombs on the AT-ATs, leaving them vulnerable as long as the Y-wings keep coming.

WALKER ASSAULT TACTICS

▶ The more Y-wings that are called into the battlefield, the longer each AT-AT walker stays vulnerable. However, just because they are vulnerable does not necessarily mean that they will be damaged. The match is determined by both phases in Walker Assault, so even if five Y-wings are called in, the Empire still has a chance to fend off all attacking Rebels. When playing on the Empire side during the walker stage, take your focus off of the uplinks. Patrol the perimeter of each AT-AT to prevent Rebels from firing on your walker.

▶ During the walker phase, use the Snowspeeders or Landspeeders to wrap up either AT-AT with the TOW-cable. Keep in mind that you only have as much time as the walkers are vulnerable to trip each walker, so start the process early. The timing for when the walkers go into their vulnerable stage does not change, so jump into a speeder before the stage starts to give yourself as much time as possible. When attacking the AT-ATs aim all of your fire at the belly of the walker, this is the weak spot and shooting this area will cause much more than normal amounts of damage to it.

▶ Time is of the utmost importance to the Rebel troops. There is a finite time in the match, let alone between the stages of the mode. Due to the interest of time, Rebel troopers become expendable. It is smart to coordinate with your team to charge uplinks and attack them in groups or from multiple sides simultaneously. However, do not waste time waiting for your team to come from the deployment area. It may be beneficial just to try your luck and see if you can take an uplink by yourself for at least a few seconds. If your team is coming from the deployment area, by the time you are found and killed after activating the uplink, they might be able to defend any stormtroopers attempting to undo your hard work.

▶ AT-ST walkers have much less armor on the back side of the vehicle, so shooting it from behind will take it down much faster than taking it head on.

BLIND TIME

Using Smoke Grenades can buy you those precious few seconds while either activating or deactivating an uplink; toss them liberally.

FIGHTER SQUADRON

Thrilling air battles await you in this starfighters-only game mode.

Keep an eye out for enemy transport ships that periodically attempt to take off from the planet's surface and escape the battle.
To earn bonus points for your team, destroy your opponent's transport ship before it escapes.

MULTIPLAYER GAME MODES

OBJECTIVES

Attack the enemy troop transports.

▶ Defend your troop transports.

▶ The side that takes out the most enemy ships wins.

OVERVIEW

ake the fight to the sky with Fighter Squadron. The objective of this game mode is to take out as many ships as you can and destroy he enemy transport ship when given the opportunity. Don't ignore your friendly ship when your team's troops are being transported, s they are worth the most amount of points. You can defeat ships with the X-wing, A-wing, TIE fighter, TIE interceptor, and (naturally) he Millennium Falcon and Slave I. Use these ships to dogfight your adversaries as well as the bots that occupy the sky. Focus strongly n taking out enemy players, as they are worth more points for your team than bots, though the true value is in the transport ships.

FIGHTER SQUADRON TACTICS

Shooting down bots is good for racking up quick points because they are easy to kill, but it takes three bots to equal the amount of points you receive for killing an enemy player. Take down your targets as quickly as possible to rack up points in between transport phases. This gives your team a boost going into the phases, making victory much easier to achieve.

Transport ships are by far the most important part of Fighter Squadron. A single transport takedown rewards your team with 10 times the score that a single enemy player defeat would grant you. With enough fighters, the transports should go down rather quickly, but it's important to get to them as rapidly as possible. You can bet there will be defenses inbound fast. TIE fighters are much faster than the Rebel starfighters, but the Rebels can take a little more of a beating with their shield bonus. Use this tactic when attacking or defending the transports.

▶ There are many tokens in the center of the map, normally at low altitudes to create a bit of a challenge when you attempt to collect them. There are Repair tokens, Refresh tokens that refresh your ship's power-ups, and (most importantly) one Hero token that spawns the collector in that team's hero ship when collected. Whether it be Han Solo and Chewbacca in the Millennium Falcon or Boba Fett in the Slave I, having a hero on the battlefield more than benefits your team. Use these hero ships to take down the transport ships exponentially faster, pushing your team even closer to victory.

BLAST

0   03:03   0

DLT-19
HEAVY BLASTER

Blast is a classic battle to the death without objectives.
The first team to score 100 points or score the most kills at the end of the time limit wins.

OBJECTIVES

Defeat the enemy.

▷ The side that takes out the most enemies wins.

OVERVIEW

In Blast, you are faced with no outside problems besides navigating the terrain and battling your enemies head to head. The biggest challenge in playing Blast is choosing your loadout and which Star Cards you should bring with you. Each map is very different, making the decision between changing Star Cards a strategic one. Take your time, and choose wisely. The first team to reach 100 points or the side with the highest score by the end of the time limit is the winner. Keep this in mind before rushing into places you where are most definitely not going to succeed.

BLAST TACTICS

Use the partner system to its fullest and stick with your partner as often as possible. There is no greater strength then having a wingman by your side when charging into any situation. Because you can deploy on your partner, stay aware of his or her health. If your partner goes down, you might want to take cover. If you take cover long enough and your partner deploys back where you're located, you have another chance to take the position you had just attempted.

Picking your blaster is one of the more important choices you must make before the match starts. Every map is a little different, which makes this decision incredibly tactical. Locations like the Imperial Station on Endor or the Rebel Base on Hoth may require short-range weapons like the CA-87 and SE-14C to take down your opponents. In the bigger locations like Jawa Refuge or the Sulphur Fields, you should use blasters like the T-21 to fire at long range without losing too much accuracy and deal a high amount of damage per bolt.

Your blaster is incredibly important, but it must be accompanied by Star Cards, including Asset, Charge, and Trait Cards. The Explosive Shot Charged Star Card is normally a great default choice when you can't think of any other card that might benefit you more. This card carries a set amount of charges until you purchase more or collect some on the battlefield. It also charges your blaster bolts with explosive AOE damage that is great for outnumbered situations where you can't shoot two enemies at once. Don't forget about using the Jump Pack or Personal Shield to even out an unfair battle.

Use cover whenever possible, as there is some on every map. Cover can not only be an incredible asset but might also make a difference by helping you win a match based on a single death or kill.

DROP ZONE

This fast-paced, action-packed mode assigns a single objective: gain control of the drop pods that fall from the sky.
Claim a drop pod and earn valuable resources for your team.

OBJECTIVES

Activate the drop pod to start claiming it.

▶ Defend the drop pod while it is being claimed.

▶ The side that claims the most drop pods wins.

OVERVIEW

Drop Zone is the ultimate test of strength and domination of any one point on any map. The objective for Drop Zone is to take control of a drop pod in a given location. The twist is that the location where these drop pods will actually fall can be virtually anywhere on the maps this mode is playable on, and that area is always random. The best way to play this mode is to always keep moving and never stand still for too long. This technique both keeps you safe from attackers who remember where you were when you killed them and leaves you ready to move when the next pod drops. Once the pod has dropped from the sky, your next move is to actually claim the pod by pressing the Action button directly on it. When you're capturing, you must wait for a timer, which leaves you vulnerable for a short amount of time. Once that timer is finished, a much longer timer starts (the capture timer). You must protect that drop pod until the timer is fully expired before you can claim the loot that dispenses from it. The goal is to capture five different pods for your team in order to win the match.

DROP ZONE TACTICS

The drop pod's randomized location means that you must always stay frosty and keep on your toes; at any moment, the drop pod could be found in any direction. The pods don't always drop one after the other, either. It's possible that if a single drop pod is not claimed after a certain amount of time, another will drop, leaving two unclaimed drop pods available at once.

Sometimes the easiest way to capture a pod is to lock down the location it has dropped in before you even attempt to activate it. Communicate with your team, and set up a perimeter around the drop pod before activating it to ensure that you can protect it with full force. However, you should read the situation because sometimes the pressure is so constant that you may not be able to lock down the area first. You might need to constantly filter in friendly reinforcements. Assess what's happening, as every team is different.

Once a drop pod has been captured, beware that anyone (truly anyone) can claim the loot that has dropped from it. If you are the only one around the captured pod, try picking them up and use every power-up, if only to prevent the enemy from having access to them.

Using Star Cards like the Squad Shield or Personal Shield can give you those extra few seconds of survivability it takes to activate the drop pod for your team. This helps in hot situations and can even turn the tide for your team. If the other team is very close to capturing a pod, your activation will reset the timer.

DROID RUN

The fast-paced action here involves three moving objectives: droids. Interact with a droid to begin the capture process, and then defend your droid to prevent the enemy from stealing it back.

OBJECTIVES

Activate the droids to start claiming them.

▶ Defend the droids as they are being claimed.

▶ The side that claims all three droids wins.

OVERVIEW

Droid Run is a balance between greed and tactics. To win a Droid Run match, you must claim all three droids. Greed can be a virtue, encouraging you to take risks in order to win, but it can also cost you the match if you are not careful. The three droids are located fairly symmetrically around the map, and it takes a good amount of communication and an aggressive attitude to finish the match with victory. All three droids roam around a very specific location, but you must remember that they still roam. This can place them in very different strategic areas depending on where they have wandered.

DROID RUN TACTICS

The droids roam around the area where they are located, which can be both good and bad for you as you try to defend or capture them. There are times when they will be in more cover than normal, which are usually the best times to take them. However, this isn't the best way to take them if you have to wait for it.

Be greedy, but be smart about it. Sometimes going after that last droid could mean the win for your team. If you have a strong suspicion that the enemy is not anywhere near capturing either of your other droids, you might as well go for it. The worst that could happen is that you get killed and redeploy closer to your friendly droids.

Using the Star Card Jump Pack allows you ultimate mobility. As long as you have Jump Pack available, you can attack your opponent or unclaimed droids without fear of returning to your droids in time. The Jump Pack will not get you all the way back to your friendly droid if you are directly next to another one, but you can still close a great distance with the Jump Pack. Another Jump Pack tactic on Droid Run is using it to get a vantage point on the battlefield. This makes it easier for you to call out enemy movements to your teammates and help to protect your already claimed droids.

After a droid has been captured, it can be captured right back just as easily. This can hinder your progress if you are being greedy and pursuing the other droids. Beware of this situation, and make sure that if you are going to get greedy, your team is there to back you up.

CARGO

Run and gun while stealing cargo from the enemy and preventing your own cargo from being captured.

OBJECTIVES

Bring the enemy cargo to your base.

▷ Defend your cargo from the enemy.

▷ The side with the most cargo in the end wins.

OVERVIEW

Cargo is similar to an average capture the flag game, but it is slightly more complex. Yes, the point of this game mode is to capture the enemy's cargo and bring it back to your base, but every time your team or the other steals a piece of cargo, they are literally doing just that. When a piece of cargo is stolen from your base, you lose that cargo piece until it is returned. Although the first team to collect 10 pieces of cargo is the winner, each team starts with five. There is a finite amount of cargo on the battlefield, so this game is similar to capture the flag, but it is also a game of tug-of-war.

CARGO TACTICS

There are two general tactics to playing Cargo on any map, and the first one is the run and gun tactic. Run and gun is literally just that: it is your job to attack the enemy base, do everything possible to take the cargo, and bring the cargo back to your team's base. You can do this in many ways, but one of the more favorable strategies is running around the outside perimeter of the map, avoiding any of the major action that may create a challenge for you.

The other general strategy is a strong defense, or camping method, as your victims may claim. One of the best defenses in *Star Wars* Battlefront is not finding one great spot from which to sit and take out enemies, but finding several that you can rotate through to watch multiple angles and avoid getting flanked by incoming foes. Of course, it is much easier to defend a location if you have friends helping you. This is a great opportunity to use the partner system and decide that you want your duo to stick strictly to defense. With the right communication, your defense can become impenetrable.

When running with the cargo, remember that you cannot use a Jump Pack to launch yourself forward, as you are too heavy. The Jump Pack is a great asset to use in Cargo for making it to the other team's base or protecting your friendly cargo carrier, but as soon as you have the cargo, you are forced to run all the way back.

HERO HUNT

A single hero is up against a squad of enemies. The hero player is chosen randomly, but all players get a chance to be the hero during a match. Whoever has the most kills at the end of the time limit wins the game.

OBJECTIVES

Defeat the hero to become the hero.

▸ Whoever defeats the most enemies wins.

OVERVIEW

Hero Hunt is one of the most unique modes in *Star Wars* Battlefront because it pits a team of hunters (whether they be stormtroopers or Rebel troopers) against a single hero character that includes both heroes and villains, depending on the planet. The hero character will play Luke Skywalker, Han Solo, or Leia Organa when playing on Tatooine and Hoth, or Darth Vader, Emperor Palpatine, or Boba Fett on Endor and Sullust. Each player can play a hero character while the troopers attempt to hunt them down. Hero Hunt becomes a test to see how vulnerable the heroes and villains of the *Star Wars* universe actually are.

HERO HUNT TACTICS

Playing as the hero means playing to that character's strengths. You don't know which hero you will be controlling when you become the hero character, but once you find out, it becomes your job to adjust. Melee characters should stick to close-quarters situations, while blaster-type characters might play the outdoors a little more.

Troopers are the hunters, and even though you want to get the kill so you can become the hero, you still must work with your team. Most hero characters need to be ambushed either from a distance or right around the corner and played to their weakness. Generally, explosives are most likely to damage hero characters. Most can either escape blaster fire or deflect it right back at you, which could mean your death.

Use items like Seeker Shot to take the hero character on from a distance, while keeping you as safe as possible. If you want to survive the battle, fire and expend with Seeker Shot and all weapons in general. Without a doubt, you are at a disadvantage, even when outnumbering the hero character. Staying on the move helps keep your survival rate up, giving you more chances to down the hero character.

As the hero character, a good team of hunters will attempt to ambush you. Luckily, almost every hero character has an ability that can be used to escape dire situations. Don't be afraid to attack head-on, but read the situation and escape if necessary.

HEROES VS. VILLAINS

In this round-based combat mode, all heroes battle each other, with their teammates as backup. Three players from each side are randomly chosen as heroes; dying causes them to respawn as normal soldiers. Eliminate all enemy heroes to win the round.

MULTIPLAYER GAME MODES

OBJECTIVES

Defeat the villains.

Protect your heroes.

The side that takes the most rounds wins.

OVERVIEW

In Heroes Vs. Villains, the most powerful beings in the galaxy face off on the battlefield with the aid of their trooper teammates. Each team has three hero characters and three troopers until the hero characters are killed. After they die, they redeploy as troopers. The objective is to keep at least one of the heroes or villains on your team alive while you take out the three opposing heroes. Do everything in your power to keep your team's heroes alive, and take your opposition on in match-ups that should statistically work in your favor.

HEROES VS. VILLAINS TACTICS

Because of the power behind each individual hero and villain, this game mode is mostly about match-ups. Some heroes can easily take on a specific villain but get destroyed by the others. There are ways around this, but that depends on how comfortable you are with the character you are controlling.

In most situations, Han Solo and Boba Fett are evenly matched. However, head to head with Emperor Palpatine may skew in favor of Han. Emperor Palpatine fares rather well against Luke Skywalker because his Force Lightning deals a constant amount of damage that Luke cannot block. Take each match-up very seriously—every movement and every head-to-head combat sequence matters.

Do whatever it takes to avoid engaging in a two-on-one situation, especially if Princess Leia or Emperor Palpatine is part of that two-person squad. Both Leia and Palpatine are primarily support characters and can directly aid any characters nearby. Not only does grouping with another hero or villain help Leia's and Palpatine's effectiveness, but gathering their troopers can create a formidable squad. Each character can drop supplies for their teammates and protect them with the Enhanced Squad Shield or a Chain Lightning blast to throw the enemy off balance.

Troopers are expendable in this game mode, so don't be afraid to sacrifice yourself if it helps protect your friendly hero. In the same vein, don't get sucked into a trap where you are drawn to a trooper when a hero character is waiting to attack you.

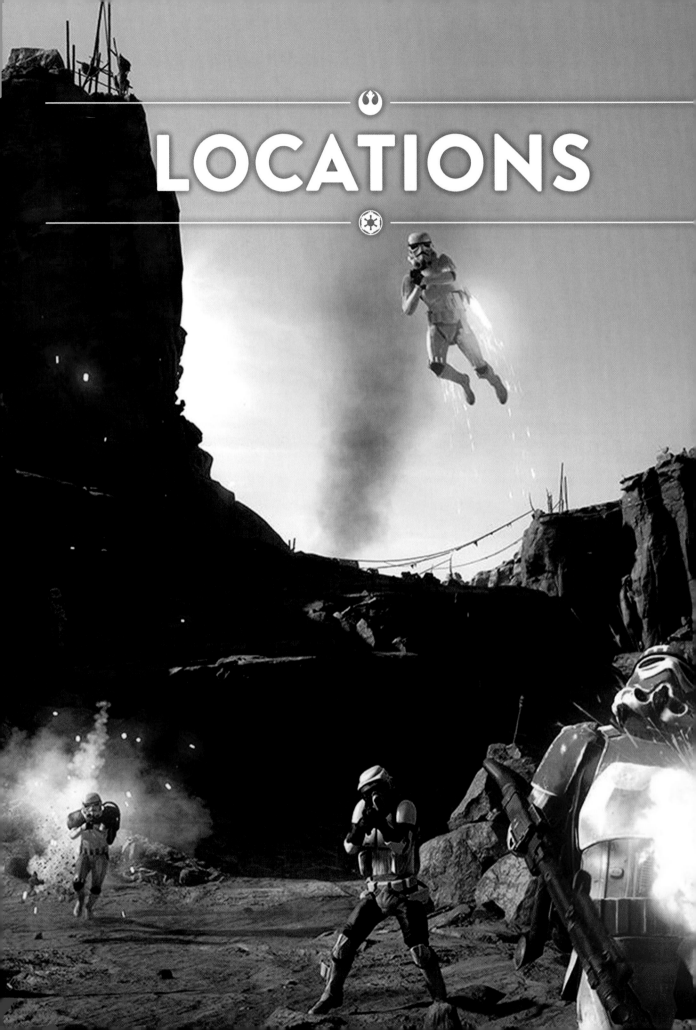

LOCATIONS

TATOOINE

The desert world of Tatooine, the home planet of Luke Skywalker, is a vast place full of sand and crawling with some of the lowest of low criminals and smugglers. Covered in both sand and large rock formations, Tatooine is a planet that can betray even the most careful of explorers if they are not fully prepared. The planet orbits two suns, Tatoo I and Tatoo II, making for an extremely bright and hot surface. While it is livable, Tatooine is not a place of comfort. Additionally, the indigenous beings known as Jawas and the Tusken Raiders, are not exactly the most friendly. Watch your back at all times, and keep your head on a swivel—you can consider relatively everything deadly, leaving a small chance of survival.

Known for having caves and a small amount of huts for you to hide inside, Tatooine is primarily a planet played outdoors. This forces you to act quickly and find cover in a moment's notice before you get shot. This desert planet contains four multiplayer locations, all of which are extremely bright and hot even after the suns have set. Each location has its own tactical advantage, whether it's using vertical movement to get over and around your opponent in the Jawa Refuge or employing the Rebel transport's underbelly to set up ambushes for your enemy at the Dune Sea Exchange. The Rebel Depot is small and presents a minimal amount of room for flanking your opponents. However, the Rebel Depot has many ledges and layers that you can use to get the upper hand on an enemy. This leaves the infamous Jundland Wastes as an extremely large location with an exorbitant amount of opportunities where you can get around the enemy undetected.

JUNDLAND WASTES

Supremacy

CONTROL POINT: EMPIRE	⬤
CONTROL POINT: REBELS	⬤
CONTROL POINT: MID	⬤
SPAWN: EMPIRE	EMPIRE
SPAWN: REBELS	REBELS

The first location both teams must capture in the Jundland Wastes is directly in the center of the Wastes, immediately adjacent to the Jawa Sandcrawler. The capture area is very small and extremely exposed to the surrounding mountain terrain and the opposite side of the giant crawler. Keep your distance from the objective area before going in for the capture; you can be taken out from almost every direction. Use the Sandcrawler and the mountains to conceal your approach and as cover while your teammates take the control point. Employ the pieces of vehicle debris shed from the battle as excellent cover while you capture the point. Also, toss down a Smoke Grenade for added cover, asinces you are extremely vulnerable.

When the Rebels are in their first "push forward" phase after capturing the central point, the second control point is in the Jawa village, located well within the mountainous terrain away from the Sandcrawler. The Jawa village has quite a bit of cover initially, so get there quickly. Watch your corners when approaching: although there are crevasses that provide protection, enemies may also be waiting for you to round corners so they can

take you by surprise. Use the village huts to hide and set up ambushes for incoming enemy troops. Stay aware of your surroundings, as your opponents can destroy them, turning you into a sitting duck. There are four main entrances to this control point: one directly from the Imperial base, and three that can be taken from the center near where the Jawa Sandcrawler is. It is beneficial to defend these entrances from the Sandcrawler. As a Rebel, you must still defend the Sandcrawler because the Imperials need that location to advance forward, pushing you away from the Jawa village. When playing on the Imperial side in this situation, it is useful to have the Jump Pack available. Taking on the Rebels via alternate routes rather than the four aforementioned entrances to the Jawa village works greatly in your favor.

When the Imperials are in their first "push forward" phase after capturing the center point, the Rebel location is near the depot, where close-quarters combat is a real danger. When attacking this location, equip either the Smoke Grenade or Flash Grenade Star Card to disorient the enemy as you enter and clear the area. Defend all entrances and exits of the depot base to keep foes from flanking you. In this location, it helps to stay close to the capture point simply because it is extremely difficult to access the area while others are defending it from the inside. Make use of the CA-87 blaster, as it is a shotgun-type weapon that deals an extremely high amount of damage with a single shot which is exactly what you need in these tight corridors. When you are defending, watch out for the Barrage explosive launcher. The launcher can bounce grenades around corners that you may be hiding in, leaving you no time to escape. Your best defense is staying on the move or setting up proximity mines where you think the enemy might launch these grenades from.

Both sides have a distinct advantage when defending their final control point. However, if the attacking team can get in and at least secure the initial entrance of the control point, there are a lot more power-ups in a much smaller proximity. These provide an entire arsenal of weapons and power-ups, and if you use them in rapid succession, you can decimate the enemy and gain free access to attack their transport ship. Use your friendly transport ship when defending your final control point both from the ground and on the ship itself, as it can provide a great deal of cover from all directions. Just remember to keep your head moving. Even though your opponent will typically come from the direction of their control point, there are plenty of opportunities to get around your team and flank you. At the very beginning of this phase, you should keep a few troops at your final control point, but send the majority of your forces to the enemy's point. Be prepared to fall back once your adversary appears to even come close to breaking through. After you lose this final location, your team loses the battle.

DYING IS A SECOND CHANCE TO DEFEND

Dying while attacking the forward location after your team is on its last chance can be helpful. Use it to check in on defenses before attacking again, as you can be your team's only hope for victory

GO VERTICAL WITH FETT

Boba Fett's jetpack allows him to access many locations that no other character can, giving him the ability to take the best vantage points over the entire battlefield.

Walker Assault

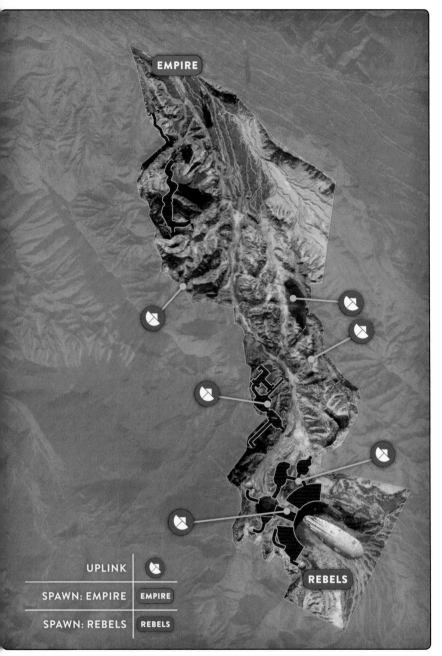

EMPIRE

REBELS

UPLINK	
SPAWN: EMPIRE	EMPIRE
SPAWN: REBELS	REBELS

Like in Supremacy, the first set of uplinks that must be activated or defended is located underneath the Jawa Sandcrawler and in the Jawa village inside the small mountain range just across the plain. It is incredibly important for the Rebel team to activate both uplinks and defend them for as long as possible in order to have the longest opportunity for taking down the AT-ATs. Because of the fairly open areas in the beginning phase of the Jundland Wastes, you should employ the Squad Shield to protect your team when capturing or defending either of the uplinks. Additionally, this is a great situation for using the Cycler Rifle after you've unlocked it. It can penetrate shields to keep the enemy from surrounding your squad.

As the Imperials, when the Y-wings come in for their first bombing run, you should use the Bowcaster, Homing Shot, and Barrage to dispatch as many enemies attempting to take down your AT-ATs with Ion weapons as possible. You also want to create large perimeters and keep spread out to ensure that no Rebels make it through the defensive lines and get to any prime locations to fire on the walkers. Once you have secured the area, push forward and attempt to move the fight closer to the next two uplink locations. This both creates an opportunity to build an early defense and shortens the Rebels' opening to attack your walkers.

The next two locations are pushed back to the smaller canyon area just beyond the Sandcrawler. In this second phase, there is more use for the Jump Pack Card than anywhere else, simply because being able to get over the terrain grants you several different access points that would not be possible otherwise.

HEAVY TURRET TACTICS

During the transition phase from one uplink location to another, use the heavy turrets stationed in specific locations

to keep the enemy at bay while your team sets up a defense.

The next two locations are pushed back to the smaller canyon area just beyond the Sandcrawler. In this second phase, there is more use for the Jump Pack Card than anywhere else, simply because being able to get over the terrain grants you several different access points that would not be possible otherwise. On the side of the Sandcrawler, the uplink is located on the pathway heading toward the depot. You can use this area as a major chokepoint for all enemies attacking on foot. Set up deployable turrets in a way that allows a long sightline. Even if you can't fend off your adversaries, those who are really paying attention will be deterred from moving down that path. The second uplink is a little tougher to attack, as it is located inside the mountain. Within

the intel base, three entrances lead directly into the room with the uplink, so watch out for Proximity Mines and heavy turrets. Use Smoke Grenades to conceal your approach and keep the enemy from locking you out.

The second attack phase of Walker Assault on Tatooine is by far the most dangerous for the Imperial walkers, as there is a great deal of cover that can be used from both sides of the walker. Rebels should take full advantage of all angles on the walkers since the action occurs directly in the center of the map. However, because of this advantage for the Rebels, Imperials should definitely be aware of this and minimize the amount of time they have to attack the AT-AT walkers.

In the final location of Walker Assault, there are two more uplink locations. Like the second phase, there is one just inside the mountain where the transport depot is located. The interior location is a lot like the mountain location from the last phase, but finding the alternate entrances as an Imperial is a little more challenging. (Those entrances are in the same direction from where the Rebels will more than likely deploy.) The alternate location to the interior uplink is located closer to the Rebel transport ship. Even though it is in the heart of their defenses, this is the easiest place for Imperial troops to attack and take over. If you're playing as a Rebel and the outdoor uplink is deactivated, fall back to the first uplink and defend it as effectively as possible. If the Imperials deactivate both uplinks, the Rebels will be in deep trouble, especially if both walkers are still healthy. Fall back and defend until you know that the outside is secure, and then move out to activate the second uplink. This is the best opportunity to use heroes and villains to clear out heavily defended locations in preparation for the final attack phase.

In the final attack phase, it may be beneficial to use as many of the air vehicles as your team has available. Use the X-wings and A-wings to defend the Landspeeders from TIE fighters as they attempt to use the TOW-cable and trip the walkers. If the AT-ATs are above 50 percent health, the TOW-cable becomes the last hope for the Rebel side. There won't be much time to attack, and a successful trip mini game can take down each walker immediately.

Fighter Squadron

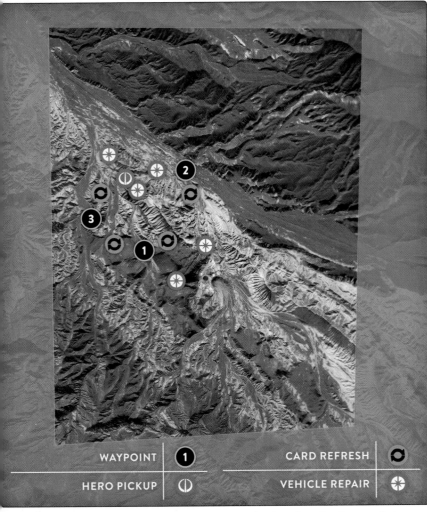

WAYPOINT	①	CARD REFRESH	↻
HERO PICKUP	⏀	VEHICLE REPAIR	✦

① Jundland Wastes is the battle arena with the most treacherous terrain of all Fighter Squadron locations. Most of the Repair and Ability Refresh tokens are extremely close to the ground, and traveling at high speeds already makes it difficult to fly through them without hitting the ground. Here in the Wastes, you must be keenly aware of your altitude and how close you are to hitting the planet surface, as well as your distance from the surrounding mountains. Because of how rapidly the elevation of the obstacles changes, keep your head on a swivel even at mid-height. There might be a mountain face ready to render your ship destroyed.

In the air, there isn't much difference from any other map while playing Fighter Squadron. However, be aware of the two suns high in the air because it is easy to lose your enemy in the bright light. Whenever you are blinded or impaired by the suns, use your stunt maneuvers to avoid taking fire.

② **③** Throughout the match, several escort instances take place. The direction in which each team's transport begins their travel across the map is always the same, but the angle that they travel in is subject to change. Pay attention to your HUD when these events begin, and bring as many members of your team as you can to that location. Get there as fast as possible to complete the mission as quickly or efficiently as you can. Since the angle of the transport's travel changes, the transport could possibly begin inside one of the canyons, making it difficult for you to track and destroy the enemy transport ship.

JAWA REFUGE

Blast

1 The Jawa Refuge is not one of the biggest locations in the game, but it has one of the largest amounts of cover and layers that compensates for that. When playing Blast, it is all about keeping your kill/death ratio the best it can possibly be in order to win. To stay alive, use the debris and vertical cover at all times. Make use of the cliffs that look over the shaded areas of the map, as there might be troops traveling underneath you. If you time it correctly, these cliffs can make for the perfect ambush locations. Contrarily, if you spot enemy troops above you, toss a Thermal Grenade or Smoke Grenade to clear them out or get away safely.

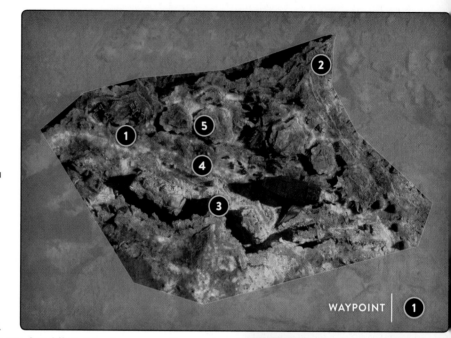

WAYPOINT | **1**

2 3 If you're a long-range player and like to use weapons like the Cycler Rifle or the Pulse Cannon, use the cliff to fire downrange to the other end of the refuge. The cliffside is quite open; you can post up on a few different levels, so scope those out and make sure not to get counter-sniped. Also, be prepared to evacuate at a moment's notice. While you can see all the way down one side, the cliffside is still wide open, making you an easy target for anyone who knows you're there.

4 Because of how complex the Jawa Refuge is, always stick together with your team. Use the larger areas of debris to fortify and defend an area to prevent the enemy team from gaining the upper hand. The partner system comes in handy while playing Blast in the Jawa Refuge because roaming the battlefield is extremely dangerous. So, when you and your team are defending a location and your partner goes down, stay alive until he or she comes back, thus strengthening your numbers. The Squad Shield is a great item to use when fighting next to your battle partner. However, the Personal Shield provides better support because it is not a power-up that you need to find out in the field. The Personal Shield is a Charged Star Card, so as long as you have purchased some charges for this particular card, you can activate the shields whenever you choose. This gives you an extra amount of health that can only help you during a close firefight.

5 Picking up and using power-ups like the Blaster Cannon or Infantry Turret can make the difference on this map, especially if placed in an area with a wide field of view. Placing an Infantry Turret above a canyon and directing it to fire down inside creates a great method of ambushing an enemy squad. If you and your partner set up one turret and then set up another in the other direction, you have a vicious crossfire opportunity, introducing a chance to rack up multiple kills.

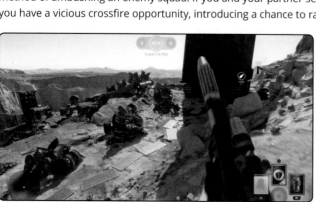

Drop Zone

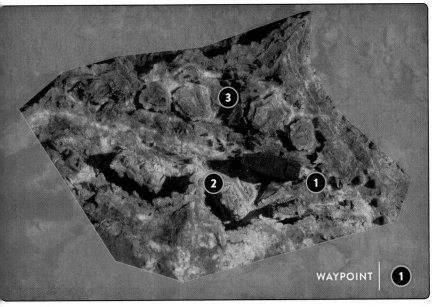

1 In the game of Drop Zone, the drop pods drop in major crossroads and normally high-traffic areas. Here, be ready to take this thought even further with an added upper-level challenge. With most maps containing upper levels, you must deal with one or two walkways that are normally in the distance. However, in the Jawa Refuge, there are multiple situations where you have to deal with enemies in all directions, including directly above your position. One of the safest ways to defend a drop pod after you've initiated the capture timer is to either drop a Squad Shield or set up an Infantry Turret in the direction you're not covering as thoroughly. The Infantry Turret's auto lock has a good system of informing you that someone is coming. For the best results, set it up looking down the longest hallway or sightline. That placement gives the turret time to lock on and kill your adversary rather than just letting you know that a foe is there. Keep in mind that these two items come randomly, and you may need another strategy that you can count on.

2 Even though some of the more useful items arrive randomly through power-up pickups, you can set up, plan, and control certain other things. The Barrage explosive grenade launcher can keep enemies at bay when you are in the last few seconds of capturing the drop pod. Pay attention to the motion tracker on your radar. As soon as you are close to making the capture, launch a few explosives in the direction where you see the most enemy pings, and wait for the repercussions of your actions. If you have the Smoke Grenade unlocked, this is a good way to disorient the attackers coming in to steal the loot from the drop pod. Now you have an advantage because if they take a shot, you know exactly where they are.

3 After you retrieve the loot, your actions are extremely important on this map. You may only have a few options when it comes to exiting the area, and choosing the wrong one can cost you dearly when attempting to get to the next drop pod before your opponent. The Jump Pack is one quick way of getting out of a tight spot. However, using another Smoke Grenade on the ground while staying close to the current pod gives the next pod a chance to drop and you the chance to get the jump on it. You won't have to wait for a respawn or go in the wrong direction (which makes it even more difficult to arrive at the destination).

Droid Run

1 The first on the list of droids that you must capture for this mode is the "A" droid, located near the canyon opposite of the cliffside. If you are attacking or moving toward this droid from either of the other droids, it is located on the other side of the large Jawa Sandcrawler. Because of this, you can use the crawler to your advantage. Use a Smoke Grenade or two to create a wall of distractions and obscure the enemy's long-range vision to your position. The side of the Sandcrawler that is facing the power droid is the easiest to defend because of the smaller area to cover. If you're not going to have all three droids, the best combination is to have the "A" droid and the "C" droid. This makes cornering your opponent significantly easier than it is with the other two combinations. Applying this same logic, your adversary might also have the same idea. Therefore, if you pick up on this information, it might be an effective

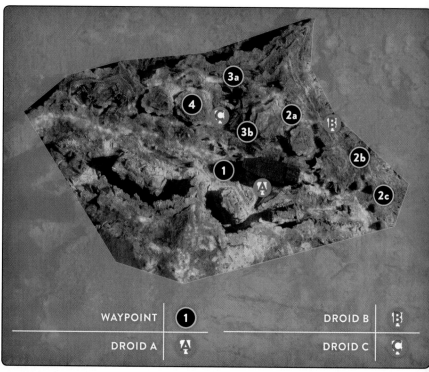

| WAYPOINT | **1** | DROID B | 🅱 |
| DROID A | 🅰 | DROID C | 🅲 |

tactic to go for the weaker combination at least temporarily. It will be less challenging to grab because of the lack of focus on defense. Remember to use the canyon behind you to get optimal sightlines on enemies attempting to attack your location. Relying on the canyon also lets you stay away from the action but remain close enough in case you are needed for an emergency capture defense.

2a 2b 2c The second droid on this map is the "B" power droid, and it's located far along the cliffside near the Jawa village. This location also has a large amount of cover, but it is extremely easy to become pinned down from enemy fire and get locked into this part of the map. There are a few escape routes if you're being closed in, but you must trust your judgment when taking any of them. Take the path of least resistance: if you don't have to be near the droid, back off a bit to avoid becoming an easy target for attackers. You and a couple of friendlies can move up the hill and take over the Jawa village. Then, use it for an elevated advantage when attempting to

defend the droid. From the Jawa village, you can head directly toward the droid to defend it, or you can move over the upper surface and head into the location over the top. Be careful when tossing Thermal Detonator and Thermal Imploders near the power droid—the ledge is quite narrow and can be very dangerous because it is difficult for enemies to escape before the explosive goes off.

3a 3b The third and final of the three Droid Run droids in the Jawa Refuge is the "C" droid, located near the cliffside and on the lower end of elevation within this map. Surrounding the droid, you can find several great locations for fortifying, defending, and waiting for your enemy to attack. Look along the cliff for a tent-like shelter unit that is incredibly useful for hiding from any foes coming from above. There is also a corner underneath the tent that you can hide behind, not warning your attackers that you might be there. However, remember that once this hiding spot is revealed to your opponent, you may need to relocate. The spot is fairly easy to flank if the other side of the droid is not defended. On the other side of the droid and along the opposite direction on the cliff is a much more open area, followed by a very sharp corner.

Unless you have friendlies covering you from the small cliff above you, this side is a prime location for foes taking you by surprise. To avoid getting eliminated, cover this side from just in front of the droid you are capturing or attempting to capture.

4 Just like Blast mode, it helps here to use the higher elevations to ambush enemies running through the lower center of the map. However, there is a major difference about this mode in the Jawa Refuge. Because this map takes place at night in Droid Run, and because of the specific locations of the droids, take advantage of the shadows and cover of darkness to use the area under the upper surface. (Note that this doesn't work in any other variation of Jawa Refuge because it is still relatively easy to see foes in the shadows considering how bright of a planet Tatooine is during the day.) Stay vigilant: even though it is dark, your opponent can still see your movements on their radar. While you are stealthily moving from point to point, don't be afraid to stop and let the enemy pass by to avoid giving away your position.

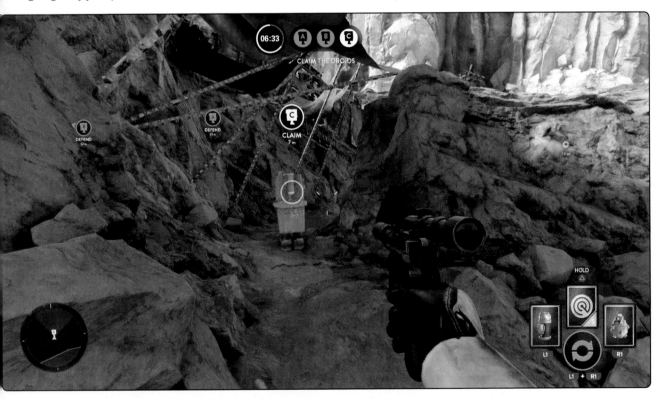

THE DARK, COLD COVER OF DARKNESS

Tatooine's two suns provide for a brightly lit planet, but at night, the shadows are still extremely useful for concealing your movements.

Hero Hunt

1 Hero Hunt on Jawa Refuge becomes a little difficult if you are the type of player who likes to find a corner of the map that you can fortify and defend with all of your might. Jawa Refuge is dynamic in the sense that there are not many corners and it is quite asymmetrical. This means that if you are playing as a hero, you should run laps around the perimeter of the map to keep the Imperials guessing and more than likely catch their flank before they have a chance to turn around and defend themselves.

2 Part of Hero Hunt is always playing the hero that you are most comfortable with and that plays to the map in the best possible and most efficient way. While all heroes are very powerful, some work better on Jawa Refuge than others. For instance, playing as Luke here is great for

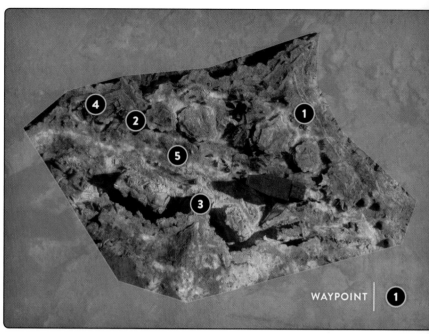

WAYPOINT **1**

taking on multiple enemies at once, but it can be overkill inside the canyons and under the top surface. Leia can use the larger canyons to set up a shield and shoot through it with her projectile weapon. However, Han is your best bet on this map. He has a very powerful blaster, and his high-powered shot with explosive damage can affect enemies around corners. With Han, you can charge down narrow corridors, taking down everyone in your path for a short burst.

3 The other part of Hero Hunt on Jawa Refuge is using specific locations to ambush the heroes and surprise them. Surprising heroes is the best way to defeat them because their health is a bit higher than a standard trooper's. This means that it takes more than one trooper to take them down, depending on distance and whether the hero sees you or not. Use corners and elevated sections to sneak up behind heroes. Take away the hero's advantage of getting the first shot on you, and hopefully turn this into an opportunity to deal more damage than the hero can do to you. If the hero is Han or Princess Leia, the best way to take them down is by shooting from close range with a rapid-fire blaster, as it disorients them and forces them to react quickly. However, if

you're facing Luke, you may want to surround him while also keeping your distance. The moment Luke closes the gap between you and him, you might as well stop shooting and run—there's a good chance you're already dead.

Heroes Vs. Villains

4 Heroes Vs. Villains is pure chaos no matter which map you play it on. Follow the same trooper tactics as you would in Hero Hunt, such as setting up ambushes for the opposite team's heroes or villains but also playing to the characters' weaknesses when attacking them as a trooper. Understand that even though you are expendable as a trooper, it is important to protect your allies and keep them alive. Once they're dead, your team loses.

5 There are a few good preferred match-ups. If you're on the disadvantaged side of a match-up, just be aware of it and be ready to counter by exploiting your opponent's weaknesses. Because Jawa Refuge has both close-quarters areas and mid- to long-range areas, all heroes and villains have their advantages; it truly depends on where they are in the map. On the upper surface of the Refuge, characters like Luke, Darth Vader, Boba Fett, and Princess Leia have the highest success because of their ranged attacks and speed. Han Solo can hold his own up top, but when faced against Darth Vader, he better sneak up on Vader and shoot him in the back. Otherwise, it'll be a challenge to deal damage while attacking head-on. Down below in the trenches, characters like Han and Palpatine dominate their opponents. Even though Luke can deal a lot of damage to multiple targets, Palpatine's lightning is constant and gives Luke and Leia hardly any chance to escape before draining their health to zero. On the other hand, Han Solo can keep his distance underneath and use his explosive damage that cannot be deflected by Darth Vader or out-gunned by Boba Fett. Boba Fett's blaster is powerful, but in a one-on-one fight, Han's blaster inflicts more damage with slightly more accuracy, giving him the advantage. The best thing for Boba to do in that situation is fly through an opening in the ceiling and create some distance between himself and his target.

REBEL DEPOT

Blast

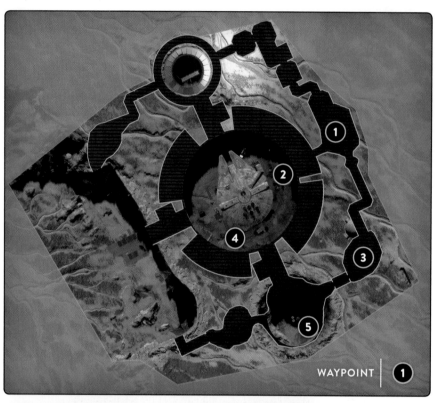

WAYPOINT | **1**

1 The Rebel Depot is one of the rounder maps, with an interior perimeter and an exterior center that make for a well-balanced map when it comes to playing Blast. If you are the run-and-gun type, there are several ways you can play Blast on Rebel Depot: circle the outside perimeter, circle the inside perimeter, or (if you like to change things up) try a mix of both an inside and outside run.

Circling the outside perimeter means that you are using close-quarters tactics. Equip a blaster with a high fire rate, like the DLT-19 or the T-21, or try something like the CA-87 shotgun-type blaster to take care of any enemies that surprise you around corners. If you happen to pick up a proximity mine on a power-up, note that setting up ambushes is not their sole use. The best places to drop a proximity mine when using the run-and-gun tactic are directly around a tight corner (like a box or turn) or in a narrow corridor (like a doorway or maintenance shaft).

2 The inside perimeter run requires a slightly different approach, as there are points during the run where you are exposed on multiple sides. Unlike circling the outside, this tactic works best when you are teamed up with a partner. Being able to watch both flanks from a short distance, you and your partner can cover each other's blind spots, taking the Millennium Falcon's exterior by storm. Just like the interior on the outside perimeter of the map, there are general preferred areas for dropping proximity mines, such as in front of doorways and behind box corners. Drop the mines on the corners facing the direction in which you are running. Anyone who catches a glimpse of you may come out to shoot you in the back, and what is waiting for them could potentially save you.

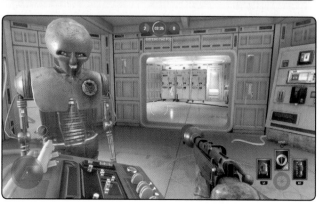

3 Running the perimeter of the map in Blast is a very effective tactic, but depending on the enemy, there are situations where you should stop and lock down a location and block any opponents who may have the same idea. Locking down a location also allows for a defensive setup. With such a setup, you run the chance of frustrating your adversary, causing them to make mistakes—possibly even the same mistake repeatedly. Dropping Infantry Turrets and Blaster Cannons becomes extremely effective when they're aimed at choke points.

4 5 A few locations quickly become highly valued because if you have at least one of them, your team can funnel enemy troops through a minimal amount of passageways, lining them up like target dummies. The X-wing hangar with the destroyed X-wing has only three entrances. As long as a few members of your team are on board, it is very effective to lock this hangar down. Whatever you do, don't break ranks. Another location is located on the opposite end of the map, in the outdoor cargo area. Here, using the same tactics is almost as effective because of the same amount of entrances. Note that this area is slightly less effective simply because it is a little easier to get the high ground just above. Watch your entrances, and take a peek at the ledge above you every few seconds to make sure that you're not about to get a Barrage thermal grenade launcher dropped atop your head. If you're feeling adventurous and you happen to have a team that you really mesh well with, try taking over the Millennium Falcon hangar and posting troopers at locations overlooking the hallways. Your opponents will begin to spread out because in the hallways, the number of enemies in the group have little to no effect because of the bottlenecks. Unless they all attack at the same exact time, you have a large game of whack-a-mole on your hands.

Drop Zone

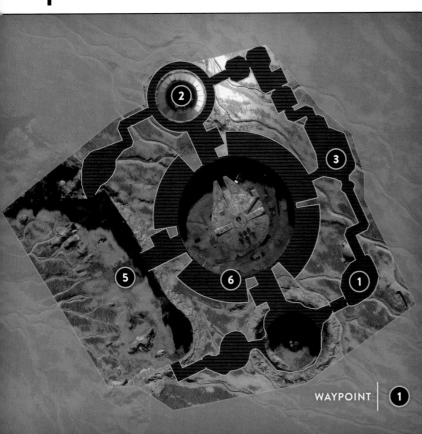

WAYPOINT | **1**

1 One of the most important things to know about playing Drop Zone on Rebel Depot is that a large percentage of the map is indoors, which means there is a relatively small amount of space for drop pods to land. Think about this map like so: even though the map is quite asymmetrical, there are five distinct areas where you can check in and have a jump on getting to the pod before the enemy does. These areas include the X-wing hangar, the intelligence center, the outdoor cargo hold, the depot entrance, and the Millennium Falcon hangar, which sits directly in the center of the map. Each of these areas has a chance to drop a pod, making them the most important locations.

2 The X-wing hangar has an opening above it, and the drop pod can deploy directly next to the X-wing. There is not much variance in the exact location it drops while in the hangar itself. As long as you are near the destroyed X-wing, you are close enough to claim the drop pod for your team without resistance. After you have claimed the pod, you have a couple ways to defend this location during the capturing phase. Keep at least one other team member with you during this phase, and use the partner system. You must cover three separate directions, and it's much easier to do that with a wingman. If available, drop an Infantry Turret in the direction that is of lower priority to cover; this is normally the direction that the majority of your team is in. If your team is close enough, you'll be able to see them on your radar. Drop down the auto-firing turret, and pay attention to what you originally are supposed to guard, while the turret guards the final unguarded area. If you can, keep up communications with your partner, and make sure that you drop back and stay safe if your partner goes down. As long as you're still alive, he or she can potentially deploy on your location

DON'T GIVE THE ENEMY YOUR PROVISIONS

Once the drop pod is captured and opened, your team earns a point. However, your opponent still has full capability of claiming the power-ups that come from the pod. Protect it as best as you can, and don't let your foe reap the benefits of your previous success.

3 The next zone over is the intelligence center to the starboard side of the Millennium Falcon. It may not seem like there are any places where the drop pod can fall from to make it into this location, but there are a couple very narrow openings in the ceiling—just perfect to drop supplies through. Just like the X-wing hangar, there are three directions you must watch when defending the location. However, the ceiling is much lower and the corridors are a lot tighter, making the CA-87 shotgun-type blaster more effective here than in any other section of the map. Use the chokepoints to defend this location, and set up deployable turrets to mow down any opponents that round the tight corners, leaving them no chance of escape. Attacking the intelligence center is the most challenging. Use Seeker Shots and Smoke Grenades (in that order) to have a chance at poking a hole in the enemy's defense.

4 The third location is quite a bit more open than the previous locations. Thanks to its wide open skyline, it is technically outdoors. This open format allows you to jump to the top level and get the advantage over the defenders. If possible, use a Jump Pack to get up there from the Millennium Falcon. If you're in the middle of capturing the drop pod from the outdoor cargo hold, don't risk getting to the top level. Accessing it isn't a simple task, nor is it possible from that side of the cliff. Because of this danger, some of the best locations from which to defend the drop pod are the interiors, either the hallways on the sides or the vehicle entry underneath the cliff itself. The location that allows the easiest return to the pod is the central entryway from the Millennium Falcon hangar. However, it is also in the direction where the enemy most likely attacks from. The Personal Shield is very useful when you are attempting to get to the drop pod in a pinch. Anything might be waiting for you, and the shield gives you a few seconds to react to whatever is there.

5 The depot entrance is by far the most open area of the map. However, with the boundary keeping you from leaving and running out into the rest of Tatooine, it can appear deceivingly bigger than it actually is. There is no defined wall, but you can go beyond the main line of debris, which makes for a great ambush location. Hiding behind the debris that lines the border of the map gives you two advantages: you avoid being directly in the line of sight, and you remain completely hidden until you choose to reveal yourself. Since you are out of any enemies' line of sight as they enter this area, you have the advantage of waiting for them to enter your chosen ambush location and striking at your discretion. There is always the chance of a vigilant opponent coming to look for you before attempting to capture the drop pod, so stay frosty and be ready for anything.

6 Finally, the biggest and most difficult location to hold in the Rebel Depot is the Millennium Falcon hangar, which can be accessed from any other area of the map. This location is always a bit chaotic, but as long as you can get the high ground on the Falcon or one of the cliffs, you will have a major advantage. Keeping the high ground is both challenging and requires some help from your teammates. You won't be able to capture any drop pods while up high, but it is your job to keep them protected and call out any locations that your opponents are attacking from. The drop pods can drop anywhere around the Falcon, so be ready to set your sights on every angle. Also, be ready to jump as quickly as possible; by default, your foes roam this area anyway.

Cargo

1 The Rebel Depot is definitely one of the more advanced places to play Cargo on. The tight corridors make it difficult to get past any defenses the enemy team might have set up in preparation for your return with their cargo. Alternatively, if the cargo carrier can get lucky or directly outsmart the other team, he or she can return to base without laying eyes on a single adversary. The same goes for defending cargo. You should always be aware of where your opponents are and where they might be defending from (or where exactly they are defending). Either way, all tactics in this mode on this map require a ton of teamwork before you can defeat the other side.

2 Playing as the Rebel Alliance, your team's cargo is located in the outdoor cargo hold, which sits toward the stern of the Millennium Falcon. There are three different directions to be aware of, but whenever you're playing Cargo, you and

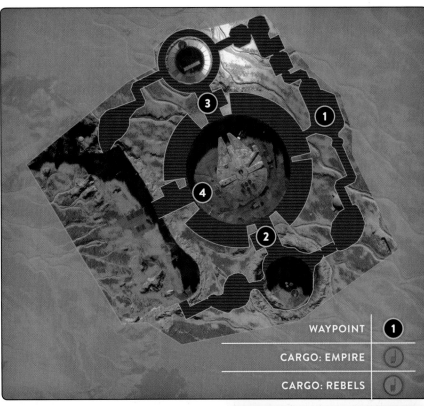

WAYPOINT	**1**
CARGO: EMPIRE	
CARGO: REBELS	

your team should know what everyone is doing and which tactics you plan to use. If the majority of your team is playing the midfield and has a fast pathway to your friendly cargo hold, you might want yourself or other friendlies to defend the side paths from inside the corridors and from a little farther up to keep the enemy as far from your cargo as possible. However, if your team is scattered and perhaps on full-charge offense, the defender should stay as close as possible to your friendly cargo and remain out of sight. Within the cargo hold, "out of sight" means either behind some of the boxes spread out in this area or in one of the corridors to the side (granted, there you have something or someone watching your back).

3 Fighting for the Empire is fairly similar, but the big difference is that you have fewer options of hiding and keeping protected while near the cargo than you do in the side corridors. The cargo for the Empire is located in the X-wing hangar off the bow of the Millennium Falcon, and the entrance to the hangar is slightly narrower. However, there is not a wall that obstructs the entrance, unlike the outdoor cargo hold on the Rebels' side of the Rebel Depot. You can shoot straight into the X-wing hangar, creating somewhat of a free fire area near the cargo. Because it's likely for the hangar to get quite hot, you should defend from the sides. Here, there are a couple of rooms that provide some areas where you can move around and set up proper defenses against attackers. However, because it is not as difficult to attack this side of the map, this also means that a good way to prevent the enemy from looting your team's cargo is to take over and hold down the center Millennium Falcon hangar. Use that leverage to quickly dispatch any attackers from this location if they happen to get inside the X-wing hangar, or cut them off before they get to their side by running down the horizontal center of the map.

4 Avoid worrying too much about the neutral center of the corridors on the sides of the map, unless you and your team have a plan. Controlling the hangar that the Millennium Falcon is located in gives your entire team the advantage in moving to either side to defend your teammates as they make off with the enemy's cargo, or kill the enemy stealing yours and return your own cargo, keeping the enemy team from scoring. The port side of the Falcon leads to the depot's entrance, the most open area, which leaves a lot of room

for unknown and unexpected firefights. You never know if someone might be waiting out there for you, so taking the cargo this way is extremely unpredictable. Still, it is much easier to protect if planned in advance. If the status of the depot entrance is unknown, the safer path is the starboard side of the Falcon simply because you can see much of how well it is defended before you go too far.

Hero Hunt

1 Hero Hunt in the Rebel Depot is heroes against stormtroopers, or in this case, sandtroopers. As the stormtroopers chase you around the Millennium Falcon, there are dozens of locations and ways to avoid and/or ambush them, depending on the character that is chosen for you to play. If you are playing as Luke, Han, or Leia, your tactics should change dramatically, as these characters are built extremely differently. As with all modes on Rebel Depot, there are five prime locations that give both teams an advantage when used in a few specific ways.

2 Luke Skywalker has a few extremely powerful strengths that can eliminate the entire team if you catch them off guard. Using Luke's full swing, you can take out every enemy standing nearby, so a small room or intelligence area can lead to a massacre. Consider how narrow the corridors leading from room to room are. If you can lure the entire team into a single hallway, deflect blaster bolts straight

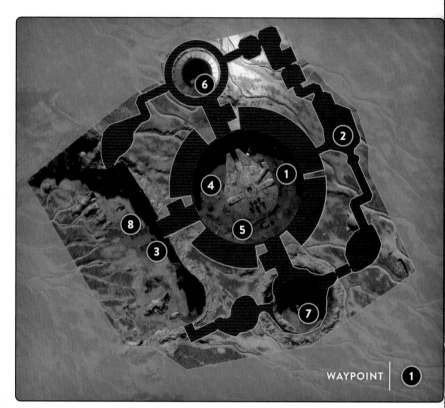

WAYPOINT | **1**

back at them, leaving them no room to avoid your fire. If the stormtroopers get wise and stop shooting in order to throw grenades or explosives, Luke can use his Force Push to heavily damage the enemy troops. He can then use his Saber Charge ability to immediately go after the survivors.

3 If you are playing as Han Solo, you want to use the outdoor locations (like the cargo hold or the depot entrance) and keep the enemies at range. Han's blaster wins any potential gunfight challenge. Use Lucky Shot to take down a group of troopers in a single shot, or at least heavily damage the majority of them. This makes it much easier to kill the group and win the bigger fight. Occasionally, you may be forced to run from a fight when the entire group of stormtroopers is firing on you from one location. Remember that when you're stuck in a tight situation and don't have any chance but to fight, use Shoulder Charge to rush through your adversaries, hopefully trampling a few along the way. If you don't get all of the troopers in your path, you at least have a choice of escaping, as you are no longer pinned down and stuck in a difficult spot.

4 The Rebel Depot does not favor Princess Leia, but there are still many ways to survive and use her abilities to kill the enemy. Leia's supply drop doesn't help your success in Hero Hunt, but dropping the Enhanced Squad Shield and immediately popping Trooper Bane lets you shoot through the shield. You can kill each trooper with one shot while limiting their options for attacking you. The Enhanced Squad Shield can be useful for several situations (like the one just mentioned), but it can also be used as a trap. For the most part, the only way to attack Leia is to destroy the incredibly powerful shield, which takes a good amount of time, or to enter the shield and force a close-quarters combat situation. Use that knowledge to lure a stormtrooper or two into the shield, and then outshoot the trooper, knowing that you have a great deal more health than he or she does. Use the narrower spaces on this map to your advantage, and employ the shield tactic when you are caught in a pinch, both indoors and out.

Heroes Vs. Villains

5 The balanced, Rebel Depot lends very well to this mode, allowing all the characters to use each of their abilities to its full capacity. For the most part, the heroes use very similar tactics as they would in Hero Hunt. However, there are a few slight differences that might make or break your victory. For instance, when you are playing as Princess Leia, keep in mind that your shield not only grants you more cover, but it is also the best way to counter Boba Fett's powerful blaster as he launches above you. As Han, you should use Lucky Shot, as it is something that causes a great deal of damage and that enemies can't deflect. Using Rapid Fire against Darth Vader or Emperor Palpatine can only get you into trouble, though, as they can deflect that high amount of damage right back at Han.

6 In this mode, you can play as Darth Vader on Tatooine. Using his Saber Throw is one way to deal with both Han Solo and Princess Leia. It is difficult to kill either hero with Saber Throw, but it inflicts more than enough damage to give you a chance to close the gap between Vader and them, giving yourself the advantage of close quarters. The center underneath the transport ship's hull is Vader's most useful area. This location brings in most enemies close, taking away any disadvantages that Vader has at range. Lure your opponent into a tight location like this one, and then use Force Choke or Heavy Strike to take down your adversary with ease.

7 Boba Fett is a man to be reckoned with here in the Rebel Depot. On this map, players can perfectly stay at range the entire match if desired and still be effective. Post up on the Millennium Falcon located to the north side of the map, and take advantage of being able to go anywhere within seconds by using your jetpack. Once you have an idea of where the enemies are, you might want to save some jet fuel and let it loose to get the high angle on all of them. If they can't see where you are right away, you have the advantage of getting a few shots on them before they do see you, and then bugging out before being attacked. Launching Wrist Rocket as your first attack toward any hero gives you quite the advantage when it comes down to damage per second on your opponent. The Flamethrower attached to your forearm may not be quite as useful on this map as your other abilities, but if you're caught in a pinch, it could get you out of a close-quarters situation against someone like Luke Skywalker.

8 When playing as Emperor Palpatine on this map, keep in mind that you have a very powerful deflect ability that comes quite in handy when facing heroes like Han Solo and Princess Leia. As the Emperor, your best strategy is sticking as close as possible to other villains. Because you are close, you can support them by casting Chain Lightning at multiple enemies. This can either cause your opponent to bug out or attempt to close the gap on you, only to be ambushed by your partner standing closeby. Remember to escape or help protect another villain with Force Dash.

DUNE SEA EXCHANGE

Blast

❶ Playing Blast on Dune Sea Exchange is one big free-for-all in the sense of how open it is. There are several key locations on this map, but it is possible to get a line of sight to any location rather quickly. The transport ship is directly in the center of the map. Surrounding it are the Khetanna sail barge, the sternside cargo crates, the shipping dock, and the bowside cargo crates. All of those locations are almost symmetrically placed around the transport ship, which acts like a centerpiece for the entire map.

❷ The transport ship in the center has become the structure that provides the most cover, but also the most action. It has a small temporary base set up directly underneath the hull and provides cover for both fighters passing through and those hiding to ambush the aforementioned fighters moving from one end to the other. You can also hide behind a few machines. Although there is not a whole lot of room, these locations do come in handy when you don't want someone who has no idea you are there to see you.

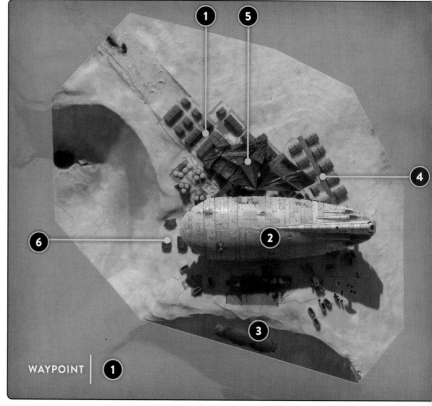

The area under the ship extends the entire length of it, so use this to fire on troops directly on the opposite side of you.

❸ Looking out to the port side of the transport ship is a Khetanna sail barge that is docked against the clifflike edge of the sand dune. It is attached to the ground via a bridge extending from the ship itself. You can use the barge to get a wide-angle view of the entire starboard side of the transport ship, including some from both the bow and stern. Pay attention to the machines directly next to the Khetanna, as they are tall enough to cover a foe's approach on your position. The machines are set up in a way that allows you to either move around them or pass in between them. Accordingly, you have a few different options for using them as cover when you move around the map. It's also important to notice the walkway built directly above these machines, which can likewise give you a great view of this side of the map. However, because it is located at a slightly elevated location and lacks adequate cover, you are a sitting duck if you stay up there too long.

4 Moving to the stern of the ship, you can find a collection of large cargo crates. These crates don't provide for a great amount of cover, but they do conceal your movement because of the slope that they are set on. It may not be a great idea to spend too much time here, and it isn't very easy to see where the enemy is aside from using your movement detector. Still, if you have no choice, you have plenty of space to use some power-ups there. Try setting up an Infantry Turret or calling in an Orbital Strike outside the perimeter of the cargo crates to at least give you an idea of someone approaching. Hopefully, you can manage a kill or two and give yourself an opportunity to escape, punching a hole in any fortification your opponent might have.

5 The shipping dock is the most complex location of the Dune Sea Exchange, as it has a walkway similar to the one near the Khetanna. This walkway can also leave you exposed if you stay up there too long, but there is much more cover just in case you are spotted. Directly below the walkway, you can find a few more machines next to another load of large cargo crates. This area provides the most cover and functions just like a simple maze. Use it for losing an enemy during your blaster's cool-down or any abilities that may be on a cool-down timer. You can also jump on top of the cargo crates to surprise an opponent directly in your vicinity. However, don't jump on the crate unless absolutely necessary: a jump reveals your location to more foes than just the one you're attempting to avoid or sneak up on.

6 On the bow (almost directly in front of the ship) is a large load of open supply crates that are slightly different than the cargo placed uniformly in the sand. With less of a structure on this side of the map, you shouldn't pass between the crates, but you can use them for cover. Note that these supply crates are slightly shorter than the other cargo crates, so crouching is your best way to stay hidden. Use this area to take the longer-range shots: it is located in the most "corner-like" part of the map, and you can see down two ranges and hide after each shot.

Drop Zone

1 As one of the more open maps in all of Tatooine, Dune Sea Exchange has multiple locations available where pods can drop. A few locations encourage strategies that match up very well to other possible drop pod positions on the map. Such positions include the cargo crates underneath the secondary transport ship, the control dock, the bow of the main transport ship, and the stern of the ship between the spread of open supply crates.

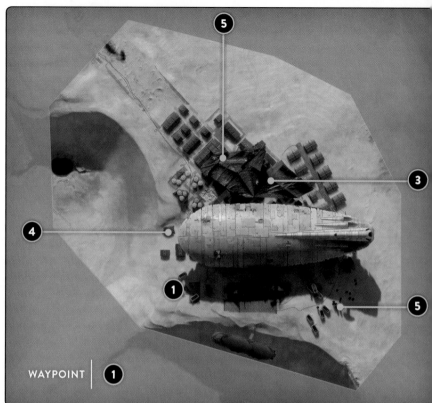

WAYPOINT | **1**

2 The cargo crates located to the starboard side of the center transport ship and in between that ship and the barge have little to no cover and are a great place for a Squad Shield. You can use the large cargo crates to take cover from attacking enemy troops, but it's not the best way to avoid being fired on entirely. As mentioned, the Squad Shield allows you and your team a few more seconds when you attempt to begin the capture sequence. Avoid setting down too many power-ups just to capture one drop pod. Although the entire point of the mode is to capture drop pods, if your team uses every power-up it has, you could be left vulnerable and less powerful when you go for the next drop pod. This area and a couple others lack the structure for you to feel safe and locked down when defending the drop pods. Once you have initiated the capture, your success is not even close to being guaranteed.

3 The next key location is not too far from the last one. As you move closer to the center transport ship, you can find a dock with a walkway. This section features two layers that you must stay aware of to avoid getting shot from a place where you just didn't think to look. Drop pods fall all around this location, and it is helpful to use the walkway to set up an overwatch for your team. Overwatch is key while your teammates go for the capture. You can get a great deal of kills and rack up defense points, in turn bringing your team one step closer to victory. If you find yourself getting picked off from a distance, or if the enemy team has taken over the walkway, try getting in underneath the elevated location. Then, stay out of their sight while you shoot them in the back.

4 The spread-out bow of the ship is a great place for using the Jump Pack to get from cover to cover as quickly as possible. Take note of the Khetanna sail barge slightly off to the side of the bow—it provides a great vantage point for sniping attackers. This area requires the largest amount of communication with your teammates because they won't always be in your line of sight or possibly even near you. Spread out and play to the terrain of the map's location. Call out enemy positions frequently, giving your team an idea of where to send their blaster bolts and explosives.

5 A load of electronic beacons and supply crates is stationed near the stern of the center main transport. Very similar to the cargo crate staging area, this location also lacks a large amount of cover, although there are still objects that you can use. However, unlike the large cargo crates, these blocks of several beacons are tall enough to afford you some cover when moving while standing. You don't need to crouch, but be careful not to move around too much. Showing up on the enemy's radar because of excessive movement gives away your position anyway. Toss Impact Grenades toward the drop pod you are trying to capture, as long as you can guarantee that there are no friendlies around. The Impact Grenade has a lower range of explosion but leaves your opponent no time to escape, as they are in the capture timer and are guaranteed to be in close proximity to the drop pod.

Droid Run

1 Droid Run on Dune Sea Exchange is mayhem, especially when two teams fight over the same droid. Because of the map's layout, there is a natural center of action as the three objective droids roam around the Rebel transport ship. The transport ship acts as a dangerous shortcut to each droid, so move at your own discretion, and avoid danger if you can. Use the outer peripheral objects and structures to stay out of the major line of sight, thus limiting unnecessary deaths while attacking or defending droids and key locations on the map.

2 The "A" droid is located just in front of the bow of the transport ship. It tends to roam in between the turret heads, near the large cargo crates. Try capturing this droid when it is in the center of the turret heads because that provides the most cover for incoming lateral fire. The turret heads are not very tall, so crouch while you capture the droid to avoid being seen. The capture speed is rather fast, so if you see the opportunity, go ahead and take it. Then, escape immediately to find some

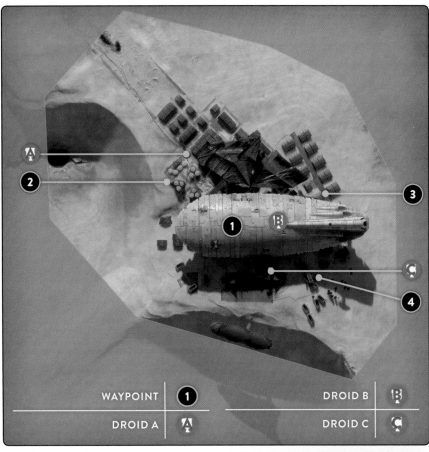

WAYPOINT	1		DROID B	B
DROID A	A		DROID C	C

real cover, as you must now protect the droid from the enemy. This area requires the most defense because it is one of the easier locations to access and see from a distance. There are some tented cover units nearby. You can use them to conceal your location, but keep an eye on the droid so that it is not stolen from under your nose.

3 The next droid that needs capturing is "B," located on the starboard side of the transport ship. In this capture (and in the "C" droid capture, as well), certain sections of the droid's roaming path can leave you more exposed than others. The "B" droid roams directly around the walkway that is part of the supply dock, but because of this, it can roam into open territory and leave you exposed to enemies on the other side of the ship. However, there are a few large stacks of cargo crates that more than cover you, and the droid does roam near them. Capture the droid as it moves behind the stacks to be fully protected from an entire side—leaving the chances of being shot from a blind side much less likely.

4 The "C" droid location on Dune Sea Exchange happens to be on the port side of the center transport ship, and this droid roams the partial length of the ship itself. The area where the power droid roams is important to know and understand because there are safer points than others when you attempt to capture this droid. As the droid begins heading toward the stern of the ship, it becomes a lot more exposed to both the center of the map and most of the starboard side of the ship. It's best to capture the droid when it is in the most forward section of the ship. This part provides a little more cover than the droid's other roaming area, but you still aren't completely protected from most angles. Avoid spending too much time waiting for it to roam. Know that you are exposed when the droid is in the rear section of its walking path, and have your team watch your back.

Hero Hunt

1 Like all locations on Tatooine, you play as the Heroes and sandtroopers on Dune Sea Exchange. Dune Sea Exchange is excellent for Hero Hunt because although it may feel quite large, it is actually small compared to most maps. This makes it easier to find the sandtroopers (or the hero, for that matter). As a sandtrooper, you must take the heroes on from all angles and avoid getting caught while clustered up in one area. (That shouldn't be a problem on this map.) This area feels large because it contains many places that separate into various sections of the map, including large electronic panels, metal walkways, cargo crates, and other debris. Because of the multiple sections, you and your fellow sandtroopers should know how to call them out as quickly as possible so you can take down the enemy hero.

2 Playing as Luke Skywalker gives you the ultimate power to loop around most of the obstacles found on Dune Sea Exchange. Get behind the enemy sandtroopers and use the Saber Rush

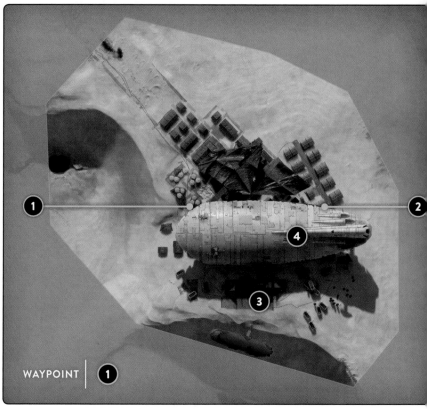

WAYPOINT **1**

to catch them with a killing blow from quite a far distance. Jump high in the air before employing the Saber Rush to arrive at some locations much more quickly, giving the hunters even less time to set up an ambush or attack. When looking for places to use your Heavy Strike, check out the space underneath the hull of the center transport ship; the enemy has a hard time avoiding this attack.

3 Han Solo thrives on maps like Dune Sea Exchange. There isn't as much cover here as on many other maps, but there is more than enough for Han to use while blasting his way through the hunting sandtroopers. Using abilities like Lucky Shot can give you an advantage while playing as Han: these abilities have a high radius of explosive damage, which helps when you're trying to hit enemies behind cover. Considering that most of the cover on Dune Sea Exchange is shorter than average, shooting Lucky Shot right over the top and hitting the other side of the cover typically damages or even kills adversaries hiding from your fire.

4 If you are deployed as Princess Leia, your biggest strength is the use of your Enhanced Squad Shield; where there isn't much cover, you can make your own. For the most part, you must create as much cover as possible as often as possible. While playing as Leia, you are relative to a stronger trooper and must play as if it were simply a one-trooper-versus-all situation. You have many advantages when it comes to health and damage, so use them, but don't get carried away. Leia is quite fragile when there are no heroes to support.

Heroes Vs. Villains

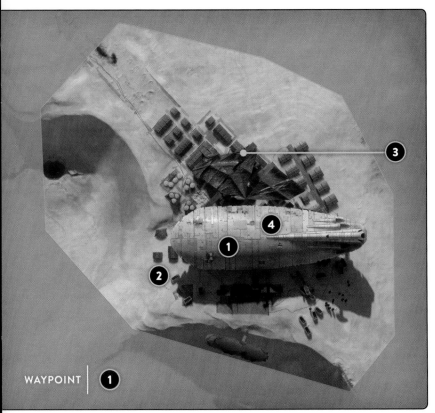

WAYPOINT | **1**

1 The balanced, open Dune Sea Exchange lends very well to this mode, allowing all the characters to use each of their abilities to its full capacity. For the most part, the heroes use very similar tactics as they would in Hero Hunt. However, there are a few slight differences that might make or break your victory. For instance, when you are playing as Princess Leia, keep in mind that your shield not only grants you more cover, but it is also the best way to counter Boba Fett's powerful blaster as he launches above you. As Han, you should use Lucky Shot, as it is something that causes a great deal of damage and that enemies can't deflect. Using Rapid Fire against Darth Vader or Emperor Palpatine can only get you into trouble, though, as they can deflect that high amount of damage right back at Han.

2 In this mode, you can play as Darth Vader on Tatooine. Using his Saber Throw is one way to deal with both Han Solo and Princess Leia. It is difficult to kill either hero with Saber Throw, but it inflicts more than enough damage to give you a chance to close the gap between Vader and them, giving yourself the advantage of close quarters. The center underneath the transport ship's hull is Vader's most useful area. This location brings in most enemies close, taking away any disadvantages that Vader has at range. Lure your opponent into a tight location like this one, and then use Force Choke or Heavy Strike to take down your adversary with ease.

3 Boba Fett is a man to be reckoned with here in the Dune Sea Exchange. On this map, players can perfectly stay at range the entire match if desired and still be effective. Post up in the Khetanna located to the north side of the map, and take advantage of being able to go anywhere within seconds by using your jetpack. Once you have an idea of where the enemies are, you might want to save some jet fuel and let it loose to get the high angle on all of them. If they can't see where you are right away, you have the advantage of getting a few shots on them before they do see you, and then bugging out before being attacked. Launching Wrist Rocket as your first attack toward any hero gives you quite the advantage when it comes down to damage per second on your opponent. The Flamethrower attached to your forearm may not be quite as useful on this map as your other abilities, but if you're caught in a pinch, it could get you out of a close-quarters situation against someone like Luke Skywalker.

4 When playing as Emperor Palpatine on this map, keep in mind that you have a very powerful deflect ability that comes quite in handy when facing heroes like Han Solo and Princess Leia. As the Emperor, your best strategy is sticking as close as possible to other villains. Because you are close, you can support them by casting Chain Lightning at multiple enemies. This can either cause your opponent to bug out or attempt to close the gap on you, only to be ambushed by your partner standing closeby. Remember to escape or help protect another villain with Force Dash.

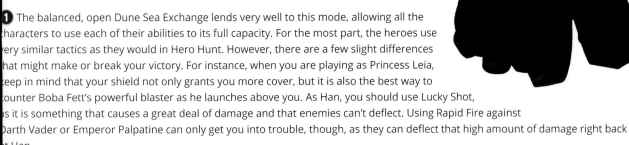

ENDOR

Covered in grassy plains, small oceans, some very uneven terrain, and (above all else) forests, Endor is more specifically referred to as the Forest Moon of Endor. Endor is home to the Ewoks, which are known for aiding the Rebels in their battles against the Empire. The planet is quite devoid of humanoid life but is extremely thick with vegetation and small animals. The wildlife may seem adorable, friendly, and sweet, but they can be quite dangerous, as most are predatory. The Empire has set up bases here, and now the Rebel forces have come to destroy their resources and strategic locations with the help and resistance of indigenous lifeforms.

Endor is covered in many sorts of flora, such as tall redwood and pine trees, thick short-growing bushes, and a tremendous amount of ground cover. If there were a planet that provided the most natural cover for troopers to hide behind and use as tactical advantages, this would be the one. The extremely tall trees make it difficult for snipers to shoot from long distances, as they obstruct most views. However, this is not impossible, especially in the clearings where small bodies of water may be. Take note of the complex tree bridges and stairs that the Ewoks living in these areas built. They are very useful, considering the angles that you can fire from. In these sections, you must remain aware of what or who might be near you. Even though your radar might indicate that an enemy is standing right next to you, he may be several meters above you thinking the same exact thing. Take time to look around before moving into the open. The longer you stay in cover, the better chance you will have the opportunity to see your opponent make that exact move, revealing them directly in front of your crosshairs.

FOREST MOON OF ENDOR

Supremacy

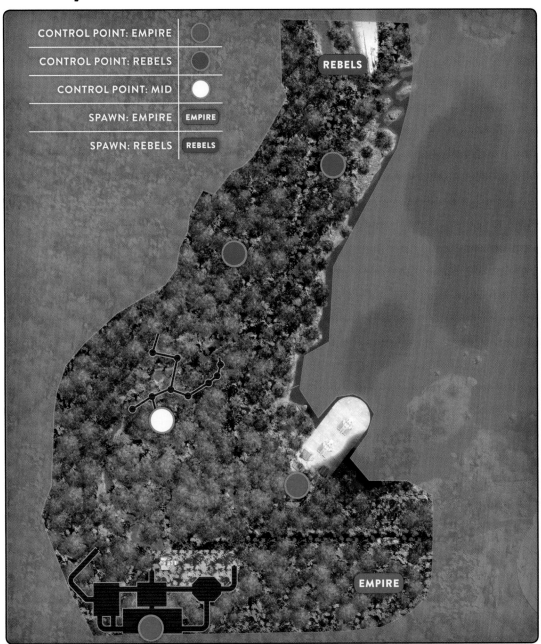

CONTROL POINT: EMPIRE	○
CONTROL POINT: REBELS	●
CONTROL POINT: MID	○
SPAWN: EMPIRE	EMPIRE
SPAWN: REBELS	REBELS

REBELS

EMPIRE

The center of the map and the first control point available for capturing is up in the trees, sitting on top of one of the Ewok-built stairs. Both fortunately and unfortunately, you can capture the control point from multiple elevations as long as you are located inside the capture circle. The fight over this control point can dictate the pace of the match, as the point is contested quite often simply because of its location. One of the most strategic areas from which to take this control point is one of the bridged sections across from the actual control point.

From here, you can defend the location from anyone attempting to contest it while your team tries to take it. This strategy also applies after you have taken the point and must protect it while your team needs to advance onto the next point.

During the Imperials' first "push forward" phase, be aware of any enemies standing underneath the initial control point. As mentioned previously, the area can be taken from several different locations, most of these are blind. The next area to capture is the forward Rebel camp. Multiple cargo crates and supplies surround this area, leaving plenty of structures available for cover. When attacking this position, keep your eyes on the surrounding forest, as many sightlines lead directly into this location. Popping a Smoke Grenade can protect you from snipers and definitely protects you from the Seeker Shot. One thing to remember during Supremacy on Forest Moon of Endor is to use the structures and crates as camouflage—your stormtrooper gear blends in rather nicely.

Next up is the Rebels' final stand: another forward camp. This time, it's located on a shallow cliffside adjacent to the lake. The challenge when attacking this area as an Imperial occurs during the "push forward" phase because there are many places to hide along the way to this final Rebel control point. Rebels should use these hollowed-out trees as major cover and ambush points. But remember that although running through one of them is great for concealing your approach, it is also a easy way to get ambushed upon exiting the tree. When you are defending this location, note

ROYAL SUPPORT

Leia's Enhanced Squad Shield defends your teammates while they help you capture any of the enemy points. However, it can also help protect your squardmates from adversaries firing on your position from above while you focus on incoming fire on the ground.

that the Rebels want to be pushed forward. Keeping the enemy as far away from the point as possible is what saves your team from defeat. With that being said, it is also important to avoid being flanked around the side that is opposite of the lake. The lake can keep your team somewhat protected because you can see what's down there, but the forest can help conceal the enemy, making defense a little bit more of a challenge.

Going the opposite way of the center point happens when the Rebel forces have the advantage and have pushed the Imperials back to their outpost. This next control point is located inside the outpost. Having the control point indoors may seem like an advantage to the defending team, but remember that once you have broken the enemy's defenses, it becomes just as difficult for them to take it back. Inside the capture area is a turret. This is a very important piece to the map because it points directly at the main entrance, which is where the majority of enemy troops enter from. There are a couple other entrances to stay aware of, however. Use proximity mines and deployable Blaster Cannons to either set up a crossfire or an even more formidable defense system, covering all possibilities into this outpost. It is also beneficial to defend from the outside if there are too many teammates inside. In that situation, if one Rebel gets lucky, your entire squad could be finished in one fell swoop.

Finally, the Rebels have pushed the Imperial forces back to their transport ship. Without a way to successfully flank the enemy, there is not much you can do besides face them head-on. But that's fine in this situation—the platform where the Imperial transport ship sits is quite open, exposing the Empire's forces rather easily. Be aware that this area is not as easy as it seems, even with the lack of places to hide. Because this location is so open, it is a prime spot for the use of AT-ST walkers with extremely high firepower and defensive capabilities. Equipping Ion Torpedoes and Ion Grenades is one of the only things that can bring down these walkers without wasting a ton of troops. The AT-ST is not the most maneuverable vehicle, but it can turn its upper body quickly enough to cover its surroundings. Fire your torpedoes and then find cover immediately, since the driver will find you and take you down if he or she spots you.

Walker Assault

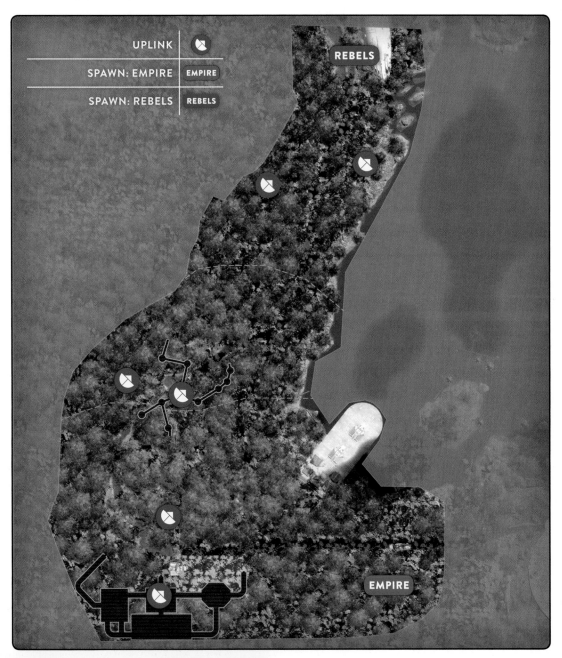

Due to the very dense canopy on this forest planet, there is only one single AT-AT walker when playing Walker Assault on Endor. The large trees provide cover for Rebel forces as they attempt to get close to the walker during its vulnerable phase, but beware of the high-powered blasters mounted on the AT-AT's turrets. During the first phase of Walker Assault on the Forest Moon of Endor, you can use several bunkers to get from section to section while staying protected from the walker. The Empire troopers also use these bunkers to stop your forces from getting close to their walkers. For the Imperials, the bunkers can come in handy when you're guessing where the enemy will be, but it is also a good place to simply watch and set up defenses just outside the entrances. When your opponents are inside the bunker, there isn't much they can do to your mission; it's when they leave that you have a problem.

As with all versions of Walker Assault, there are two uplinks that the Rebels must capture in order to temporarily disable walkers (in this case, a single one). The first of two uplinks in the first phase is located in one of the middle bunkers just inside the entrance. There are several ways into this part of the bunker, but the main entrance is very close to the uplink. An effective way to defend this uplink is from the door or hallway closest to your team's "side" (meaning the side of the map closest to where you deployed from). This strategy gives you the best angle on where the majority of enemy troops come from, but it still leaves you in a slightly vulnerable location. Whenever possible, you should

push past the objective and defend in front of the uplink. This technique provides a much tighter chokepoint, and if enemy troops come in through another way, they are not likely to turn your direction until it's too late.

The second uplink in this first phase is located just across the creek from the first, directly under a fallen tree. The second uplink is a lot more vulnerable to attack from vertical angles, but it is much easier to hold once a side has taken control of it. Unfortunately for the Rebels, once the AT-AT gets close to this uplink, it very effectively bombards the location to ensure that forces from either side will not be able to secure this location. It is most effective to activate this uplink early and attempt to hold it as long as possible. It takes your team fewer troops to hold the interior uplink, so with a little teamwork, your team can take over both uplinks early and hold them for the entire first phase.

The second phase in Walker Assault on Endor has a slightly different setup. The indoor opportunities are gone at this point, and long range becomes the friendly tactic (unlike the first phase). The first of the two uplinks is located in between a few very large, thick trees. The trees form a cove-type shelter that looks like it was made for a speeder to drive straight in and take control of the uplink from the Imperial side. Behind this uplink is a tall hill that anyone can climb, although it is a little easier to stay protected when playing as a Rebel because of the exposed side of the hill that the Rebels deploy from. Use the hill for both attack and defense, but remember that Imperials are a little more vulnerable when defending from the hill.

TIMELY SPEEDER

Use the speeder before the phase change to get to the next zone before anyone else has the chance.

The second uplink in the second phase of this match takes place high above in the trees on one of the Ewok-made wooden platforms. Approach this uplink from a distance by using one of the other stairways to access the high elevation before heading over to the uplink. This may give you a better sight of who might be defending the location before you arrive and get blindsided. The area containing the uplink is quite complex as far as the levels go. Take advantage of this when attacking by checking everything before heading to the uplink; it saves you in the long run.

Once the uplink is under your control, take over these areas and levels to gain full dominance. As difficult as it may have been for you to check everything, it will be the same for your opponents, so you should have the advantage of spotting them first.

The final phase can be extremely challenging for both sides, and its difficulty solely depends on taking control of the uplink area quickly. Both uplinks during this phase are extremely exposed and sit inside the camps near the Rebel transport ship, which happens to be the target for the Imperial AT-AT walker. Taking control of these uplinks does not guarantee your victory because they are incredibly difficult to defend; this goes for either side. One of the best strategies for the Rebel team is maintaining some space between your hideout and the uplink. There isn't much cover that can protect you from a Thermal Grenade or two, so keep some distance, and take out any enemies going straight for the uplink.

SWAMP CRASH SITE

Blast

1 In the Swamp Crash Site, you must use everything you possibly can as cover and as a means of protection. Use the trees, the downed starship, the rocks, and the changes in elevation to keep yourself from being seen. Not many planets give you the opportunity to stay stealthy and hidden in the same way that Endor does, so use the brush and shadows to your advantage to flank the enemy. Playing Blast is all about getting the most kills. Because of this, you and your team must also have the fewest deaths. Stay hidden, and pick your battles carefully. The treacherous terrain and thick forest can betray your senses, and the moment you are not careful is the moment you get shot in the back.

2 Some of the better weapons to use in a mode like Blast in the Swamp Crash Site are the mid-range blasters. Blasters like the E-11 or the DLT-19 give you the advantage of having a large spectrum of accurate moments with any situations you may be caught in while on this map. Items like the Smoke Grenade or Seeker Shot are challenging to use here because the areas are so vast. They may even give your position away, killing the element of surprise. Instead, assets like the Pulse Cannon or the Cycler Rifle can keep you at range and out of dangerous firefights while still snagging kills for your team.

3 The best place to use these assets are on top of the elevated walkways along the edge of the map, and looking downrange and downhill toward the transport ship.

For those who are not the stealthy type, looping the outer perimeter of the map can also provide active cover in the way of having an entire flank covered at all times. Because long-range Star Cards and mid-range blasters are so incredibly useful here, running along the outer perimeter of the map helps your team from being taken out at longer ranges. It also gives you the opportunity to take your opponents out, thus protecting your teammates with an active offense.

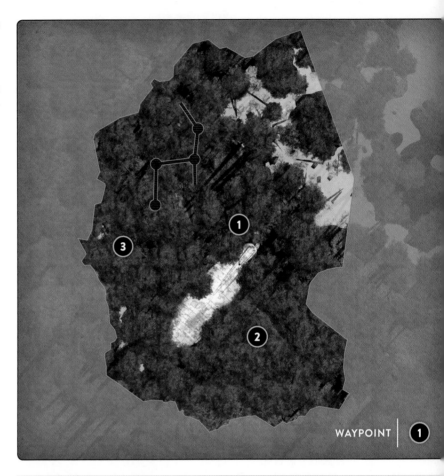

WAYPOINT **1**

DANGER CLOSE

Use your radar to track any enemy motion. Even if you don't see an adversary, use an Orbital Strike when possible to clear out any area that might contain foes. Given that it is difficult to see the enemy, this is a worthwhile risk and a likely heavy point boost.

Drop Zone

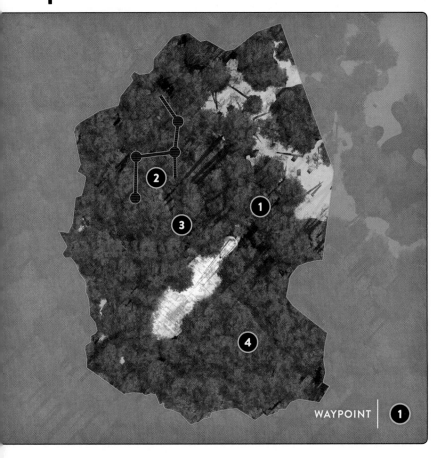

The Swamp Crash Site on Endor has a mostly closed canopy and plenty of objects on the ground that prevent drop pods from falling just anywhere. Luckily, there are still multiple opportunities for the drop pod to land. In fact, because of how dense this map is, it is quite illusionary as to how many locations there actually are.

1 A drop pod can potentially land almost anywhere around the downed transport ship, but one of the more important spots is near the stern and in the center of a spread of countless pieces of debris and cargo. Because of the large crash, there are about a half-dozen destroyed trees and what appears to be a previous explosion of ship parts and cargo. Each of these items and debris acts as a great resource for cover and tactical advantage. The drop pod lands directly in the middle, leaving it more vulnerable than the perimeter around it. That's why it is important to claim the pod as quickly as possible and escape to go find cover. Cover this drop pod from a short distance instead of immediately next to it. This helps you stay hidden and avoid opponents taking you out with long-range weapons.

2 The next location is in the middle of a small creek that has developed into a waterfall. The waterfall is not very big and can be easily traversed, but one of the Ewok bridge tree structures surrounds it. The structures that are built high in the trees make this place extremely dangerous, mostly for attackers. The main goal of securing this area should be taking control of the tree bridge because it has the ultimate overwatch on the drop pod location. The drop pod usually lands symmetrically between the trees and directly in the center of the creek, making for another extremely vulnerable location. Take over the high ground to eliminate the vulnerability, and own this section of the map to collect your loot.

❸ Between the last location and the ship is the possibility for another drop pod. Though it would be incredibly fortunate for a pod to drop immediately after the tree bridge area, you shouldn't count on it. The next location is directly outside the pathway that leads underneath the transport ship and extremely close to the center of the map. Naturally, significant foot traffic leads that way. The drop pod for the current location also drops straight in the middle of the creek. You might want to stay close to the pod; there is not much cover around that isn't in the middle of a popular pathway for all the troopers on the battlefield. The difference between this area and the last is that a large fallen tree nearby can act as a blind spot for any enemies coming from the transport ship proper. To optimally control this location, use the ledges and the brush to hide your approach and your defense. If you know that an adversary is attempting to take back the drop pod, walk over the fallen tree to give yourself an elevated advantage.

❹ On the opposite side of the ship, the terrain has a few drastic elevation changes. On the high side, a large clearing follows along the creek. This clearing has great possibility for drop pod locations, but they all can be defended from the edge of the clearing and in the brush. Take advantage of the large trees in this area because there isn't much else to hide behind. The popular location for the pod to land in is the intersection of several paths, presenting a great opportunity for you to use a Squad Shield. You can protect yourself and a few teammates while you take control of the pod and collect any additional power-ups you might find. Beware of the hill on the other side of the creek, though. While it is a tight space, it can hide a trooper or two waiting to make the jump during your most vulnerable moment.

Droid Run

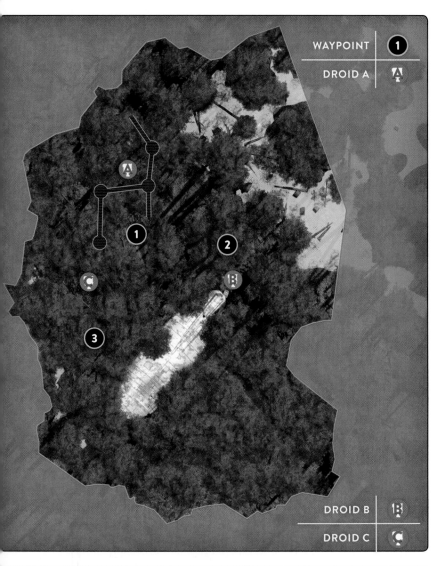

WAYPOINT	1
DROID A	ⓐ

DROID B	Ⓑ
DROID C	Ⓒ

COVERED MINES

Proximity mines emit a bright flashing red light when they are planted on the ground. However, if the proximity mine is placed carefully in an area with a high amount of foliage, the red light can be dampened, hiding the mine from the blind eye.

❶ As with all versions of Droid Run, you must find three capturable droids. They are stationed in three semi-symmetrical locations all over the Swamp Crash Site. The first of the three is appropriately labeled "A," and like the rest, it is a Power Droid. The map is slightly oriented on a hill, and as you move down the creek, you are also moving downhill. This "A" droid is located at the bottom of the hill and likes to roam along the creek in between the trees. The best time to begin your capture attempt is when it's at the lowest point on the hill and hidden behind some of the larger trees. The droid also likes to roam beneath the Ewok tree bridges, which makes for a great spot to watch over the entire area. Take control of the droid, and head through the high ground for the most optimal defense. An Infantry Turret can help you on one of the bridges by firing while the Power Droid is in your blind spot.

❷ The next droid that you can capture here is in a slightly narrower spot that does not allow for much defense other than the two entryways into the location. Fortunately, this means that once you've captured the droid, it takes a minimal defensive team to defend it. Any more, and it might actually hurt the offense that your team needs for other droids. The "B"

Power Droid is located between two sets of large cargo crates. One of the best ways to defend this location is using a Pulse Cannon from down the hill. There are a few sightlines to the droid as it roams up and down the pathway between the crates, making for a great use of long-range blasters and assets.

❸ "C," the final Power Droid, is actually located in the swamp at the top of the hill, which is the most challenging area of operations in the Swamp Crash Site. The difficulty increases here because the swamp acts as one giant kill box simply due to a lowered elevation and how it performs as a focal point to its surroundings. Unfortunately, once you've captured this droid, it takes a great deal of skilled shooting to defend it from anyone coming in and attempting to take it from you. You must be able to hide and ensure that the enemy does not find you before going after the droid. This location is key for holding the advantage on the map because it can act as a central area for friendlies to deploy. Copious natural cover surrounds the swamp, and the more allies present, the less likely the enemy is going to have a clear chance to capture the droid.

Hero Hunt

1 Hero Hunt on Endor is one of the two planets where the heroes are actually villains: you are hunting down Darth Vader, Emperor Palpatine, and Boba Fett. There are very specific ways to deal with and counter these villains while playing on Swamp Crash Site because most of the map appeals to a select number of play styles. Swamp Crash Site is mostly an open-air map that lends well to ranged attacks and requires close-range combat to be lured into very specific parts of the map.

2 Darth Vader has a bit of trouble when fighting on this map simply because he is a melee character who requires closed spaces for optimal effectiveness. The best place for Darth Vader to fight in is underneath the transport ship in the middle of the map because of the corridor's narrowness. The same goes for the area near the wreckage of the large cargo containers. When hunting Vader, the best weaponry to equip is high-powered mid-range blasters that allow you to keep your distance while being able to escape from his lightsaber at will. A Jump Pack gives you the quick option of escaping if you are caught in a pinch.

3 Whenever you are hunting down Emperor Palpatine, you don't want to bunch up with the rest of your friendly hunters because of his Chain Lightning

WAYPOINT **1**

ability. Minimize the Emperor's effective damage by keeping your distance between each other, and take him down from all ranges. Even though Palpatine does not have significant range on his Force Lightning, there are many chances where you definitely want to be up close and personal with him. While he is distracted by one of your teammates, use the CA-87 on him to take away a large chunk of health, giving him little chance to be able to defend from you. Beware of his Saber Defense ability, though. As soon as you see it go up, stop firing immediately to allow your team to gather on his flank. The main tactic for defeating Emperor Palpatine here is ensuring that he is always out in the open. Use the trees and natural cover to keep yourself protected from his lightning while you overwhelm his position before he can escape.

4 Boba Fett is by far the most dangerous villain in the Swamp Crash Site because he can get anywhere as soon as he wants. Boba Fett's jetpack can take him to the Ewok bridgeways, granting the element of the high ground while also letting him escape before any troopers have the chance to even get close. Boba Fett's biggest weakness is that his blaster becomes a little less powerful and accurate at long ranges. This means that if he does take the high ground, having long-range assets and blasters equipped gives the hunters slightly more of an advantage over the villain. Whenever possible, use the Pulse Cannon and the Cycler Rifle.

Heroes Vs. Villains

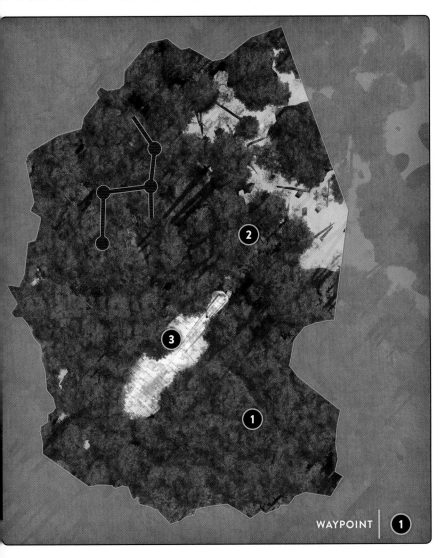

WAYPOINT | **1**

Playing Heroes Vs. Villains in the Swamp Crash Site on Endor leaves tactical advantages to a select few characters. However, all characters have their own weaknesses, and because of this map's layout, such weaknesses may differ from any other map where this mode can be played. Some of the stronger characters for this map are Han Solo, Boba Fett, and Princess Leia, while Darth Vader, Luke Skywalker, and Emperor Palpatine may be left at quite the disadvantage.

1 This map lends well to both Boba Fett and Han Solo because their specialties are mostly ranged abilities that allow them to take enemies down without being in the range of their lightsabers or lightning abilities. Han's Lucky Shot and Boba's Wrist Rocket cannot be deflected, so when they use both the high ground and long sightlines, these two characters can be virtually untouchable. However, because they are strongest on this map, know that they must individually counter each other to protect the rest of their team.

2 The next two most effective characters in the Swamp Crash Site are Princess Leia and Emperor Palpatine. They are designed to both support their fellow teammates and deal with mid-range foes. Leia and Palpatine should always stick to their fellow troopers, as they act as bodyguards and can protect them. Leia and Palpatine can then return the favor by using Enhanced Squad Shield or by taking down an entire squad of troopers with Chain Lightning. If a hero or villain decides to come and attack either of these two, the entire squad of troopers alongside Leia's or Palpatine's own firepower should be able to handle it.

3 Finally, there are the two melee characters, father and son, Darth Vader and Luke Skywalker. Although these two have been labeled as the least advantaged on Swamp Crash Site, they are still two of the strongest characters in the game. If players who are comfortable with these two characters are controlling them, they can be extremely dangerous, even here. Playing Luke or Vader means that you must be tactical and diligent as you move around the map. Because of the range capabilities in this locale, always pick your battles with prejudice. If there is a hero at mid or long range, don't use Saber Throw to attempt to take him or her down. Odds are that unless your opponent is almost downed, you will put yourself at a major disadvantage. The same tactic generally applies to Luke, as well. Follow your enemy or attempt to cut off their current path. If you can catch your opponent by surprise, no character in the game can take on either of these lightsaber-wielders head-on at close range.

IMPERIAL STATION

Blast

1 The Imperial Station on Endor is quite the symmetrical map, making for one of the fairest places to play Blast on. Because of the way the station is configured, there are three main locations: two facilities and a landing pad that acts as the mid-ground between the two buildings. The match does not stay geometrically balanced the entire time, but there is a good chance that the initial first minutes will work that way. Take your time, and don't move around aimlessly. Random movements do make a difference when there are so many corners that enemies can hide around.

2 The facilities on either side of the landing platform are almost identical, having two floors and a few corridors on the back side that are all connected by stairways. Starting from the top floor is a long hallway that can both act as a sightline when you're hiding around the major corners awaiting an enemy's arrival and as a way to stay in cover when you're being attacked from the outside. The top floor acts as a great overwatch area when you are covering your teammates from above. Use it to call out enemy troops and newly respawned power-ups so that the other team cannot collect and use them against you. Be aware that it is very possible to be flanked while you're up there. Either work with a partner, or set up proximity mines and Infantry Turrets to deter the enemy and protect your six.

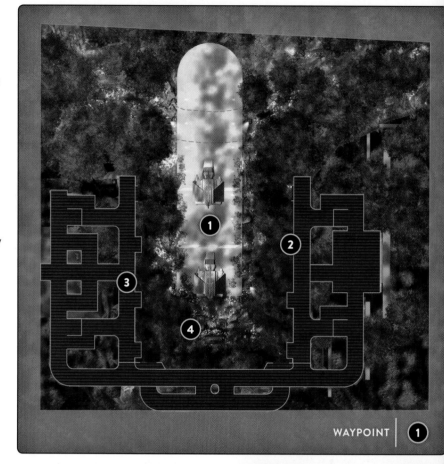

WAYPOINT | **1**

3 The lower floor of each facility is one of the most important areas to control, since it is the gateway to almost all points of cover at the Imperial Station. You can use the large doors as a tactical on/off cover system. Simply pop open the door and take a few shots to slow down the enemy. The moment your foe starts attacking you, back out and let the door provide major cover. You can move around the bottom floor and make your way to the top in a few ways. Just above the main entrance is a balcony that has direct access to the top floor, but the only way to get to the balcony is by using a Jump Pack. The other way to reach the top floor is to move through the bottom floor toward the back and through the corridor to the stairs.

4 The center of the map contains a great range of possibilities as far as combat goes. The landing pad includes two Imperial transport ships that are tall enough for you to peer underneath them. With a Jump Pack, you can leap from ship to ship if want to use them as another form of cover. However, it is entirely effective to use both the ships and the boxes set down on the landing pad itself. This is where the majority of the action happens at the Imperial Station, so get familiar with these forms of cover and use them to your best ability. The other area that can be used in the center of the map is located just off the side of the landing pad in the grassy area. There is quite the drop off the edge, and you can use that alone to toss a grenade or two onto the landing pad itself. Use this as an alternate route when the landing pad just gets too hot.

Cargo

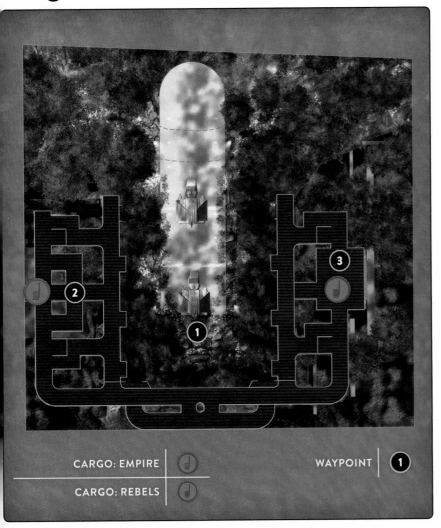

CARGO: EMPIRE	🎵
CARGO: REBELS	🎵

WAYPOINT	❶

① Cargo at the Imperial Station on Endor makes for a relatively short run when making the line from cargo storage to cargo storage. However, there are added challenges because of the map's width. Because the run from base to base is short, players have the quick impulse to run straight down the middle, taking the shortest route possible to make the run even shorter and thinking it might be an easy grab. On the contrary, there are many places to hide in the center section of the map between the facilities that allow players to camp the middle and watch for any cargo carriers. One of the best tactics for this map is the "chaos tactic." Wait for chaos to ensue (because it will), and use it as cover and distraction to take the route around it. You'll make it past the enemy without being noticed.

② The Imperial cargo storage is located in the reactor room and has a great amount of ceiling room. This allows those with Jump Packs to get a height advantage when trying either to surprise defenders or avoid a bad situation with attackers and keep the advantage. There are three different entrances into the reactor room, and you must defend each one of them if your team is to avoid having your cargo taken. The tricky part about defending the reactor room is that the doors give you very short notice before enemies are in the room with you. Take cover behind some of the crates on the walkways, and don't forget to duck behind the cargo itself if you need to fall back to safety.

TOO HEAVY FOR FLIGHT

The cargo carrier cannot use the Jump Pack Star Card, so keep this in mind when you're attempting to quickly return to base.

③ The Rebel cargo storage is a tad different from the Imperial reactor room, with the biggest difference being the amount of room there is to move around. The Rebel cargo storage is located on the other side of the map and inside an intel room that includes very low ceilings and is a complete waste for Jump Packs. The Flash Grenade is one of the best Star Cards to use in this room, both for defending and attacking. Since the room is such close quarters, it's very likely that a single Flash Grenade will affect the majority of the soldiers in the room, allowing you to easily take advantage of the situation. The intel room also has three entrances, but the major difference is that the cargo storage is extremely close to one of the doors. If you have multiple defenders, you should set one defender outside the closest door and one directly behind the cargo itself. This gives your team a protected view of the cargo and allows you to have the advantage of covering a full flank.

Hero Hunt

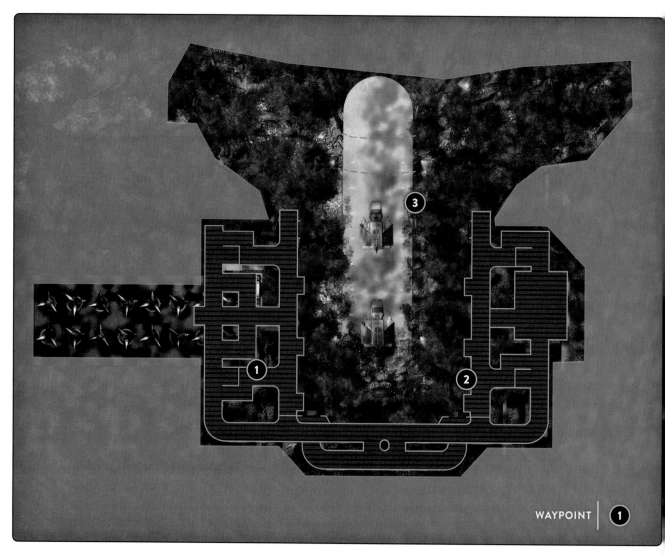

Playing Hero Hunt on Endor means that the Rebels are hunting the villains of *Star Wars* Battlefront. Adjust your tactics to their fighting styles. Vader is by far both the best villain to play in this map and the most difficult to kill, followed by Emperor Palpatine and Boba Fett. Use their tactics as the knowledge to beat them, and play to their weaknesses to make things a tad easier while hunting them down.

❶ Darth Vader is a melee character, and because of the size of the Imperial Station, he flourishes. He is almost invincible as long as he is indoors. Because Vader can deflect almost any bolt that comes flying toward him, the best course of action is to always get behind him and prevent Lord Vader from deflecting your bolts back at you. He has an extremely powerful Heavy Strike, but he does not have a lunge, which means you must lure him outdoors slowly and carefully. Do this, and you will have Vader at a major disadvantage.

❷ Emperor Palpatine also has quite an advantage in the Imperial Station because of the indoor, close-quarters combat. Because of the Emperor's Chain Lighting, never line up for him. Either take him on two at a time (one from each side), or launch explosives like the Thermal Grenade or Contact Grenade at him for quick damage. When you attack Palpatine, it's important to use an alternative damaging method because he can also block blaster bolts. To damage him quickly, shoot the explosive cans located inside the corridors.

❸ While hunting Boba Fett, you may have to completely change up your previous tactics because of the map's layout. However, it works to the hunters' advantage. Treat the landing pad in the center of the map as a giant kill box, using crossfire between your team to trap Fett within these parameters. Splitting up the team and putting them on the top floor of each of the facilities can do one of two things: the player controlling Boba will either try to take cover and shoot the hunters from the center, or he will enter the inside and chase them down. Unfortunately, the bounty hunter has quite a bit of health, making it extremely difficult to take him down head-on. If he chases you into the facility, use the Jump Pack to get out of there, and regroup with your team to attack him in full force while you have him trapped inside. If he decides to stay outside, make sure your fire is relentlessly pinning him down from both sides, giving him no choice but to keep moving and distracting him from firing on the hunters.

Heroes Vs. Villains

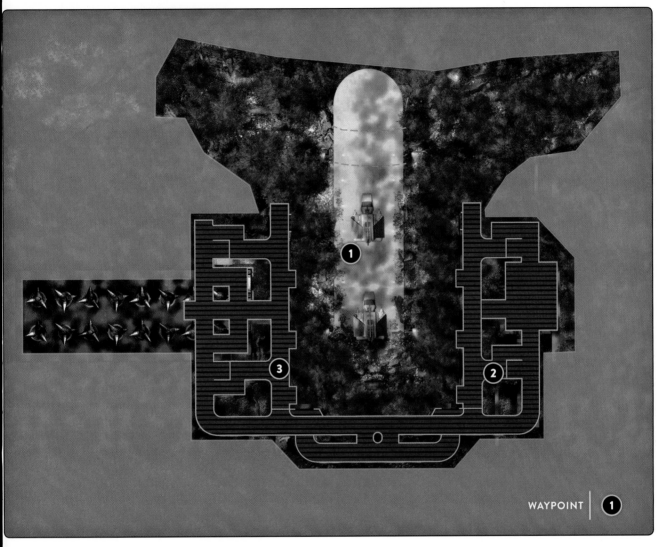

WAYPOINT ①

① Heroes Vs. Villains at the Imperial Station makes for one of the most epic battles in *Star Wars* Battlefront. Because of the close-quarters combat that is inevitable at the Imperial Station, the melee characters are more than dangerous, but everything depends on positioning. While it is very easy to take down the enemy when using Luke Skywalker or Darth Vader, the elevation and levels make a huge difference, as players can change with the flick of the wrist.

② Watch out for the proximity of Luke Skywalker or Darth Vader. If you are caught within their reach, it's likely you will be removed from the match quite quickly. The best thing for the troopers on each team to do is to lure them to an ambush location where other heroes or villains can take them out. With Vader's Saber Throw, distance may not be your savior. Use the sharp corners to draw your opponents toward you and meet them with several of your own forces. Keep Vader at a distance to do as much damage as possible before your squad is completely wiped out by the Heavy Strike. Skywalker has a similar Saber Rush, but it isn't identical and must be handled a little differently. Simply moving around the corner may not keep you safe; he might not kill you with the Saber Rush as you hide behind the corner, but he will get to said corner much faster, leaving you zero time to set up an ambush. Instead, try tempting him to use the Saber Rush directly into a barrage of explosives, or use a Smoke Grenade to escape from him.

③ Emperor Palpatine has a great advantage while inside these corridors and stairways. He can use his lightning and take constant health from his enemies as long as they are in range. Since there are not many ways to escape once you are deep enough inside, his lightning lasts for quite a while before his opponents can get away. The counter to Palpatine is Han Solo because he can Shoulder Charge Palpatine, taking him down a few pegs. Han may sacrifice a few points while charging, but he can disorient Palpatine as he runs him down. At this moment, Solo must make a hasty escape and rest so he can then take the Emperor down with Lucky Shot. It's up to Palpatine to prevent Han from getting away with his antics and Force Dash after him, keeping the distance close.

HOTH

This cold, icy, and mountainous planet is the home of tauntauns and wampas, but it also hosts the very important Echo Base. The temperatures can be unforgiving, and it is hardly habitable, but this may be why the Rebellion decided to build their covert base here in an attempt to keep it secret from the Empire. Eventually, the Empire found Echo Base, but it was ultimately lost to them during the battle on Hoth. Echo Base housed an extremely important shield generator. The surface is very bright, making few things easy to see while fighting on Hoth, especially the snowtroopers' white attire. With Outpost Beta still standing during Star Wars Battlefront, you can live the epic moments against AT-AT walkers, snowtroopers, and the defending Rebel Alliance.

Other than a few extremely large mountain ranges, Hoth greatly lacks natural cover. For the most part, you are left out in the open as you attempt to push forward on your enemy's position. With the exception of the Rebel Base on this planet, you should make the most of the cover-providing Star Cards like Personal Shield and Squad Shield. It is also a good idea to equip the Berserker Trait Star Card. This Trait gives you a bonus when regenerating your health, which is good if you just barely survive while you are out of cover. By contrast, the Rebel Base on Hoth is indoors, and with the amount of debris, cargo crates, and ships housed inside, there is plenty of cover for you to work with. Take aim, shoot straight, and move quickly, and you should have no problem playing any mode here on Hoth.

OUTPOST BETA

Supremacy

CONTROL POINT: EMPIRE	●
CONTROL POINT: REBELS	●
CONTROL POINT: MID	○
SPAWN: EMPIRE	EMPIRE
SPAWN: REBELS	REBELS

REBELS

EMPIRE

The first control point is located inside the outpost, well within the interior's confines. This central control point is arguably the most important because not only does it kick off the match in a single direction, but it can dictate the pace of the rest of the match. Additionally, the first control point has many walls. Once you have captured it, it is much easier to defend than attack. Getting here first and as quickly as possible gives your team a huge advantage toward winning the entire match. There are several entrances to this interior control point. However, they are extremely narrow and quickly become chokepoints, rendering the enemy's numbers meaningless.

If the Empire captures the first and central control point, they will receive the "push forward" message and initiate that phase. During that phase, the battleground shifts, moving all of the power-ups around and opening up the next control point farther up the outpost. The next control point is located directly outside the side entrance to the outpost, on a patch of snow without much cover. There is not much cover in the control area itself, but there are two different stable turrets closer to the mountain and lined with a short trench.

When you're attempting to either defend or take this control point, this trenched area is key and should be top priority whether your team controls the point proper or not. As long as there is one teammate in the trench, any trooper attempting to capture the area can easily be taken down.

If the Rebels capture the first and central control point, they will receive the "push forward" message. The battle then shifts, turning this point and the area directly outside into the lower area of the outpost. This next location for the Rebels to capture is a little more central to the map's barriers, creating a lot of room around the capture area (excluding the mountain between the point and the Imperial transport). A trench borders the control point fairly nicely and can be used for close protection of your team as they capture the control point. Drop a Squad Shield on the edge of the peninsula where the control point rests to protect both those capturing and protecting from the trenches. While the space is tight, this technique is extremely effective when there isn't someone to watch your flank.

The final control point that the Empire must capture and the Rebels must defend as their last stand to avoid instant defeat is located directly underneath the Rebel transport. The area that is used to capture the point is in between the last point and the ship, meaning that it is in front and adjacent to the trench. A single trench leads directly underneath the transport ship, clear to the other side of it. Rebels should use this trench to defend the point as heavily as possible because it provides close-quarters defense. However, beware of how large the area around the ship actually is. With all of the cargo crates and landed starfighters, the enemy could be hiding around any corner, and flanking this position is definitely possible.

Finally, the control point that determines victory for the Rebel Alliance or defeat for the Empire sits parallel to the crashed AT-AT. This control point is not half as open as the final control point on the Rebel side, but it leaves less opportunity for the Imperials to be able to defend the point from a distance.

Lobbing Thermal and Contact Grenades into this location can clear out a few enemy troopers, lightening the defense while the Rebels come in to take over. In the same vein, there is still a narrow back side that you can use as a flank or a defensive position that is not directly on top of the control point itself. Use angles and sightlines to make this location most useful, and either side can succeed relatively easily.

Walker Assault

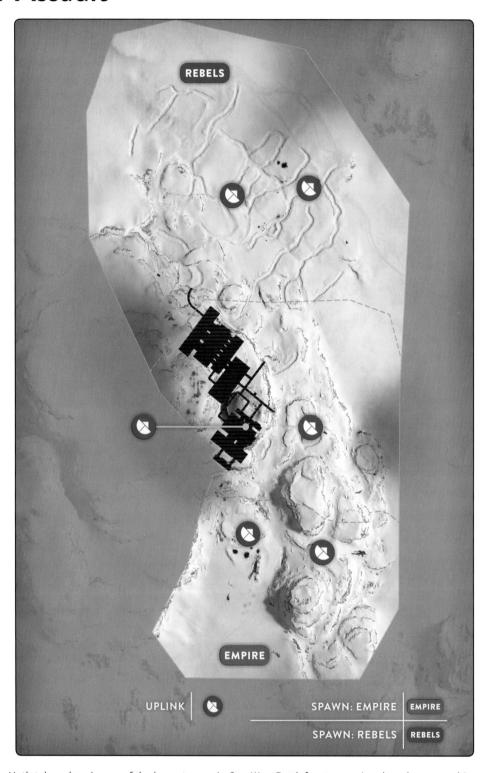

REBELS

EMPIRE

UPLINK		SPAWN: EMPIRE	EMPIRE
		SPAWN: REBELS	REBELS

Walker Assault on Hoth takes place in one of the largest areas in *Star Wars* Battlefront, meaning that almost anything goes in terms of what to use or how to use it. Keep in mind that using short-range weapons are useful in this instance, but only for a brief period. Air vehicles are extremely useful on this map. Use them wisely and don't waste time, as every boot in the snow makes an incredible difference. There are two AT-AT walkers on Hoth, and even though they eventually walk alongside each other, they start off very far apart. Be aware of this during the first walker phase.

The first uplink that you can activate is parallel to the already downed AT-AT and is surrounded by a single trench and two powerful turrets. The area where this uplink is located appears to be a forward turret camp the Rebels have established to fight against walkers, and it is made to be defended. As the Empire, watch for Rebels hiding inside the trench and awaiting your approach after they have activated the uplink. It is now the Empire's job to deactivate the uplink and use some of the same tactics. Although the area is very open, Smoke Grenades are quite effective when you're either activating or deactivating the uplink. Keep in mind that a Thermal Grenade is also effective at killing most of what is in the area that the Smoke Grenade can cover.

The second uplink in the first area of operations is located just on the other side of the large canyon that the closest AT-AT walks through. This area is very similar to the first except for the fact that it is not located in a narrow, smaller canyon. Instead, the uplink is in a much wider area while still inside the trench that runs through the location. This allows for a little bit of cover while you're either activating or deactivating the uplink. While you're operating near this uplink, watch out for the two trenches right next to each other. These trenches allow enemies to approach the uplink undetected if they are careful. Use your radar, or equip the Scout Trait Star Card to stay hidden from their radar.

Once the first uplink phase is finished and you have either defended the walkers or dealt as much damage as possible, it becomes time to capture and defend the next two uplinks. The battlefield begins to become a little narrower as the AT-ATs get closer together. As this happens, the uplinks become closer to the center of the map. The first one is located on the ridge of the large cliff in the map's center. From there, you can see where the farther walker is quite easily now. That poses a challenge for the Rebels, as the AT-ATs fire on troopers if they are in range and in their line of sight. This uplink is not near any trenches. In fact, it is wedged inside a small divot in the snow and exposed to the side the Empire deploys from, creating a bit of a challenge for the Rebels attempting to activate it. Deploy Infantry Turrets and Vehicle Turrets to deter your opponent as you activate the uplink, and then escape to find cover and protect it.

The next uplink is the first uplink that is located indoors, at least technically. The uplink is actually just inside the outpost itself, directly next to the main hangar entrance. This area is easily accessed from outside, but that does not mean it is completely vulnerable. While capturing this uplink may be a little difficult and tricky, defending it is much easier.

Again, one of the best methods to cover your exact location while activating or deactivating the uplink is by dropping a Smoke Grenade at the uplink itself, and then completing your action as quickly as possible. Once you have made your move, relocate farther inside the hangar itself, and use the tremendous amount of cover provided. If you're playing as a Rebel, defending from inside will also protect you from walker fire and Orbital Strikes.

By this time, the walkers should be heavily damaged. Even if they aren't, though, this third phase of the match is by far the most important. If the walkers have not taken many hits, the Rebels should capture the uplinks for as long as possible. This gives anyone skilled with a Snowspeeder a chance and a good amount of time to use the TOW-cable and take down both walkers the cleaner way.

The last two uplinks are located in the large intricate system of trenches that the AT-ATs must pass to get within range of the shield generator. Surrounded by a great deal of turrets, along with natural and equipment-made cover, this phase lends much better to the Rebel side. But Imperials still have a chance since they can also use the trenches for stealth and cover when approaching the Rebels. Regardless, it is vital for the Empire to drop as much firepower on this trench system as possible, hoping to slow down the Rebel Alliance's attempt at ruining their plans.

Fighter Squadron

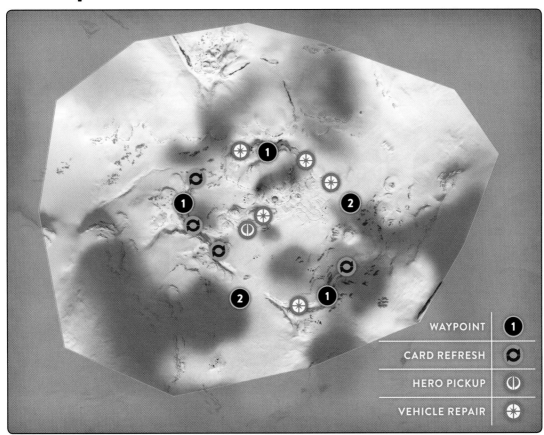

WAYPOINT	1
CARD REFRESH	↻
HERO PICKUP	◐
VEHICLE REPAIR	✦

As you fly into the airspace of Outpost Beta on Hoth, one of the first things you notice is the thick clouds of snow that sit directly in the mid-level view. Fortunately, the weather is sunny, and once you are outside of the thick vision block, the air is extremely clear. This is both a burden and a tactical piece of gold. With Fighter Squadron, there is almost always someone on your tail and a target that you want to pursue. Use the clouds to escape your adversaries. If they can't see you, they can't hit you with blasters, and torpedoes can't lock on to anything blocked by cloud cover, either.

1 There are extremely deep (but narrow) canyons all around this map, and they happen to be where the pick-ups are located. Because of this, only the best pilots will thrive while flying close to the surface. The canyons are a great place to repair if you are heavily damaged. They are also helpful for testing your tail's skills by flying through and seeing if they can keep up. On the other hand, if you are not comfortable piloting your starship just yet, avoid these canyons and do whatever it takes to splash your target before they make their way down there.

2 Fortunately, the transport ships do not travel near the surface too often, which makes things slightly easier to navigate when you're attempting to either destroy or protect the transports. The downside to the transport ships traveling in the open is that they are accessible to everyone on the battlefield. Many starships will be flying around, creating chaos in your airspace.

ICE CAVES

Blast

Playing Blast in the Ice Caves is like shooting at the blaster range: the caves are narrow, and troopers don't have many places to go once inside them. If you chose just one map where you needed to have the right blaster to kill your enemies as efficiently as possible, it would be the Ice Caves. Weapon choice is important because your cover is generally corners and a few objects that Rebel forces may have left there. Other than that, there is not much to hide behind. Stay near the corners, and only move from spot to spot once your blaster is fully cooled down and you are fully focused.

1 The caves are a great way to dominate the other team if you and your partner drive your force through them, but any more than two players, and your team could suffer major casualties with one wrong move. Don't be afraid to retreat if one of you gets taken out. As long as you stay alive, your partner can redeploy on your position, and you can reassert your dominance on any location.

2 The caves are not the only area of operations at the Ice Caves on Hoth: there is also a place where an X-wing has landed and is being stored. This area is large enough to store another X-wing, essentially dictating that multiple players are going to be located in this area because of its layout. Although there is plenty of cover out here, avoid getting pushed up against the cliff because there might be no escape.

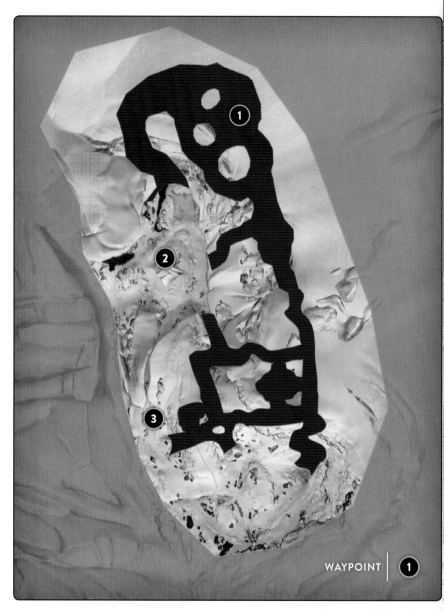

WAYPOINT | **1**

3 You can find another open area just through the tiny narrow canyon adjacent to the X-wing storage location. Here, you have a few options. This is a decent place to post up and garrison with a few teammates, as there are several entrances that might require more defenders than just you and your partner. You can also use this to find a place to flee once you are alert to the action. Finally, you can use the hill that leads you to the top of the narrow canyon and get a height advantage on the two open areas. The tiny canyon is far narrower than you might guess, so while it is a shortcut from place to place, be sure that it's safe before you enter. It is quite easy for you to get stuck and ambushed when you're inside.

Drop Zone

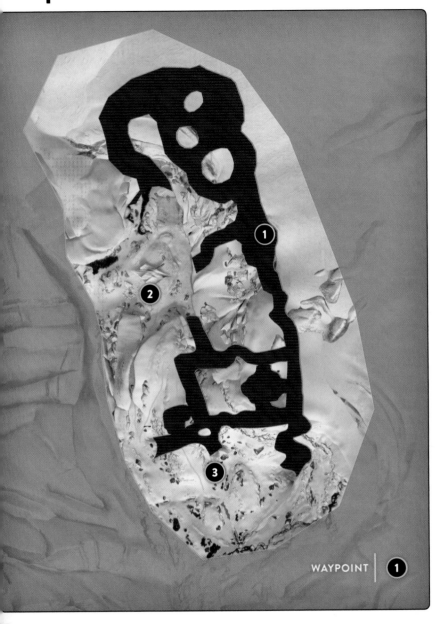

1 There are not many locations that are viable for a drop pod to land, but there are more spots than you might expect. One of these areas is found inside the caves, through one of the small openings in the top of the cave. Like a few others, this location has a three-way intersection, which leaves the challenge of both narrow corridors in the caves and the need to cover all three paths while you're attempting to capture the pod. Because of the caves' complexity, the best way to defend an interior pod after you have initiated the capture sequence is beyond the immediate location and around corners in the caves. These places give you longer sightlines and the ability to retreat if things get too hot.

2 Drop pods typically drop outside, at least more often than not. However, the pods still tend to drop near cave entrances. For that reason, defending from inside a cave and stopping anyone from leaving to grab the pod provides great assistance to the players guarding the immediate vicinity. Those in the immediate area should encamp some distance away from the pod and watch it from behind cover.

WAYPOINT | **1**

3 Setting up permanent defenses (or at least long-lasting defenses) outside is not a waste once the pod you are capturing has been captured completely. More pods will drop outside, and it's not impossible for the next pod to drop in almost the same exact area. It won't literally drop in the same place, but it could drop nearby, leaving little room required for adjustments.

Droid Run

In the Ice Caves, you win Droid Run by controlling checkpoints. The caves are quite narrow, and the droids tend to roam either outside the caves or in the caves' bigger areas. Controlling these chokepoints means that group numbers are rendered meaningless. Whenever possible, set up turrets and Blaster Cannons to defend your stronghold.

1 The first droid likes to roam around the covered X-wing outside the caves near the cliff. Fortunately, no matter where this droid roams, it's usually in a safe spot. The best way to surprise an enemy hanging around the X-wing is actually to use the Jump Pack and fly directly over the X-wing, hopefully catching your foe by surprise. Use the entire area around the X-wing (including the nooks and crannies around the cave entrances) to hide and use as cover while protecting this droid. You won't be able to get any more space anywhere on the map than right here.

2 The second controllable droid in the Ice Caves is located in a much more complex area than the other two droids. Instead of being positioned at an intersection between three tunnels, this droid roams through the smaller crevasses and complex tunnel system. This makes for a slightly more difficult capture and is why this is one of the more important droids to acquire. Because of how little space there is, you might want to stay directly on top of the droid for the best defense. Avoid getting too far away from the capture area, as it is quite easy for an enemy to come in and swipe the droid from your control. However, as long as you have an eye on the droid, it is also easy to defend it.

3 The final droid in the Ice Caves, labeled "C," is located under one of the bigger ceiling holes inside the caves. Since it is under this larger hole, you have quite a bit more space to work with. This area is also an intersection, with a few different entrances you must worry about. You can put the Squad Shield and Infantry Turrets to good use, although things may get a bit hectic. Use the partner system to stay close to your squad, and keep the area populated. Don't lose the control that is vital to your success.

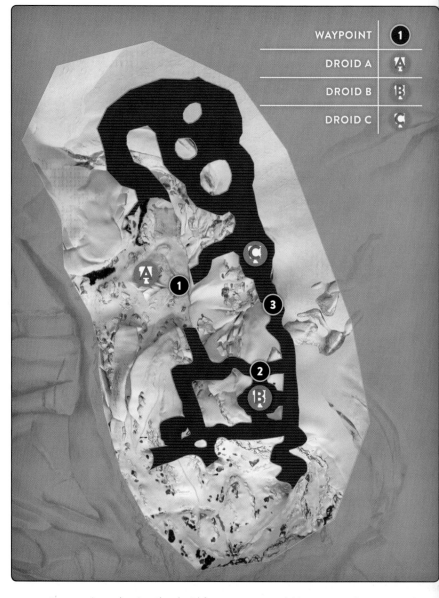

WAYPOINT	1
DROID A	A
DROID B	B
DROID C	C

Hero Hunt

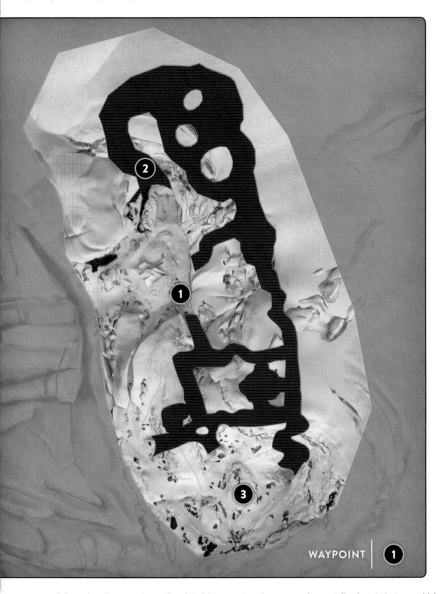

1 When you play Hero Hunt in the Ice Caves, the first thing to consider is who exactly is the most dangerous hero you will face in this location. On Hoth, the heroes that you are hunting down are Luke, Han, and Leia. Because of the way the Ice Caves are constructed, all of the heroes tend to shine here. However, one hero really stands out: Luke Skywalker dominates the battleground with his heavy blows and melee combat. If you're stuck in the caves with Skywalker, you might as well head back out. The only ways to defeat Luke are to back out and bring him outside, or to close him in and force him to fight on both sides. However, getting too close on either side to Luke means your certain death, so don't close in too far.

2 The second most dangerous hero in the Ice Caves is Han Solo. Even though Han specializes in medium-distance fighting, watch out for his Shoulder Charge that can take out anyone who gets in his way. That being said, players typically want to get in close while playing as Han Solo, which is good for you as the hunter. Han has a powerful Lucky Shot and can fire his blaster pistol extremely rapidly, but it is incredibly inaccurate up close. If your opponent decides to come in close, take advantage of this and get in tight, overwhelming your target with a barrage of blaster fire.

3 Finally, the last challenge is handling Leia Organa and her incredibly defensive capabilities. Princess Leia has an Enhanced Squad Shield that normally is used for shielding multiple people. However, with the Enhanced Squad Shield, the player controlling Leia can make the battlefield focused wherever Leia wants. There are corners and corridors all over this map, and if a situation gives her the advantage, she can drop the shield and create a one-on-one or one-on-two situation where she has a good chance of winning. With Trooper Bane letting her shoot through the shield, Leia Organa can drop the shield, kill a couple enemies as they charge her, and outlast the remaining troopers who make it into the confined area that she has created.

Heroes Vs. Villains

Ice Caves is mostly made for close-quarters combat. Even though this map lends well to every hero against normal troopers, some heroes and villains are a much better match than others.

1 Because of the tight corners and caves, most situations won't allow for Han Solo to better Darth Vader. If the player controlling Han has a two-on-one situation available, that's the best time to strike—unless Han can catch Vader outside and keep the foe at a distance while firing Lucky Shot at his feet.

2 Obviously, melee characters like Luke Skywalker and Darth Vader thrive in this close-quarters environment, but be wary of Emperor Palpatine's Chain Lightning against multiple enemies who cannot escape the confines of the Ice Caves. The rule of thumb is to run away from these three hero characters and try to round corners as often as possible to avoid Luke's Saber Rush or Vader's Saber Throw.

3 When you're playing as Boba Fett, your best course of action is using the limited high grounds, such as the top of the X-wing or the tip of the narrow canyon outside. These high places might be the only areas that Boba can quickly access when no one else can. However, they only stay safe for a short amount of time, and there are not many of these locations. If you're caught in a tight situation, use Flame Thrower to deal some quick damage to anyone around Boba, hopefully causing the foe to give him some distance as he escapes to get a better angle.

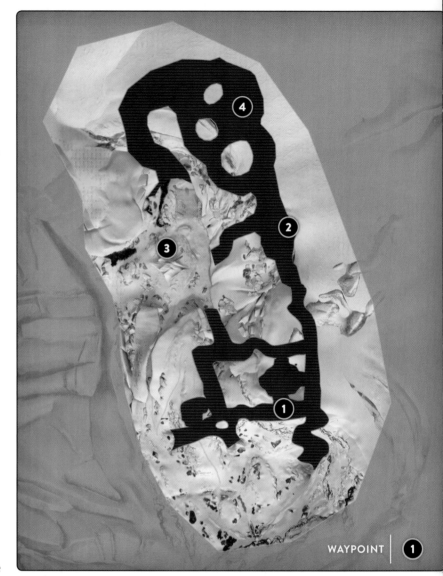

WAYPOINT | **1**

4 Leia Organa is the trickiest of characters on this map. Because she can dictate her own battlefield, Leia does great against troopers, but her defense against hero characters is a little weak. Like Han, if you're playing as Leia, you also want to do your best to stay outdoors. At the very least, keep your distance from the enemies and try not to close the gap (if there is one). Trooper Bane may not kil a hero opponent in one shot like it does with troopers, but it does inflict a great deal of damage. This gives Leia a possible upper hand at the beginning of a duel.

REBEL BASE

Blast

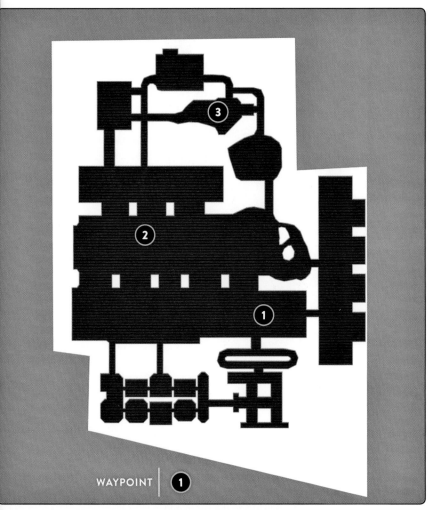

WAYPOINT | **1**

STICK AND MOVE

Try not to kill more than a few enemies at a time from a single position. Because of the short-range explosive tossing, your opponents can flush you out or blow you up very quickly once they know your location.

1 Playing Blast in the Rebel Base can be utter chaos. The Rebel Base is a complex yet extremely closed-off space with a ton of objects and debris scattered all over the ground floor. Because of how much stuff is actually available in the base, there is a great deal of cover that you can hide behind and use as coverage for movement. With all this cover, you can avoid getting hit by a long-range shooter that you just didn't see, and make it harder in general for your target to shoot back at you. However, the reason for this map's chaos in Blast mode is not because it is indoors or small—it's actually because of how much cover there is.

2 The cover in the Rebel Base is vast and lets multiple participants survive in a hot zone, which is precisely why chaos ensues. Thermal Detonators and Thermal Imploders are the deadliest of weapons inside the Rebel Base because anything with a blast radius that you can lob over the short-statured objects is going to get you kills.

The objective of this game mode is for your team to rack up the highest amount of kills before your opponent does. This can become difficult when multiple players are located in central hot spots. Some of these central hot spots include areas of the map like the main hangar and the storage facility. Snowspeeders, X-wings, and the Millennium Falcon are all stored inside the main hangar, and these are all incredibly useful objects to use as cover. You can climb atop the Millennium Falcon using a Jump Pack, but be careful. If an enemy spots you up there, you become a very easy target.

3 Using weapons like the CA-87 or the DH-17 blasters gives you a great advantage when running and gunning. When you're running and gunning, use the perimeter of the map and rush through the peripheral rooms (like the med or science bays) as cover from stray fire. However, if you're the slow, methodical type, blasters like the DLT-19 or the A280C are great for letting you sit back in a covered location and pick your foes off one by one. If you are a slower-moving player, remember that you eventually must move from side to side if you plan to stay alive very long.

Droid Run

Playing Droid Run in the Rebel Base differs slightly from playing it on any other map, but it is mostly the same. Like Droid Run anywhere else, you want to do whatever it takes to dominate the enemy's territory by pushing them back to a corner and preventing them from capturing any droids.

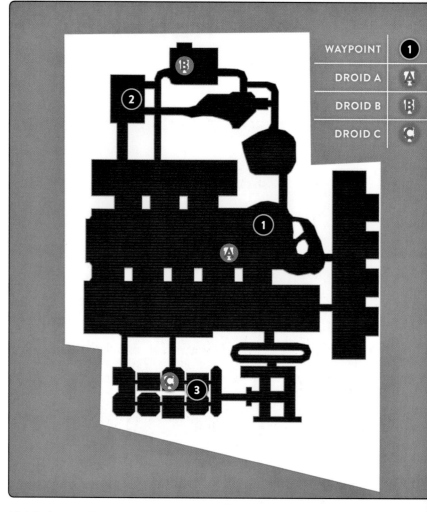

WAYPOINT	**1**
DROID A	A
DROID B	B
DROID C	C

1 The first droid, "A," is located directly in the middle of the base and roams in the walkway between the Millennium Falcon and the X-wing that sits right next to it. The problem with this area is that an enemy can come from almost anywhere, including directly above you. The droid doesn't always stay in the walkway between those two ships, though. The "A" droid also roams around the X-wing itself, creating more opportunity for you to take the droid at a less vulnerable position. But remember that even if your team is coming from a specific direction, there is always the possibility that the droid will flank you and sometimes deploy in spots you may not expect. Taking this droid is only the first challenge; defending it is the second half of the battle and is just as difficult. Keep your distance from the droid when defending it, but don't lose sight as it rounds the corner. That may be the best opportunity for your opponent to steal the droid right from under your nose.

2 The next droid is located inside one of the intelligence rooms, which is a much tighter fit for any type of battle that can occur. While the majority of your team is fighting over "A," there should always be at least one player and his or her partner watching over "B." Even though the center of the map is chaotic, you can still slip through and hone in on this location, or find your way through the side stairs. With this in mind, it is best to stay hidden yet close to the droid when defending it (as if you have a choice). The droid roams up and down the room, but no matter where it is, you can keep a good bead on it while inside the room and in your favorite spot to start out.

3 The final droid is located in the med bay and roams throughout the separate rooms. This droid's roaming path makes things a tad bit more challenging when you're defending simply because of the room changes and the way it bypasses a wall or two. You can capture this droid while safely behind a wall next to the doorway just as it passes through. This gives you the ultimate cover: you are on the side that you just cleared to get there and almost fully protected from the other side. The key word there is "almost," because this area is where Contact Grenades become your worst nightmare. Not knowing that a grenade is even lobbed at your feet before you have the chance to move can be devastating. Take a slightly more active defense with this droid. Move from room to room with it, not letting it out of your sight. If you have a proximity mine, a good place to set it is near the entrance of the farthest room that the droid might roam to, thus slowing down the enemy from overwhelming your position.

PROXEMIC BLINDNESS

Dropping a proximity mine directly on the other side of open doorways is not only a highly effective range for anyone entering through, but it is also is a great way to hide the fact that there is even a mine there.

Cargo

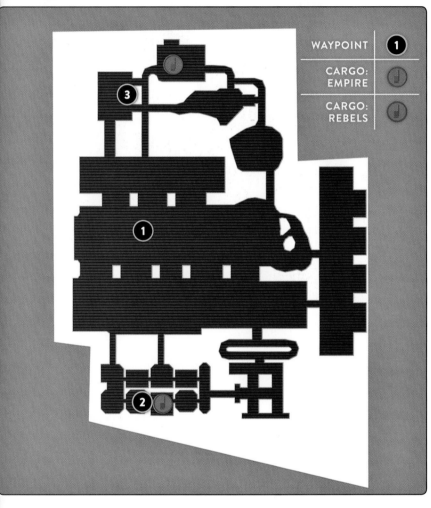

WAYPOINT	①
CARGO: EMPIRE	
CARGO: REBELS	

① The Rebel Base is the only area on Hoth where you can play Cargo, which makes for very interesting and even more chaotic gameplay. Just like Droid Run, it is incredibly important that you control the center main hangar of the Rebel Base, which acts as the gateway to both cargo storage locations. Controlling the main hangar allows your team to control the majority of the map, giving you the simple advantage of special dominance. It also forces the opposing team to be significantly more strategic when both attacking and returning to their own base with your cargo, since your team has a lot more space to work with and cut runners off before they pass the midway mark. Unfortunately, once a cargo carrier is past the midway mark, it is incredibly difficult to stop them from that point on.

② The Rebel cargo is located in the back half of the med bay. Be aware that there are two halves to the med bay, and there is a clear divide between them that is difficult to cross unless you go around it. However, a window in the middle warns you if enemies are coming around the corner or if someone is defending in that specific zone, making the window beneficial to both sides. While you return back to the med bay with the cargo, the window can give you away if a stormtrooper is hiding and awaiting your return. If you spot something suspicious, use a Flash Grenade to enter the room, and then take the cargo storage back by force.

③ On the Empire side of the map is the intelligence room, where it is much easier to defend from within the same room as the cargo because of the corners there. Use the machines and objects located throughout the room for cover and to stay hidden from attackers as you ambush them before they take your cargo. When attacking this room and attempting to grab the cargo, know that the room's orientation allows for a quick "smoke run." Drop a Smoke Grenade directly on the cargo and run straight through the room as the two entrances line up, making your way out as quickly as possible. This is a risky tactic, but with a little bit of luck, you can successfully snatch the cargo without taking a single hit.

Hero Hunt

1 A great deal like Ice Caves, Rebel Base features mostly close-quarters combat, lending very well to the hero. However, if the snowtrooper hunters can use the main hangar successfully, they can gain the upper hand on the hero character. As the hunters, don't spend too much time in any of the corridors unless you are setting up an ambush. One look around the corner from a hero, and you won't last very long.

2 From the main hangar, always keep the hero at a distance, and use the objects to place items between you two. This also takes more time because the hero must navigate an extra obstacle in order to get you. Similarly, if you can avoid the enemy and "kite" the hero around the room without him or her damaging you, the rest of your team can deal some damage as you keep the hero distracted.

3 Remember that the hangar only works well if you're facing Leia Organa or Luke Skywalker, even though they are still dangerous there. Using the corridors and smaller rooms to deal with Han Solo often proves to be more beneficial because of his mid-range build. Beware of Han's Shoulder Rush—stay close to corners to avoid his charge.

WAYPOINT | **1**

4 Hunting down Luke Skywalker greatly depends on how much room he has to operate in. Battling in the corridors that only fit two troopers is suicide against Luke because one swipe of his lightsaber can eliminate anyone in his path. The best way to take Skywalker down is to constantly put an object between you and him. This ensures that he can't Saber Rush you, as you have created a faux long-distance situation.

eroes Vs. Villains

1 Like in the Ice Caves, the two most powerful characters to play are Luke Skywalker and Darth Vader. Their melee strength and their ability to kill multiple targets in one swipe are what make the difference in any given match. However, note that in these short-range situations, most pairs of characters can take on Luke or Vader with minimal resistance. They do still require a little room to escape, and they won't have any in tight situations.

2 Emperor Palpatine and Leia Organa are the two perfect characters to pair up with Darth Vader and Luke Skywalker, respectively. Providing that extra firepower to those two-on-ones or even two-on-two match-ups is extremely useful, especially when Palpatine launches his Chain Lightning. Palpatine also thrives in the main hangar; although he does not have much range with his Force Lightning, he can perform a Force Dash. Force Dash lets Palpatine close any gap that he may have trouble reaching via his Force Lightning, giving him a major advantage when operating in the main hangar.

3 Both Boba Fett and Han Solo may have a little trouble on this map while in the close-quarters corridors. However, they both have abilities that perform rather well for avoiding or managing these situations. If he's caught in a small area, Han can Shoulder Charge through his enemy, giving him access to a way out rather quickly. If Fett is caught in a corner or tight space, he can set his adversary ablaze with Flame Thrower. The unfortunate part about Boba's main abilities is that his jetpack cannot work while he's in the smaller rooms. (Perhaps this indicates that it might not be a good idea for him to be there in the first place.) If you must travel the entire map, then by all means do so, but do it quickly and then return to the main hangar where Boba's blaster and Wrist Rocket will shine.

189

SULLUST

The multicolored, high-energy, lava-filled planet known as Sullust is home to the Sullustans, which have inhabited the underground area of the planet itself. As a member of the Galactic Republic that was later occupied by the Empire, Sullust's surface is a battleground covered in Imperial structures and forces of the Empire. Beware of its active terrain; even though the Sullustans were able to survive here, they did it under no great sense of ease. Watch your step before setting foot in any holes or craters filled with extremely hot magma.

Sullust is similar but not identical to certain parts of Tatooine. The surface is extremely treacherous, and if you're not careful and don't watch your step, you are likely to fall and take damage. This is even more true if you step into a magma-filled ditch or crater. The magma found here won't kill you immediately, but if you stay in it for more than a second or two, you won't last very long. Technically, you can use this knowledge to your advantage and quickly hide places where the enemy may not expect you to be. However, this is not recommended, and the risk is significantly higher than its rewards. Take control of the battlefield and experience some of the most complex locations and battlegrounds, including the SoroSuub Centroplex, Sulphur Fields, and the Imperial Hangar.

SOROSUUB CENTROPLEX

Supremacy

CONTROL POINT: EMPIRE	
CONTROL POINT: REBELS	
CONTROL POINT: MID	
SPAWN: EMPIRE	EMPIRE
SPAWN: REBELS	REBELS

The first location and the only one available to both teams is the center control point, which is located dead center in the middle of the Centroplex. In the center of the control point is a small reservoir of water, which is luckily safe for you to be in. Surrounding the capture point itself are very symmetrical stones and rock formations that have been created from the lava flow that was once there. Fortunately, these formations make great perches and ledges for you to use, granting both a height advantage and cover to protect the point. The area is wide, so fitting all 40 players in this immediate battle zone should be no problem. However, the fight will become chaotic, and you must be aggressive if you want to take this control point for your team.

If the Rebels take victory over the first control point, the battle then extends to the Imperial Hangar just across the main stretch that flows through the center of the map. Some very large objects and rock formations stand between you and the Imperial Hangar, so use the Jump Pack (if you have one) to rapidly traverse the land and get to the next point as quickly as possible.

The Imperial Hangar is also quite a spacious area, but aside from the large opening to the hangar, it is mostly

contained. Because of the opening in the front of the building, this is one of the most important directions to watch and should be your main priority. Yes, you could possibly be flanked if an enemy snuck in behind you, but that's part of what makes the front side so important. When defending this area as the Empire, watch out for the corridor located on the Rebel side of the hangar. That is a popular entrance for Rebels to avoid getting shot by your walkers. You can effectively defend the front of the hangar from slightly outside the hangar and the side entrance from the inside—just avoid getting cornered into one location and wiped off the map.

WALKER WATCH

Watch out for AT-ST walkers patrolling down the center stretch of the map during the transitions. Running across the center of the map while an AT-ST is standing makes for great target practice for the Empire.

If the Imperials take the first control point, the battle is then extended to the outpost a little farther down the hill. The control point for this outpost is fully interior and uses an intelligence room as the capture location. There are three entrances to this intelligence room: one from the Rebels' deployment area and two from the Imperials' side (especially after the Empire has taken the center point). Attacking this point is a bit more difficult than it sounds. Although there are two entrances on the Imperial side, they are still connected to narrow corridors. No matter how you set up, this fight always involves close-quarters combat. Use the computers and cargo crates as cover while setting up Blaster Cannons to both help defend the point and lay waste to anyone hiding inside.

If the Rebels can successfully push the Empire all the way back to their base and final control point, the rest of the match can proceed in one of two ways. The first way is that the Rebel Alliance will dominate and take the final control point within a matter of seconds. In the second way, the fight stays directly on this final stretch of Centroplex for the rest of the time remaining in the match. Both outcomes strongly depend on whether the Imperial magmatroopers can quickly set up effective defenses. To get to the final control point from the last is a simple run up the hill, avoiding walker fire as much as possible. However, once you get there, both attacking and defending this place requires an incredible amount of timing and luck. The control point is at the bottom of a multi-leveled section of the map that features both structures and rock formations. Two large structures stand on either side of the control point, and these act as a great ambush crossfire if you can find your way onto them. Then, you have a large ledge off to the side with three different layers of elevation and a fixed turret to help fend off attackers. Use every level and height advantage that you can to defend this place. The real challenge is that the control point is at the lowest section, and it is quite easy to peer down onto it.

Finally, if the Empire has pushed the Rebels all the way back to their ship, this next control point is all about cover and getting the best angle on your opponent. Unlike the Empire's final control point, there are not many levels here where you can get height advantages. However, there is a much wider area of operations, which allows for more of a distanced defense and attack style. A number of crates surrounds the control point; use them for cover and concealment. At the same time, there is an outpost that actually leads to the next control point up the hill, making it a great flanking route. This route is rather dangerous because it is incredibly easy for Rebel troopers to get inside the outpost and defend the shortcut from within. Still, it is important to have your allies inside because you don't want the Rebels using it to get around your troopers and moving to take the next point from your team. Attack this control point head-on to overwhelm the defending force and take it with all of the Empire's power. Taking things slowly and methodically might make defending the control point significantly easier for the Rebel Alliance.

Walker Assault

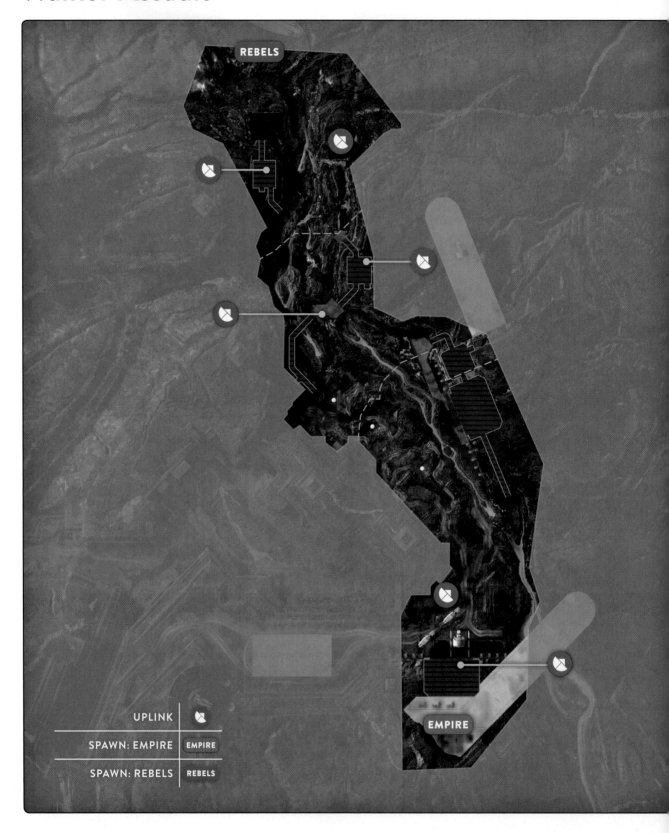

REBELS

UPLINK

SPAWN: EMPIRE | EMPIRE

SPAWN: REBELS | REBELS

EMPIRE

In Walker Assault on SoroSuub Centroplex, there are two walkers that both head through the narrow center stretch moving downhill from their base. The narrow path that the AT-ATs take doesn't make the world's difference. But unlike some other maps, the AT-ATs are much closer together here, possibly allowing a more focused attack on both targets for the Rebellion.

There are two uplink stations, with one on either side of the walkers' path. The first is inside the Imperial Hangar and up the stairs of the closest TIE fighter dock. Because the uplink is on the dock itself, it is extremely exposed to enemy fire. This makes a great opportunity for you to break out the Squad Shield or to call in Leia Organa to help protect the Rebel troopers trying to activate this uplink. The Empire's best defense on the first uplink is from down below, and using Jump Packs to access it quickly is completely necessary. Defending the uplink from the exact spot is just as dangerous as it is for the Rebels to activate it.

The second uplink in this first phase is located just across the way near the water tanks, on the edge of a very open area. Fortunately for both teams, the uplink is set close to a cliff that leads just a bit farther uphill. This cliff can be useful for the Imperials, as it gives you a great height advantage looking straight down onto the uplink to defend it effectively. Another advantage to this cliff is that it looks over the wide, open area that leads to the uplink from the Rebels' original location. The best way for the Rebels to handle this is to take this uplink first and as early as possible. It is much easier to take it from the center of the map moving toward the uplink than from head-on. If you can move in without the walkers spotting you, the Rebel forces have a better chance of getting on top of that cliff and controlling it for themselves, making the activation of the uplink that much easier.

Once your Y-wings have come in and you've dealt your share of damage to the AT-ATs, it becomes time to move to the second phase, which is typically the phase that makes or breaks your team's morale. The second set of uplinks is quite a bit different than the first. For example, the first uplink gives a definite advantage for the Rebellion, at least at the start of the phase. The uplink is set up next to a large structure that completely blocks the Empire side and is widely open to the Rebels' position. This is tactically advantageous to the Rebels at first, but as a minute or two passes, it opens up to a world of heat brought on by the Empire's vehicles. To stay protected from vehicles, use the outpost that is located immediately next to this uplink, as it can provide cover and safety for you and your teammates. The only downside is if the Empire forces camp that spot and don't allow you to come back out, you will have to deal with their vehicles in order to succeed.

The next uplink in this phase is located inside the outpost on the other side of the middle stretch. While attacking or defending this uplink, don't fear any vehicles, as they have no effect inside this location. The uplink itself is located in the center back area of the outpost, leaving it directly in the line of crossfire between the three parallel entrances. In this situation, you want to use cover as heavily as possible and peek out only to take potshots at your enemies, keeping them pinned down and out of your territory. Standing out of cover too long here will not only get you killed, but also possibly give away the immediate positions of your fellow teammates. Defend this area with Infantry Turrets and Blaster Cannons to keep the adversary at bay, then power through the walker phase to deal as much damage as possible to the enemy AT-ATs.

The final two uplinks are located both on the exterior and the interior of the mountains. The first is located near the end of the hill and directly outside the leftmost outpost in the dead center of a cargo staging area. There is no great way to defend this location because of how open the format is, but that doesn't mean it is impossible. The best way to defend or attack this uplink is by communicating with your team to set up a perimeter around the staging area and secure the outside, not letting any troopers in. With this strategy, the problem you encounter is the attack from vehicles. With that said, this is the most vital time for the Rebellion to start getting inside vehicles and blasting

some of the walkers down, relieving pressure from your troopers on the ground. You should always have either Ion Grenades or Ion Torpedoes equipped to best take down the AT-ATs, but on this map, it is even more important because of the constant attack from AT-ATs.

The last and final uplink is just across the way, inside the outpost that leads into the mountain. This uplink is another interior uplink like the one in the second phase, but the difference is that the uplink is now centered in the room. That gives the crossfire of the three entrances an even more specific meaning. This intelligence room has the same layout as the room in the second phase, but everything is flipped, as it is located on the other side of the map. Use the computers as cover, and remember that it is entirely possible for the Empire to sneak up on Rebels from behind. If you're playing as a Rebel, you won't know that because there is no door this time to warn you that enemies are on your six.

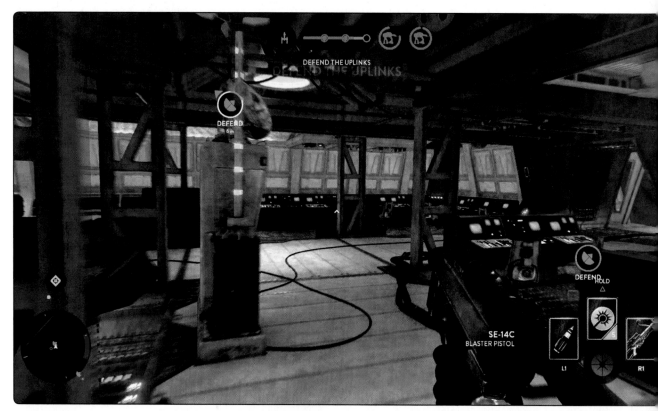

Fighter Squadron

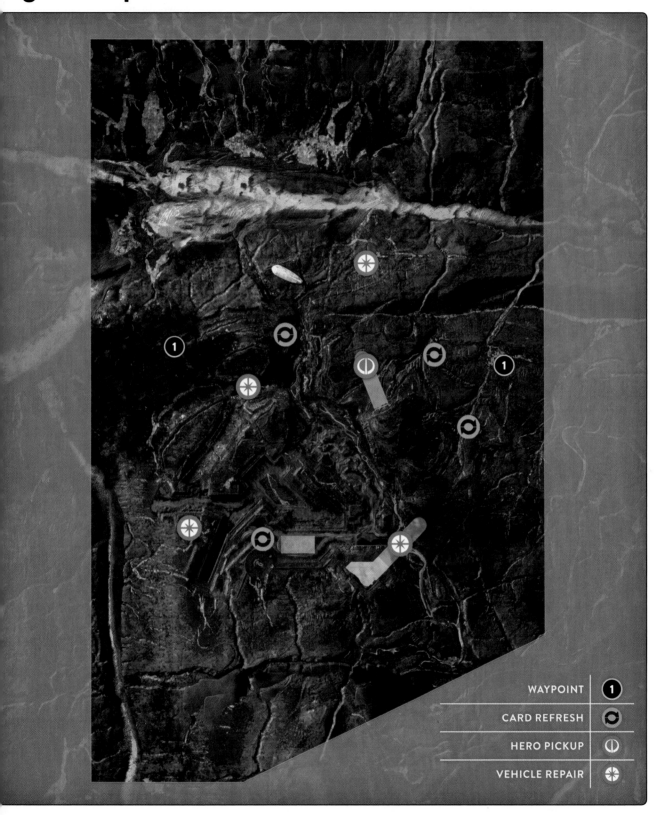

WAYPOINT	**1**
CARD REFRESH	↻
HERO PICKUP	◑
VEHICLE REPAIR	✳

Fighter Squadron on Sullust takes place directly above the lakes and rivers of lava and magma, which creates a large collection of smoke and clouds that blocks your long-range vision. Once you find your bearings and are fully in the battle, you must avoid a plethora of obstacles if you are going to collect any pick-up tokens, whether they be Repair tokens, Refresh tokens, or Hero tokens.

In the air, there isn't much difference from any other map while playing Fighter Squadron. However, take note of the plumes of smoke. When you're flying through them, be ready to use your stunt maneuvers to avoid taking fire.

1 Throughout the match, several escort instances take place. The direction in which each team's transport begins its travel across the map is always the same, but the angle that it travels in is subject to change. Pay attention to your HUD when these events begin, and bring as many members of your team as you can to that location. Get there as fast as possible to complete the mission as quickly or efficiently as you can. Since the angle of the transport's travel changes, the transport could possibly begin inside one of the canyons, making it difficult for you to track and destroy the enemy transport ship.

SULPHUR FIELDS

Blast

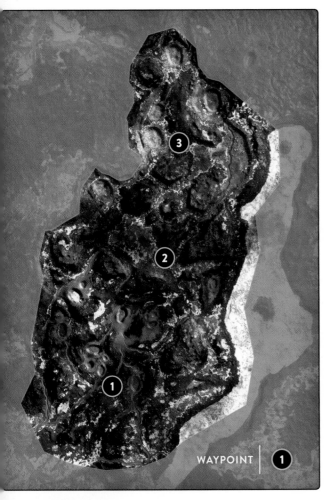

The SoroSuum Centroplex is split into three sections only separated by a level of elevation, but it also contains several terraneous objects that require a bit of finesse when you're attempting to outmaneuver your opponent. Some of the most useful Asset Star Cards to carry in your hand while playing Blast in the Sulphur Fields are Barrage and Bowcaster. Barrage helps you hide in the blind spots of some hills and launch explosives in the general area where you might have your enemy pinned down. Bowcaster is best used in the compressing areas of the map where two or three routes become one and when partners or parties come together, creating the perfect group shot.

1 The first area of the Sulphur Fields is the outer rim of the map that borders the map in the direction heading out toward the cliff. This specific area is the most open area of the map and allows for more mid-range firefights. Out here, you can find a crashed TIE fighter that makes for excellent cover and a great object to conceal your approach. Pay attention to the small, dry rivers, and watch your step in the outer rim. Most of the sulphur deposits are in this area, but they are a little smaller here and sometimes harder to see when you are focused on enemies at range.

2 The next area of importance in the Sulphur Fields is a small, flat area where the Imperial transport ship has landed. This staging area for Imperial forces is the center of the action and is where some of the more explosive ordnance is used. If you

have a Jump Pack, you can get on the hull of the Imperial transport, which gives you a generally wide field of view and can let you know where the majority of the enemy forces are coming from. Don't stay on the ship's hull too long, though, as this spot is easily given away if you are obviously peeking your body over the top. Behind the ship are a few cargo containers that border the ship, which creates a couple layers to the main transition walkway. Use the containers to ambush foes as they come by and take them by surprise. As they try to cross to the other side, your adversaries may not even be paying attention to the fact that someone might be waiting for them.

3 The final location on the map is just over the hill that the Imperial transport has landed on. This place is interesting because the outer rim and the staging area connect here, making each spot highly accessible from any location. There is a second staging area here that contains a few more crates. Another secondary area is also a little more open, though it contains some more terrain obstacles. Along with the rocks placed in spread-out locations, you also have a few of the larger sulphur pits that can damage you if you stand on them too long. This area is not the best place to linger, so try not to get pushed back here for very long.

Drop Zone

Drop Zone in the Sulphur Fields is very much a free-for-all when it comes to predicting where the most likely spots for the drop pods will be. If your team can control the outer rim of the map near the cliffside, you will likely have an advantage on the initial jump toward the next fallen drop pod.

1 One of the likely spots for a drop pod is far out beyond the Imperial transport ship and in the middle of the small river, where it appears that lava recently may have flowed through it. The river has two small ledges and a few rock formations that are perfect for cover when you are defending the pod. However, they are a tad small, making it very difficult to hide for long before the enemy spots you. Finding an Orbital Strike and firing it in this location can be very effective because of how much overhead cover the area lacks. Avoid getting too close to your teammates out here, as it is easy to become surrounded; when you approach your target, you want to be the group that surrounds them, not the other way around.

2 The next popular drop pod landing zone is located on the other side of the map, near the larger sulphur pits. Here, there is a bit more cover because of larger rock formations and the walls that surround the pits.

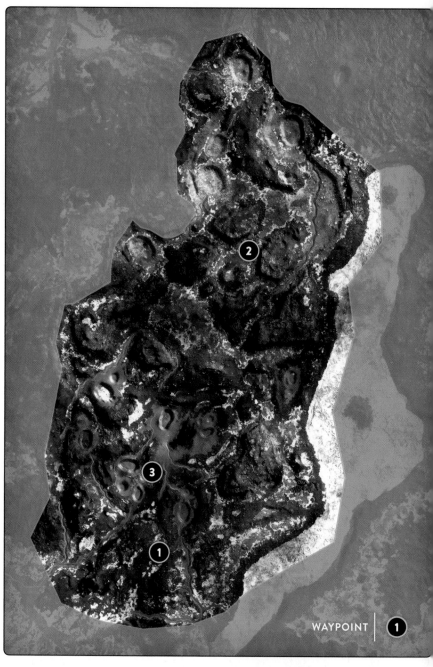

WAYPOINT | **1**

However, the damaging sulphur beneath your feet limits the amount of places where the enemy will not find you. The best way to defend this location is to push forward and set up camp behind the large cliff in the middle that creates the fork in the path just before the Imperial transport ship. Defend from this location, but watch both sides and straight above you, as your opponent could come from any direction.

3 The third key location for these drop pods is again on the outer rim of the map, but this time, it is much closer to the ship. By taking the path that is on the starboard side of the Imperial transport ship, you are led down to another wide area, but this location is easily guarded from the cliffs and ridges above it. The pods that land near here typically land in the shadow of the cliff. This creates a great opportunity for you to use the cliff as overwatch, or even use it as a piece of cover to hide under from any foes who may be attacking you from above.

Droid Run

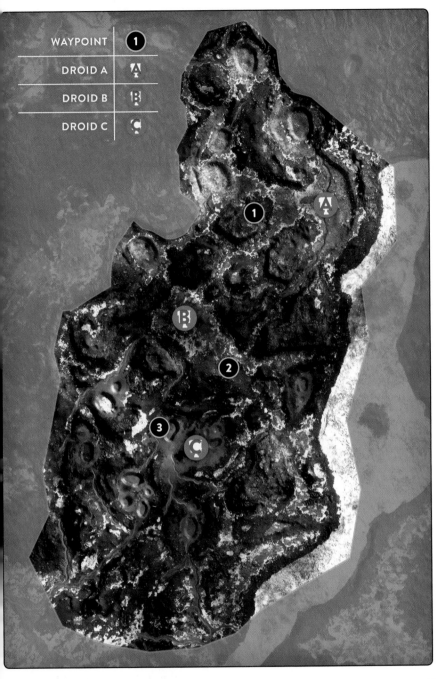

WAYPOINT	1
DROID A	A
DROID B	B
DROID C	C

1 Droid Run in the Sulphur Fields is much more like a map/mode combo where anything can and will happen. he structure of the Sulphur Fields allows you to quickly get to any part of the map from anywhere else. The progression in this version of Droid Run does not go in a sequential order. Either side can potentially control the "A" and "C" droids, but the combination of who controls what changes rather frequently. The "A" Power Droid roams around the secondary staging area that is away from the Imperial transport ship and off near the sulphur pits. You can either defend this droid from the cliff on the hill or use the cargo crates that are being staged here. Using Star Cards like Contact Grenade and Pulse Cannon can really benefit you. Being able to lob a grenade at the droid itself to ensure that no one is attempting to take it is a quick way of staying protected while also guarding your territory. The Pulse Cannon gives you a little more reach, which allows you to watch the droid from afar.

2 The "B" droid has claimed the flat landing area where the Imperial transport ship is stationed and the Empire has staged a few of its cargo crates. The amount of objects that are up on this flat piece provides an incredible amount of cover, but take note that this location has the most foot traffic. This makes the place a nightmare while you wait for the droid to walk to a safer area. At certain points, the droid may be on the side of the "A" droid, the "C" droid, or the side of the cliff that is open to all sorts of mayhem. The important lesson is not worrying about where the droid is when you attempt to take it. Just claim it, and claim it as fast as you can. Defending this droid takes an incredible amount of stamina and quick cool-down speed. Use the necessary abilities and shoot straight—one wrong move can take you out of the area very quickly.

3 Finally, the "C" droid does not roam very far but has no problem with being out in the wide open area. This droid roams around the area of the crashed TIE fighter. You won't have much cover to use, but the large TIE fighter and the cliff both provide an incredible tactical advantage. Because of its position, the droid can be spotted from a great distance away, making a long-range defense perfectly viable. You can also use the large rock next to it for a great perch that lets you grab a quick glance at whoever is attempting to take it. Avoid staying on any high surfaces out in the open in this location, as it is suicide. Still, it is a great tactic to use for quick potshots without your enemy knowing exactly where the fire is coming from immediately.

Hero Hunt

The planet of Sullust is primarily controlled by the Empire. Along with many other planets in this situation, the locals are not pleased by this and are now on the hunt for the villains who lead this army. As with all parts of Sullust, whenever Hero Hunt is being played, there will be villains who are controlled and hunted down. In the Sulphur Fields, you are hunting Darth Vader, Boba Fett, and Emperor Palpatine. By far the most challenging villain to kill here is Boba Fett, so let's start with him.

WAYPOINT | **1**

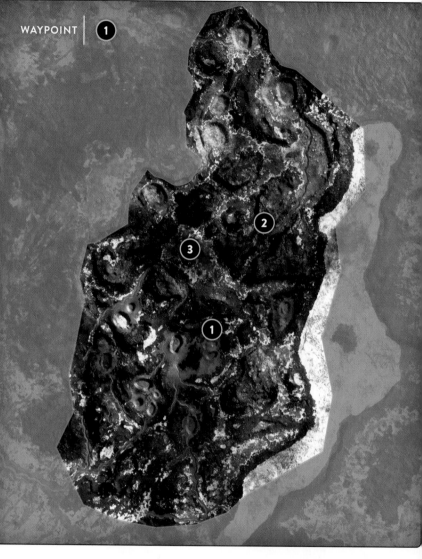

1 Fett is highly mobile and can travel to any part of the Sulphur Fields extremely quickly, making him almost unstoppable unless you play to his weaknesses. It is nearly impossible to sneak up on Boba Fett, as the player who is controlling him will most likely use the jetpack whenever possible. Because of this, you should equip high-powered mid-range blasters that allow you to keep your distance while still being able to deal major damage to him. But be very careful while using this tactic, because Boba is also equipped with a high-powered blaster rifle and can fire back. However, the range on his blaster is not the farthest, so using Star Cards like Pulse Cannon and Cycler Rifle can give you an advantage—especially because he does not have a lightsaber to deflect bolts back at you.

2 Keeping a long distance works with Boba Fett, but it may get a little trickier with Darth Vader and Emperor Palpatine. Even though Palpatine does not have a lightsaber, both Palpatine and Vader can deflect bolts and shoot them right back at you, potentially killing you if you are not careful. Dealing with these two is best completed by using mid-range tactics and lobbing explosives at them. Both characters have long-range attacks or abilities that allow them to get closer to you or attack you from their particular distance, but there is a long cool-down on their abilities, leaving you the advantage. Don't worry about these moves too much; even though they will kill you if you're caught, enough objects and uneven terrain in the area make it a little easier to avoid them.

3 Proximity mines and Smart Rockets are your best bets when hunting down the Sith Lord and his apprentice. Neither one of them has very fast movement speed, making it much easier for you to hit them. Forcing the villains to move around is also advantageous to the hunters because they want to gather your entire team into one collected area. Preventing them from doing that is what helps your team take down the enemy as quickly as possible.

Heroes Vs. Villains

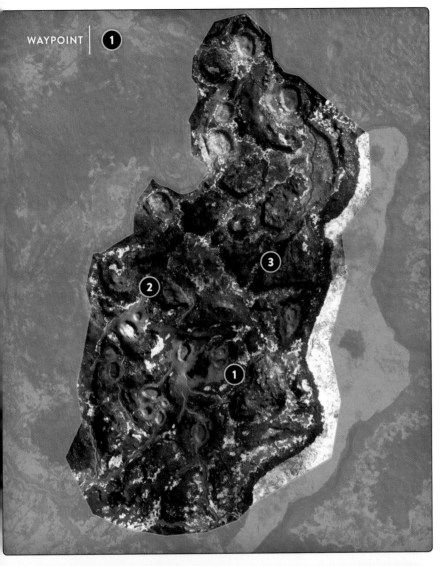

Heroes Vs. Villains in the Sulphur Fields lends extremely well to some of the ranged characters like Boba Fett, Han Solo, and Leia Organa. Playing these characters can give you an advantage over the other hero characters, but it won't automatically win the game. On this map, the weaker characters are some of the strongest characters in the game.

1 When you're playing characters like Boba Fett, you can scan the entire battlefield looking for the enemy. Being able to point out where opponents are and communicate that to your team gives you the tactical advantage. It's up to you how you organize your team in the attack, but the fact that you can see adversaries before they see you is a great plus.

2 Han Solo and Princess Leia both have powerful blasters and protective abilities that give them the upper hand against Darth Vader and Emperor Palpatine. Han can use Lucky Shot from a distance and wait for it to cool down before the enemy can get to him, which gives him a bonus health advantage when the close combat fight begins. However, with Han's speed, you may be able to keep his distance as long as you don't back up into a corner. Leia must recruit the assistance of her troopers and use their combined blaster power to deal enough damage. However, being able to protect them from Force Lightning and (more importantly) Chain Lightning helps significantly with allowing her to set up deadly ambushes.

3 All three of the remaining characters (Luke Skywalker, Darth Vader, and Emperor Palpatine) have a slight disadvantage when playing on the Sulphur Fields, but they are still completely capable of dominating each match. Because of Luke's and Vader's Saber Deflect and Palpatine's deflect ability, they can stay protected if they are caught out in the open. When you are caught, do your best to make it back to cover; you are toast as soon as your ability runs out of energy.

Blast

❶ The Imperial Hangar is one of the smallest maps in *Star Wars Battlefront*, making it one of the most chaotic maps to play Blast on. The center of the map is one giant hangar with multiple levels on catwalks, TIE fighter docks, and cargo crates. Unlike other missions here in the Imperial Hangar, Blast does not have the giant AT-AT in the center. You can see directly over to the other side from the sides, which creates a few long-range opportunities. Prepare for a great deal of blaster fire in the center of the map, especially inside the hangar itself.

❷ Also in the center of the map is a large landing pad that extends outside the hangar into the open air. You don't have anything to really use as major cover besides a few cargo crates, so this area provides a way for you to cross the map without drawing too much attention.

❸ Due to the hangar's size, two levels on the interior corridors lead to the two rooms that act as bases and allow each team to assemble its forces. If you are the type to run and gun around the perimeter of most maps, this is the path and environment you want to follow. There might be a lot of resistance from these locations, but it is mostly because players are respawning here. Odds are that you can catch most adversaries off guard, as they are not expecting to find any enemies in their "territory."

❹ No matter which strategy you choose, you must select your weapon and Star Card loadout carefully, as this map offers two very different environments that you can work in. Players who decide to bull-rush the middle and test their mettle against the big guns and straight shooters should bring a high-powered mid-range blaster and at least one explosive, possibly paired with a long-range rifle. Players who plan to run the perimeter of the map, wreaking havoc among all those not paying close attention to their surroundings, will find it beneficial to equip a short-range blaster and a Personal Shield Charge Star Card. This allows them to escape from dangerous situations when they encounter way too many stormtroopers than they bargained for.

Cargo

1 When you're playing Cargo in the Imperial Hangar, Jump Packs are extremely useful, but only before you grab the cargo. Being able to jump from end to end and float a great distance from the top floor down to the bottom lets you move down the length of the map within a matter of seconds. The only downside is that when you are carrying the cargo, you cannot use the Jump Pack, as you are far too heavy.

2 The two cargo storage areas are located in virtually identical places, making it a little less confusing when you're trying to figure out which route to take and where it will take you.

3 Each cargo storage is located in the intelligence room relative to your team's beginning area. There are three entrances to this room: one from the ground floor head-on, one leading to the upper catwalk from the side, and one leading to the ground floor from the side. To protect these areas, use the computers as cover and set up Blaster Cannons to keep the entrances under heavy fire, preventing any opponents aware of their surroundings from setting foot inside.

4 One of the best ways to escape this area with the enemy's cargo is by taking the long route around the side entrance that leads to the upper catwalk. It is somewhat dangerous because of the lack of protection and cover, but the amount of time you spend in the hangar itself strongly outweighs the danger you face from taking any other route.

Hero Hunt

Hero Hunt in the Imperial Hangar is quite complicated for both the hunters and the villains that you control on Sullust. Since there is a balance of both close-quarters combat and long-range combat, there is always the matter of positioning for each villain. Hunters, on the other hand, always face the matter of exploiting villains when they're out of position.

1 Darth Vader's specialty is close-up combat, which makes the intelligence rooms and the small corridors his home. While hunting Vader, you should stay out of these areas until you have a direct bead on him. A player who knows Vader's strengths will stay in the interior until hunters come get him. Trying to charge him is suicide, but ambushing him and surrounding him can take him down. Keep to the long hallways and take him down from both sides, preventing him from deflecting bolts toward you and your teammates. Stay close to the turns and doorways to avoid his Saber Throw, and be ready to run at a moment's notice.

2 Boba Fett favors the outside and being able to move around freely without the confines of the corridors. Beware of the open hangar, and stay indoors to best battle him while attempting to get a firing angle on his position. Having your team of hunters take different doorways gives you the better view of the hangar and also spreads Boba's attention around, making it harder for him to take you out without sustaining a great deal of damage from the surrounding troopers.

3 Finally, you have the great challenge of handling the fearsome Emperor Palpatine and his powerful Force Lightning. The Imperial Hangar is possibly one of Emperor Palpatine's best maps, as he can travel to any area and can inflict a tremendous amount of damage via all of his abilities. Using Chain Lightning in the narrow corridors can kill an entire squad of troopers, so be careful when you're traveling inside. When outside, try to always have a bead on his position. With his Force Dash ability, if you don't know where he is, there is a good chance that he is right on your six, about to toast you.

Heroes Vs. Villians

1 The balanced Imperial Hangar lends very well to this mode, allowing all the characters to use each of their abilities to its full capacity. In this mode, you can play as Darth Vader on Sullust. Using his Saber Throw is a good way to deal with both Han Solo and Princess Leia. Although it is difficult to kill either hero with Saber Throw, it inflicts more than enough damage to give you a chance to close the gap between Vader and them, granting the advantage of close quarters. The small corridors on the edges and walls of the large hangar are the most important locations for the Sith Lord. These places bring in most enemies close, taking away any disadvantages that Vader has at range. Lure your opponent into tight locations like these, and then use Force Choke or Heavy Strike to swiftly take down your adversary.

2 Boba Fett is a man to be reckoned with anywhere, but he's especially dangerous in the outdoor areas of the Imperial Hangar. On this map, he can perfectly stay at range for most of the match if desired and still be effective. Post up in the Khetanna on the landing dock located directly outside the main hangar, and take advantage of being able to go anywhere within seconds by using Fett's jetpack. Once you have an idea of where your enemies are, you might want to save some jet fuel and let it loose to get the high angle on all of them. If they can't immediately see where you are, you have the advantage of getting a few shots on them before they do see you, and then bugging out before being attacked. Launching Wrist Rocket as your first attack toward any hero gives you quite the advantage when it comes down to damage per second on your opponent. The Flame Thrower attached to Fett's forearm may not be quite as useful on this map as his other abilities, but if he's caught in a pinch, it could get him out of a close-quarters situation against someone like Luke Skywalker.

3 When playing as Emperor Palpatine on this map, keep in mind that you have a very powerful deflect ability that comes quite in handy when facing heroes like Han Solo and Princess Leia. As the Emperor, your best strategy is staying as close as possible to other villains. Because you are close, you can support them by casting Chain Lightning at multiple opponents. This can either cause your adversary to bug out or attempt to close the gap on you, only to be ambushed by your partner standing closeby. Remember to escape or help protect another villain with Force Dash.

INFANTRY

Whether a Rebel trooper or a stormtrooper fighting for the Empire, all infantry members should know a few crucial things before starting each match on Star Wars Battlefront. Each trooper can be equipped with a couple combinations of two Star Cards and one Trait Star Card, each with its own ability and advantages in various situations. Every Star Card and every blaster must be purchased before you can equip and use them. You can only purchase something if your rank is high enough for each card or blaster individually. Use this section of the guide to carefully choose what you would like to equip, and then save up for that item. As soon as your rank is high enough, you can purchase and use it on the battlefield immediately.

BLASTERS

Throughout the galaxy, not all life forms were able to wield a lightsaber. In fact, only a select few gained the knowledge of the Force and could adequately use such a mighty weapon. The most commonly equipped armament is a ranged weapon known as a blaster. Soldiers from both the Rebel Alliance and the Empire use various types of blasters to defend themselves and battle one another.

In *Star Wars* Battlefront, there are many different blasters to choose from, and choosing the right one that fits your style of play is key when attempting to defeat your enemies. Everyone on your team plays a different role when fighting for victory, but they are all equipped with a blaster. It's up to you to ensure that you are using the best one for your own tactical advantage. While all blasters fire blaster bolts, no two have the same damage output, rate of fire, range, and cooling power combination. Whether you're fighting for the Rebel Alliance against those Imperial swine or as a stormtrooper against the traitorous Rebel scum, you have access to all of the blasters you have unlocked. If you find one that works for you, use it whenever possible. However, you should try out each new blaster you unlock—you never know what new techniques you may pick up.

Each and every blaster shoots fairly straight. With any single fired shot, you will more than likely hit wherever your crosshairs are pointing. However, note that the more rapidly you fire your weapon, the less accurate it becomes. To maximize your damage, rattle off short, quick bursts at your foes. When an enemy is at a shorter range (like inside the corridors of Sullust), let those bolts fly. Even though their accuracy may diminish, blasters do not have a great deal of recoil. You can stay accurate enough to take down your opponent without missing too many shots. Pay attention to your Heat gauge, as it is very possible to panic and overheat your blaster. It is best not let your weapon overheat, but if it does, focus and complete the cool-down mini-game to quickly get it back in working condition. Failing this mini-game prolongs your overheat penalty, leaving you vulnerable.

Range is key when selecting your target or deciding whether you're in the correct position to take down your enemy. Blaster bolts are beams of high-energy particles that do not have enough mass to drop to the ground after you fire them. However, they do begin dissipating after they've traveled a certain distance. Even though your bolts won't have any drop from gravity, the farther away you are from your target, the less damage your blaster will inflict. This is where you must pay attention to your blaster's range. A blaster with a low range and a high rate of fire will not perform well when you are fighting an enemy with a long-range scoped weapon from 100 meters away. Pick your battles, and choose the blaster that was made for your style of play. That blaster may well save your life, giving your team a better chance at succeeding in any given mission.

DLT-19

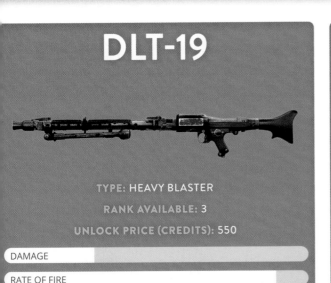

TYPE: HEAVY BLASTER

RANK AVAILABLE: 3

UNLOCK PRICE (CREDITS): 550

DAMAGE

RATE OF FIRE

RANGE

COOLING POWER

A medium-range blaster, the fully automatic DLT-19 fires downrange at a very high rate of fire. The speed at which it sends blaster bolts compensates for its damage output (which is also what makes it a medium-range weapon). For best results, use the DLT-19 in modes like Supremacy. Even though that mode is objective-based, bringing several troopers close together, the firefights are mostly mid-range fights.

DH-17

TYPE: BLASTER PISTOL

RANK AVAILABLE: 3

UNLOCK PRICE (CREDITS): 550

DAMAGE

RATE OF FIRE

RANGE

COOLING POWER

Much like the DLT-19, the DH-17 is fully automatic and performs best at medium range. As a blaster pistol, it fires at a slower rate, but it fortunately puts out a little more damage to balance this out. The requirement for accuracy is a little more stringent because of the lower rate of fire; each burst or blaster bolt must count in order for you to take down your opponent. Overall, the DH-17 is a very well-rounded weapon. Once you have unlocked it, it works very well for any type of player.

RT-97C

TYPE: HEAVY BLASTER

RANK AVAILABLE: 5

UNLOCK PRICE (CREDITS): 1250

DAMAGE

RATE OF FIRE

RANGE

COOLING POWER

This rapid-firing blaster can deal significant damage to your opponent because of how many bolts it can put out within a short amount of time. The RT-97C can fire for a bit longer than most blasters (especially heavy blasters) without overheating or having to cool down. Bring this blaster into your favorite modes and take down your enemies, as they stand no chance in a hallway or at most ranges on the battlefield.

A280C

TYPE: BLASTER RIFLE

RANK AVAILABLE: 8

UNLOCK PRICE (CREDITS): 1550

DAMAGE

RATE OF FIRE

RANGE

COOLING POWER

The A280C is a medium-range weapon that has a moderate fire rate and is the blaster that the Rebels begin with as their default starting blaster. Equipped with a mid-range scope, this versatile blaster is effective for all types of players. Taking roughly five seconds to overheat when you hold down the trigger, the A280C leaves you with plenty of time to take down multiple enemies before things get too hot. Because of the low damage on this blaster, you should aim for your enemy's head. It is important to get the most out of your attack before your target has a chance to retaliate, possibly with a more powerful weapon. Catching your opponents by surprise is your best tactic when equipped with the A280C; give your foes minimal time to locate your position and counter-attack.

BLASTERS

E-11

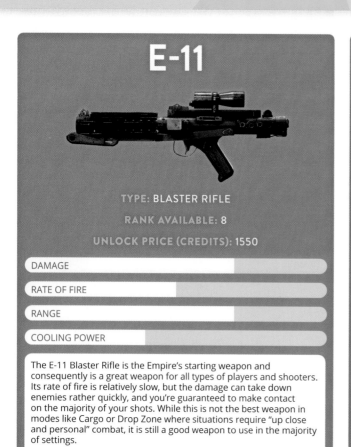

TYPE: BLASTER RIFLE

RANK AVAILABLE: 8

UNLOCK PRICE (CREDITS): 1550

DAMAGE

RATE OF FIRE

RANGE

COOLING POWER

The E-11 Blaster Rifle is the Empire's starting weapon and consequently is a great weapon for all types of players and shooters. Its rate of fire is relatively slow, but the damage can take down enemies rather quickly, and you're guaranteed to make contact on the majority of your shots. While this is not the best weapon in modes like Cargo or Drop Zone where situations require "up close and personal" combat, it is still a good weapon to use in the majority of settings.

CA-87

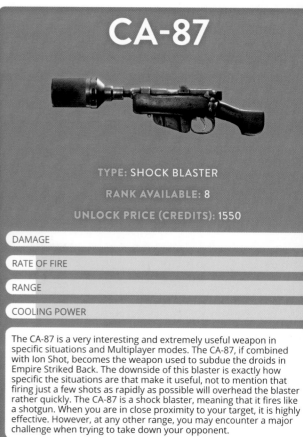

TYPE: SHOCK BLASTER

RANK AVAILABLE: 8

UNLOCK PRICE (CREDITS): 1550

DAMAGE

RATE OF FIRE

RANGE

COOLING POWER

The CA-87 is a very interesting and extremely useful weapon in specific situations and Multiplayer modes. The CA-87, if combined with Ion Shot, becomes the weapon used to subdue the droids in Empire Strikes Back. The downside of this blaster is exactly how specific the situations are that make it useful, not to mention that firing just a few shots as rapidly as possible will overheat the blaster rather quickly. The CA-87 is a shock blaster, meaning that it fires like a shotgun. When you are in close proximity to your target, it is highly effective. However, at any other range, you may encounter a major challenge when trying to take down your opponent.

T-21

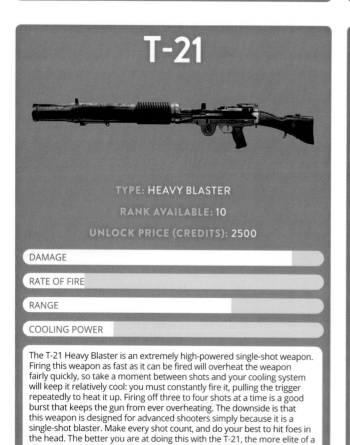

TYPE: HEAVY BLASTER

RANK AVAILABLE: 10

UNLOCK PRICE (CREDITS): 2500

DAMAGE

RATE OF FIRE

RANGE

COOLING POWER

The T-21 Heavy Blaster is an extremely high-powered single-shot weapon. Firing this weapon as fast as it can be fired will overheat the weapon fairly quickly, so take a moment between shots and your cooling system will keep it relatively cool: you must constantly fire it, pulling the trigger repeatedly to heat it up. Firing off three to four shots at a time is a good burst that keeps the gun from ever overheating. The downside is that this weapon is designed for advanced shooters simply because it is a single-shot blaster. Make every shot count, and do your best to hit foes in the head. The better you are at doing this with the T-21, the more elite of a player you will be.

SE-14C

TYPE: BLASTER PISTOL

RANK AVAILABLE: 14

UNLOCK PRICE (CREDITS): 2500

DAMAGE

RATE OF FIRE

RANGE

COOLING POWER

This blaster pistol is another weapon that works best for advanced players. The rate of fire is quite fast, but the damage is a little low. It is also a burst-fire weapon, meaning that it fires a short burst with every pull of the trigger. This helps a little with any overheating problems you may have on the battlefield. Though the burst fire does not teach trigger control, it does allow you to let the blaster cool off between shots. The SE-14C is highly effective if every shot from the burst lands on the target. Without giving your enemies a chance to recover health, hitting them with a few bursts is sure to take them down quickly.

EE-3

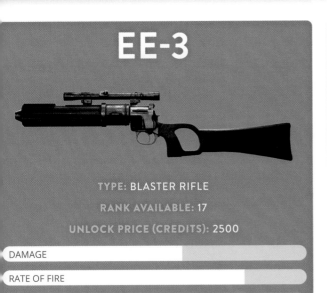

TYPE: BLASTER RIFLE

RANK AVAILABLE: 17

UNLOCK PRICE (CREDITS): 2500

DAMAGE

RATE OF FIRE

RANGE

COOLING POWER

The EE-3 Blaster Rifle might look familiar if you are a fan of the great bounty hunter Boba Fett. This is another blaster that fires in a burst style of a few bolts per pull of the trigger. However, unlike the SE-14C, this one spits out bolts a little faster, giving you less delay between bursts. This is both a strength and a weakness for the EE-3. The quick burst helps you because you have less chance of missing your target on the last bolt in the blast, assuming that the first bolt hits. However, it can hurt you if you are not paying attention to the Heat gauge. Like any fully automatic blaster, the possibility of rapid overheating applies to the EE-3. To make the most out of this blaster rifle, be careful and watch your HUD. Once you have more experience and mastery of the weapon, the EE-3 is one of the most powerful blasters in *Star Wars* Battlefront.

T-21B

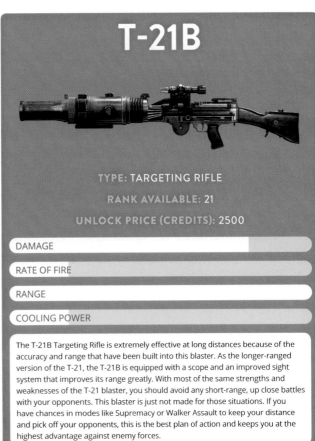

TYPE: TARGETING RIFLE

RANK AVAILABLE: 21

UNLOCK PRICE (CREDITS): 2500

DAMAGE

RATE OF FIRE

RANGE

COOLING POWER

The T-21B Targeting Rifle is extremely effective at long distances because of the accuracy and range that have been built into this blaster. As the longer-ranged version of the T-21, the T-21B is equipped with a scope and an improved sight system that improves its range greatly. With most of the same strengths and weaknesses of the T-21 blaster, you should avoid any short-range, up close battles with your opponents. This blaster is just not made for those situations. If you have chances in modes like Supremacy or Walker Assault to keep your distance and pick off your opponents, this is the best plan of action and keeps you at the highest advantage against enemy forces.

DL-44

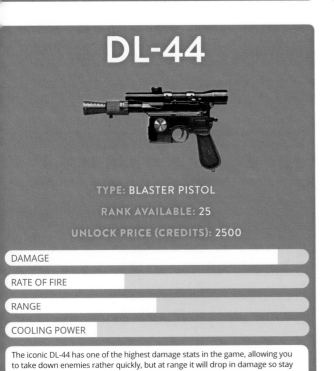

TYPE: BLASTER PISTOL

RANK AVAILABLE: 25

UNLOCK PRICE (CREDITS): 2500

DAMAGE

RATE OF FIRE

RANGE

COOLING POWER

The iconic DL-44 has one of the highest damage stats in the game, allowing you to take down enemies rather quickly, but at range it will drop in damage so stay aware of how far you are before engaging in battle. Equipped with a scope, this rifle does wonders at long range in accuracy but can also demolish your opponent in a close-quarters combat situation. One of only downsides to this weapon is that it is a single-shot blaster that over heats after about 6 shots, which forces you to make every shot count if you want it to be effective. Missing a shot or two in a firefight could really be the difference between winning and losing the battle. Keep the enemy at a medium range for the highest level of success, but know that this weapon can still perform rather nicely in any environment.

STAR CARD HANDS AND CUSTOMIZATION

Star Cards grant special weapons and abilities in Multiplayer, Battle, and Survival modes. As part of your loadout, you can take a hand of three Star Cards into a game. A hand consists of two Star Cards and a Charged Star Card. Star Cards provide a bonus weapon, while Charged Star Cards give a weapon modification or an ability like better accuracy, a personal shield, or explosive shots. Note that these cards are only available to infantry, as heroes have preset abilities instead.

As you reach specific ranks, cards are unlocked for purchase. You earn credits by completing mission stars, finishing sieges in Base Command, earning experience, and achieving awards and challenges, and you use those credits to purchase the cards. Once you have purchased them, you can upgrade Star Cards and Charged Star Cards by paying another higher fee.

Each time a Star Card or Charged Star Card is activated, it must cool down before it comes back online. The amount of time required is called its cool-down time. Charged Star Cards also require a charge for each use. The number of charges available is shown in the corner of the card. Charge pick-ups, which give you +1 Charge, are available throughout the battlefield. You can also purchase them at 25 charges for 2200 credits.

Special cards called Traits become available at later Ranks. Purchase each one for the steep price of 9000 credits to get valuable bonuses. Select one to take into a game, and then level it up with kill streaks. The level is reset at the end of each round.

Customization

When thinking about your Star Card Hand, consider your play style, the game mode, and the map. Several cards are more effective against vehicles. Others are ideal in an open environment, while some work best in tight quarters. As you unlock them, try each one out to find your preferences. You can set up a customized hand in the Star Card menu and throw your favorites in there for a quick choice.

Some cards go well together. For example, the Ion Torpedo is great against vehicles, but it takes time to get a lock. Consider also taking the Personal Shield to protect yourself or the Smoke Grenade to hide your location. For an explosive time, try the Impact Grenade, Thermal Detonator, and Explosive Shot. Then, rain destruction all over the battlefield. Marksmen should try the Pulse Cannon or Cycler Rifle. Throw in the Jump Pack to find effective sniper locations, Focus Fire to increase accuracy, or Scan Pulse to avoid getting snuck up on. Numerous options exist, so experiment to find which work best for you.

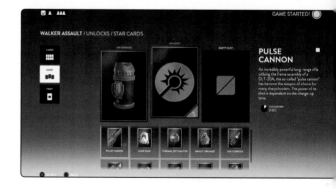

STAR CARDS

The section below lists all Asset and Charge Star Cards, along with the rank where they become available, the cost, a description, and relevant stats.

Barrage

TYPE: STAR CARD

RANK AVAILABLE: 24

UNLOCK PRICE (CREDITS): 4000

UPGRADE PRICE (CREDITS): 7000

The MPL-57 (Multi-Purpose Launcher) Barrage fires a volley of three grenades with a short delay fuse. Pressing the appropriate ability button pulls out the grenade launcher. Aim your shot and fire to send the explosives toward the target. The explosives are effective against a group of infantry. Use them to both get kills and clear out a location. When you approach an objective with enemy activity, bombard them with explosives to clear the way.

STATS

Name	Condition
Fuse	0.5 to 1 Second after Impact
Damage	55 per Grenade
Radius	5 Meters, Max Damage within 3.5 Meters
Cool-down Time	18 Seconds
Active Time	N/A
Upgrade	Cool-down Time = 15 Seconds

Cooling Cell

TYPE: CHARGED STAR CARD

RANK AVAILABLE: 7

UNLOCK PRICE (CREDITS): 2200

UPGRADE PRICE (CREDITS): 9000

When activated, Cooling Cell vents heat from your main weapon and prevents further heat build-up for a short period of time. Save Cooling Cell for times of trouble when you need extra firepower to finish off an opponent.

STATS

Name	Condition
Cool-down Time	20 Seconds
Active Time	3 Seconds
Upgrade	Active Time = 5 Seconds
Cool-down Time	20 Seconds
Active Time	3 Seconds
Upgrade	Active Time = 5 Seconds

Bowcaster

TYPE: STAR CARD

RANK AVAILABLE: 32

UNLOCK PRICE (CREDITS): 4000

UPGRADE PRICE (CREDITS): 7000

Depending on the charge-up time, the Bowcaster fires one, three, or five explosive bolts in a horizontal arc. While you hold the Fire button, five circles turn red along the right side of the HUD, signifying how many bolts are ready to be launched. Release the button at any time to let them go. The reticle also has five dots that change color as you hold the button. White dots mean that the bolts are more likely to miss their mark, while red means that an enemy is currently targeted. Once you have shot, you must wait 18 seconds before using it again, so make every shot count. The Bowcaster is best saved for a group of foes, so you can take full advantage of multiple bolts. Watch out while charging the weapon, as you are vulnerable to attack. Your health is visible with the crossbow drawn, but the scanner is hidden. The Bowcaster works extremely well with the Jump Pack, allowing the player to fire the weapon down on enemies from mid-air. The explosive bolts just need to hit the nearby ground to damage them.

STATS

Name	Condition
Fuse	Explodes on Impact
Damage	50 per Bolt
Radius	3 Meters, Max Damage within 2 Meters
Cool-down Time	18 Seconds
Active Time	N/A
Upgrade	Cool-down Time = 15 Seconds

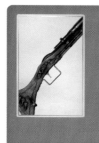

Cycler Rifle

TYPE: STAR CARD

RANK AVAILABLE: 28

UNLOCK PRICE (CREDITS): 4000

UPGRADE PRICE (CREDITS): 7000

Designed to fire solid projectiles, this crude but reliable rifle is excellent at hitting targets at extreme ranges and penetrating energy shields. Aim down the sights to zoom in on your target. The weapon has a very long range, but because it is a solid projectile, it suffers from bullet drop. Be sure to aim accordingly. A great addition to any sniper loadout, the Cycler Rifle excels against any soldier, even those protected by shields—making it a great choice against jumptroopers. Note that crouching makes you a smaller target for enemies, but it does not improve your accuracy.

STATS

Name	Condition
Damage	90 (Lethal with Headshot)
Cool-down Time	15 Seconds
Active Time	N/A
Upgrade	Cool-down Time = 10 Seconds

Explosive Shot

TYPE: CHARGED STAR CARD

RANK AVAILABLE: 18

UNLOCK PRICE (CREDITS): 2200

UPGRADE PRICE (CREDITS): 9000

Explosive Shot temporarily supercharges your primary weapon to fire explosive bolts. The ability adds explosive damage to your blaster for 7-10 seconds. Activate it just before taking on a group of foes, and then quickly fire bolts at them. Note that your weapon still overheats.

STATS

Name	Condition
Cool-down Time	20 Seconds
Active Time	3 Seconds
Upgrade	Active Time = 5 Seconds
Cool-down Time	20 Seconds
Active Time	3 Seconds
Upgrade	Active Time = 5 Seconds

Flash Grenade

TYPE: STAR CARD

RANK AVAILABLE: 20

UNLOCK PRICE (CREDITS): 4000

UPGRADE PRICE (CREDITS): 7000

This non-lethal explosive creates a bright energy flash and loud noise to disorient opponents. While the grenade does not cause any damage, it is still extremely helpful in any mode. Any trooper close to its detonation is disoriented by a white screen and deafening sound. Note that the explosion can affect you if you throw it too close to your position. Enemies cannot track you in this condition, so take advantage of the situation whether you are on the offensive or attempting to escape.

STATS

Name	Condition
Fuse	0.5 Seconds after Impact
Damage	0
Blind Effect	Max 5 Seconds (dependent on distance to flash)
Radius	5 Meters
Cool-down Time	16 Seconds
Active Time	N/A
Upgrade	Cool-down Time = 12 Seconds

Focus Fire

TYPE: CHARGED STAR CARD

RANK AVAILABLE: 7

UNLOCK PRICE (CREDITS): 2200

UPGRADE PRICE (CREDITS): 9000

This gyroscopic modification stabilizes weapon accuracy for a short time, greatly lowering the spread on all primary blasters. Though this Charged Star Card helps your accuracy no matter which blaster you carry, it is ideal for a marksman with a long-range rifle. Try combining it with a heavy blaster like the DLT-19 and briefly turn it into a highly accurate weapon. It only lasts seven or 10 seconds, so activate it when you know you have a shot.

STATS

Name	Condition
Cool-down Time	20 Seconds
Active Time	7 Seconds
Upgrade	Active Time = 10 Seconds

Homing Shot

TYPE: STAR CARD

RANK AVAILABLE: 11

UNLOCK PRICE (CREDITS): 4000

UPGRADE PRICE (CREDITS): 7000

This homing shot can lock on to enemy soldiers from afar. Activating the card equips the launcher. Aim at your opponent through the scope until the launcher gets a lock, and then fire. With a successful lock, the shot seeks out its target. You are vulnerable during this process, so take appropriate precautions.

STATS

Name	Condition
Fuse	Explodes on Impact
Damage	100
Cool-down Time	18 Seconds
Active Time	N/A
Upgrade	Cool-down Time = 15 Seconds

Impact Grenade

TYPE: STAR CARD

RANK AVAILABLE: 6

UNLOCK PRICE (CREDITS): 2200

UPGRADE PRICE (CREDITS): 7000

Having a smaller blast radius than a Thermal Detonator, the Impact Grenade explodes directly on contact with any object. Keep this in mind when tossing the explosive. The indirect damage from a nearby explosion can be enough to eliminate an enemy, or at least cause him to flee.

STATS

Name	Condition
Fuse	Explodes on Impact
Damage	130
Radius	4 Meters, Max Damage within 1 Meter
Cool-down Time	16 Seconds
Active Time	N/A
Upgrade	Cool-down Time = 12 Seconds

Ion Grenade

TYPE: STAR CARD

RANK AVAILABLE: 4

UNLOCK PRICE (CREDITS): 600

UPGRADE PRICE (CREDITS): 7000

The Ion Grenade delivers massive damage against vehicles, shields, and droids—detonating when one is within range. This explosive is a good loadout choice when you're playing against vehicles in modes such as Supremacy, Walker Assault, or Survival. The device will not detect enemy soldiers.

STATS

Name	Condition
Fuse	7 Seconds from thrown or instant vehicle comes within range
Radius	7 Meters
Cool-down Time	16 Seconds
Active Time	N/A
Upgrade	Cool-down Time = 12 Seconds

Ion Shot

TYPE: CHARGED STAR CARD

RANK AVAILABLE: 7

UNLOCK PRICE (CREDITS): 2200

UPGRADE PRICE (CREDITS): 7000

With limited supplies of armaments, Rebel forces often made battlefield adaptions to their weapons. A notable case was the development of an insert that allowed normal blasters to fire ion-charged bolts for short periods of time.

This modification allows your primary weapon to fire ion-charged bolts, making it very effective against shields, droids, and vehicles. The ability is only available for seven or 10 seconds, so activate it as soon as you have a shot at your target. At that point, rapidly tap the Fire button to take full advantage of the weapon. This greatly reduces damage to humanoids, lowering your weapon's damage by 50%.

STATS

Name	Condition
Cool-down Time	20 Seconds
Active Time	7 Seconds
Upgrade	Active Time = 10 Seconds

Ion Torpedo

TYPE: STAR CARD

RANK AVAILABLE: 9

UNLOCK PRICE (CREDITS): 3000

UPGRADE PRICE (CREDITS): 7000

A modification of the popular MPL-57 weapon system engineered to fire Ion Torpedoes. Extremely effective against vehicles and stationary weapons.

The homing Ion Torpedo is designed to deal heavy damage to vehicles, droids, and stationary weapons. This launcher locks on to its target, but it takes time to do so. Be careful during this time, as you are vulnerable to attack.

STATS

Name	Condition
Fuse	Detonates on Impact (Explodes after 8 seconds without hitting target)
Damage	Destroys droids and turrets, damages vehicles
Cool-down Time	15 Seconds
Active Time	N/A
Upgrade	Cool-down Time = 12 Seconds

Jump Pack

TYPE: STAR CARD

RANK AVAILABLE: 16

UNLOCK PRICE (CREDITS): 4000

UPGRADE PRICE (CREDITS): 7000

Although the Jump Pack does not allow for sustained flight, it offers troops a reliable alternative to move quickly across the battlefield.

The back-mounted Jump Pack utilizes burst thrusters to allow its user to jump over large distances. It is well-suited for traversing obstructions and evading danger. This card allows you to reach locations that are otherwise inaccessible. In Battle and Survival missions, the Jump Pack is required to find all of the collectibles. Jump before triggering this ability to gain an extra boost.

STATS

Name	Condition
Fuse	Explodes on Impact
Damage	130
Radius	4 Meters, Max Damage within 1 Meter
Cool-down Time	16 Seconds
Active Time	N/A
Upgrade	Cool-down Time = 12 Seconds

Personal Shield

TYPE: CHARGED STAR CARD

RANK AVAILABLE: 22

UNLOCK PRICE (CREDITS): 2200

UPGRADE PRICE (CREDITS): 9000

To minimize casualties, the Empire modified the Droideka Shield Technology for use by ground troops. Although it hindered the use of weapons, it proved popular and was adopted by the Rebel Alliance.

The Personal Energy Shield provides protection from energy weapons. However, it offers no defense against kinetic weapons like Cycler Rifles and grenades. It provides you with several seconds of protection, which is plenty of time to escape from danger or finish a task where you are vulnerable. A 20-second cool-down is a long time between uses, so activate it wisely.

STATS

Name	Condition
Health	250
Cool-down Time	20 Seconds
Active Time	7 Seconds
Upgrade	Active Time = 9 Seconds

Pulse Cannon

TYPE: STAR CARD

RANK AVAILABLE: 6

UNLOCK PRICE (CREDITS): 2200

UPGRADE PRICE (CREDITS): 7000

An incredibly powerful long-range rifle utilizing the frame assembly of a DLT-20A, the Pulse Cannon has become the weapon of choice for many sharpshooters. The power of its shot depends on the charge-up time. Aim with the gun's powerful zoom, hold down the Fire button to charge it up, and then release the button. This is great for open environments, where long sight lines are possible. Make every shot count.

STATS

Name	Condition
Damage	100 Max Charge
Cool-down Time	18 Seconds
Active Time	N/A
Upgrade	Cool-down Time = 15 Seconds

Scan Pulse

TYPE: CHARGED STAR CARD

RANK AVAILABLE: 13

UNLOCK PRICE (CREDITS): 2200

UPGRADE PRICE (CREDITS): 9000

This 360-degree pulse burst reveals enemy soldiers, even if they are behind cover or out of sight. Activating the ability sends a pulse out in all directions. Any adversary hit by the pulse appears on your scanner. This is an extremely valuable Charged Star Card in many game modes. Use the ability when you're uncertain of enemy placement, such as when approaching or defending an objective.

STATS

Name	Condition
Radius	50 Meters
Cool-down Time	8 Seconds
Active Time	7 Seconds
Upgrade	Cool-down Time = 5 Seconds Active Time = 10 Seconds

Scout Pistol

TYPE: STAR CARD

RANK AVAILABLE: 4

UNLOCK PRICE (CREDITS): 600

UPGRADE PRICE (CREDITS): 7000

The light sidearm is effective at taking out opponents at close range, though it quickly loses its capabilities at longer distances. Equip this weapon on maps that feature plenty of close combat. Fires a two-shot burst.

STATS

Name	Condition
Damage	70 per Bolt within 10 Meters
Cool-down Time	9 Seconds
Active Time	N/A
Upgrade	Cool-down Time = 6 Seconds

Smoke Grenade

TYPE: STAR CARD

RANK AVAILABLE: 13

UNLOCK PRICE (CREDITS): 4000

UPGRADE PRICE (CREDITS): 7000

The Smoke Grenade provides dense smoke that blocks visibility and lock-on weapons. Hide your location from snipers, powerful vehicles, and foes attempting to disrupt your objective. It also allows you to escape from an enemy lock-on.

STATS

Name	Condition
Fuse	0.75 Seconds after Collision
Radius	8 Meters
Smoke Time	15 Seconds
Cool-down Time	20 Seconds
Active Time	N/A
Upgrade	Cool-down Time = 16 Seconds

Thermal Detonator

TYPE: STAR CARD

RANK AVAILABLE: 2

UNLOCK PRICE (CREDITS): 100

UPGRADE PRICE (CREDITS): 7000

Leia Organa, disguised as the bounty hunter Boushh, threatened to use a Thermal Detonator during her rescue attempt of Han Solo from Jabba the Hutt.

As the most popular and widely used grenade in the galaxy, the Thermal Detonator is easy to use and provides deadly results. The explosive is great against a group of infantry but ineffective against vehicles. As the first available Star Card (and a relatively inexpensive one), it's well worth purchasing just so you have an explosive to take into matches.

STATS

Name	Condition
Fuse	2.25 Seconds after thrown
Damage	100
Radius	7 Meters, Max Damage within 3 Meters
Cool-down Time	15 Seconds
Active Time	N/A
Upgrade	Cool-down Time = 10 Seconds

TRAITS

The five Traits are listed below, along with the rank where they become available, the cost, and the effect at each level. The level increases with kill streaks and is reset after each round.

Bodyguard

RANK AVAILABLE: 15

UNLOCK PRICE (CREDITS): 9000

Rigorous training and a brief career as a bodyguard in the Outer Rim have made you a lethal warrior capable of handling extreme situations.

Level	Condition
1	Decreases explosive damage by a small amount.
2	Decreases explosive damage by a medium amount.
3	Decreases explosive damage by a large amount and blaster damage by a small amount.

Bounty Hunter

RANK AVAILABLE: 26

UNLOCK PRICE (CREDITS): 9000

The Galactic War creates many veterans looking for opportunitie Fighting for the highest bidder, they see each battle as a chance to gain new riches.

Level	Condition
1	Low chance to get a Power-up with each kill.
2	Medium chance to get a Power-up with each kill.
3	High chance to get a Power-up with each kill and resets cool-down with each kill.

Scout

RANK AVAILABLE: 15

UNLOCK PRICE (CREDITS): 9000

During a brief stint in an elite reconnaissance unit, you learned how to use stealth tactics to find and eliminate the enemy.

Level	Condition
1	Sprinting does not show on enemy scanner.
2	Sprinting and firing your primary weapon does not show on enemy scanner.
3	Sprinting and firing your primary weapon does not show on enemy scanner, and killing an enemy resets weapon heat.

Sharpshooter

RANK AVAILABLE: 26

UNLOCK PRICE (CREDITS): 9000

Trained as a sharpshooter by a small team of rogue elite snipers, you enjoy operating alone and harassing the enemy from afar.

Level	Condition
1	Headshot kills reduce current cool-downs by a small amount.
2	Headshot kills reduce current cool-downs by a medium amount.
3	Headshot kills reduce current cool-downs by a large amount.

Survivalist

RANK AVAILABLE: 15

UNLOCK PRICE (CREDITS): 9000

As an orphan, you were raised by the Wookiee Berserkers on Kashyyyk, where you learned to revel in combat and quickly get back into the fight even after the most serious of injuries.

Level	Condition
1	Health regeneration starts a bit faster.
2	Health regeneration starts faster.
3	Health regeneration starts much faster, and you replenish a small amount of health with each kill.

POWER-UPS/ FIELD PICK-UPS

Scattered throughout the battlefields of most game modes, power-ups and pick-ups are one-time use items that offer special weapons, vehicles, and abilities. Always keep an eye out for them, because they can be game-changers.

POWER-UPS

A Power-up is represented as a specific circular icon at a set spawn location on the battlefield. Once you collect it, a power is randomly selected and placed in the lower card slot on your HUD. Press the Power Ability buttons to activate the skill, which is held in the Power slot until you use it. If you find another power-up that you would rather have, simply walk up to it and press the Use button to swap. Some of these powers are extremely strong; use them wisely.

Blaster Cannon

A stationary blaster that can be placed anywhere there is space. It operates just like the E-Web blasters. It has a shield and stays at a location until destroyed.

STATS

Name	Condition
Shield Health	200
Rate of Fire	275 RPM
Damage	35 plus 25 explosion damage
Radius	1.3 Meters

Card Refresh

Instantly refreshes Star and Charged Star Cards in a hand. Use up your arsenal to take full advantage of this power-up.

Infantry Turret

Automated defense that targets infantry. It remains active until destroyed. Look for populated locations for maximum effect. Objectives, chokepoints, and power-up locations all work well.

STATS

Name	Condition
Lock Time	1.5 Seconds (3 Seconds beyond 40 Meters)
Rate of Fire	425 RPM
Damage	10

Orbital Strike

An artillery barrage that rains destruction on a chosen outdoor location. Aim your shot until the blue reticle lines up with the desired target, and then fire. An aware opponent has time to flee, though. Great against a mob of soldiers or an objective. In an objective-based game, don't worry if kills are not acquired, as clearing out an enemy position is often the first priority. Max damage is ensured unless target exits danger zone. Note that an Orbital Strike cannot be used inside.

STATS

Name	Condition
Radius	18 Meters
Damage	100 per projectile

Proximity Bomb

Drop the bomb near objectives or any location you want protected. The powerful bomb detonates when anyone gets too close. A beeping sound alerts you that it's active. If you hear a high-pitched beeping noise, you have entered the trigger area of a hostile Proximity Bomb—get out of there!

STATS

Name	Condition
Proximity	7 Meters
Fuse	1.5 Seconds when Triggered
Damage	150
Radius	7 Meters, Max Damage within 5 Meters

Sensor Droid

Gives you a support droid equipped with a blaster. Imperial forces receive a Viper Probe Droid, while Rebels get an Astromech Droid. Both are weak to ion damage. Each droid has two special abilities: lock on and fire upon soldiers as well as other droids and a scan pulse that makes enemies visible for all teammates.

R5 DROID STATS

Name	Condition
Type	Ground Droid
Lock Time	1
Rate of Fire	500 RPM
Damage	20

VIPER DROID STATS

Name	Condition
Type	Repulsor
Lock Time	1
Rate of Fire	200 RPM
Damage	20

Smart Rocket

This powerful rocket/missile hybrid locks on to vehicles, but it can also be quick-fired against infantry. Locks on and tracks vehicles if fired in general direction. Try to fire from cover to minimize damage taken.

STATS

Name	Condition
Fuse	Explodes on impact
Damage	500
Radius	3 Meters, Max Damage within 2 Meters

Squad Shield

Activate to put up a small circular shield for 90 seconds, big enough for several players. Anyone inside cannot shoot out, but it does block blasters, explosions, and grenades. Both friends and foes can destroy the transmitter that projects the shield.

STATS

Name	Condition
Health	1000

Thermal Imploder

A high-damage grenade with a big area of effect. This has an extremely large radius, which works great against groups of enemies. Be careful that you don't end up in the explosion yourself.

STATS

Name	Condition
Fuse	1.5 Seconds after impact
Damage	200
Radius	11 Meters, Max Damage within 7 Meters

Vehicle Turret

An automated defense that targets vehicles with rockets. It remains active until destroyed. Look for a semi-protected location to place the turret, keeping in mind that it needs to get shots on the machines.

STATS

Name	Condition
Lock Time	1 Second
Ammo	10
Reload Time	10 Seconds
Damage	Take down AT-ST if all ten rockets hit

FIELD POWER-UPS

Vehicle and hero power-ups are found on the battlefield in Supremacy and Walker Assault modes. A unique icon indicates the item being collected. Once you've picked one up, you have 15 seconds to activate the power with the Power Ability buttons before it disappears. Since you are vulnerable to attack, find a safe place to use the power.

 **Air Vehicle**

Available in Supremacy and Walker Assault. As Rebel Alliance, find an X-wing, A-wing, or T-47 Airspeeder power-up. As Galactic Empire, find a TIE fighter or TIE interceptor. Use Power Ability to switch to the air vehicle.

 **AT-ST**

Available for Galactic Empire in Supremacy and Walker Assault. Switch to an Imperial AT-ST, which is destroyed once it is defeated or when you exit.

 **AT-AT**

Available for Galactic Empire in Walker Assault only.
–Take command of the three weapons on an AT-AT.

 **Hero**

Available in Supremacy and Walker Assault. Once you collect it, activate the power-up to choose from three heroes, depending on your faction. Rebel Alliance chooses from Luke Skywalker, Han Solo, and Princess Leia. Galactic Empire picks from Darth Vader, Emperor Palpatine, and Boba Fett.

PICK-UPS

Pick-ups are different than power-ups since their benefit is automatically applied when collected. Charge pick-ups are found in most game modes, while the others are limited to specific modes.

 ## Charge

Available in most game modes, including Battle and Survival missions. Once it is collected, you gain +1 Charge.

 ## Extra Life

Available in Survival only. Gives you an extra life.

 ## Ability Refresh

Available in Fighter Squadron only. Fly your ship through the icon to reset abilities for immediate use.

 ## Hero Vehicle

Available in Fighter Squadron only. This Jedi icon transports you from your starfighter to one of two hero vehicles. Rebel Alliance gets the Millennium Falcon, while Galactic Empire uses Slave I.

 ## Vehicle Repair

Available in Fighter Squadron and Beggar's Canyon Training mission. Fly through the icon to heal your air vehicle.

VEHICLES AND TURRETS

INTRODUCTION

Air and ground vehicles play a significant role in both Walker Assault and Supremacy, while Fighter Squadron is all about the starfighters, making it well worth your time to learn how to operate them all. The four training missions that introduce you to the X-wing, Speeder Bike, AT-ST, and T-47 Airspeeder are a great place to get started.

Most vehicles are restricted to one faction or the other with the exception of the Imperial Speeder Bike, which Rebels can operate as well. Turrets are not exclusive to either side and can be used by anyone, except when you are playing as a hero.

A vehicle's primary laser cannons overheat with extended use, as a curved bar beneath the reticle indicates. The meter turns red as you continue holding the trigger. Firing in bursts keeps them from overheating, but if they do reach that point, the weapon becomes unusable until it has cooled off. This loses valuable time, which can result in you missing out on a kill in a dogfight. Vehicle abilities also require a cool down, just like a hero's ability or a soldier's Star Cards.

In Supremacy and Walker Assault, you can abandon a vehicle at any time by holding down the Use button. Control then returns to your infantry character. Take notice of when you are needed back on the ground and should return to your original soldier. Control is lost while abandoning your vehicle, so be sure that you are not headed to your death before you can exit.

Vehicles can tip a battle in your faction's favor, but know your place. If your current objective requires you to remain as a soldier, then forgo the opportunity and continue the ground fight. Be aware of what is happening around you, in the air, and below you.

VEHICLE POWER-UPS

In Supremacy and Walker Assault, vehicle power-ups are scattered all around the battlefield. They appear on your heads-up display once they are within range. Pick one up and activate it to get the opportunity to take control of that vehicle. Try finding a safe place to do so, as your soldier is vulnerable during this time away.

Each time you collect a vehicle power-up, you must decide whether to keep your boots on the ground or take to the skies. Assess the current situation, and make the decision based on your faction's current needs. Are there enemy starfighters that need to be taken care of? Does the current objective require more help on the ground? You only have 15 seconds to use a vehicle before the power-up is lost.

VEHICLE REPAIR, ABILITY REFRESH, AND HERO VEHICLE PICK-UPS

Fighter Squadron employs three different pick-ups. Ability refresh instantly cools the ship's abilities, making them available for immediate use. Fly through the hero vehicle pick-up to switch to the Millennium Falcon or Slave 1, depending on which faction you fight for. Vehicle repair pick-ups recover health when your aircraft has been damaged and are also available in the Beggar's Canyon training mission.

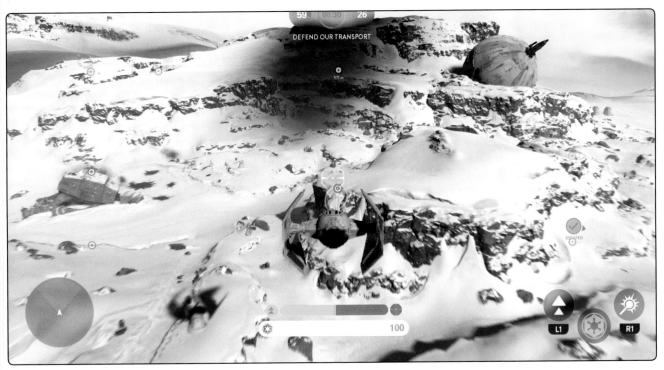

GROUND VEHICLES

Only three vehicles (all from the Galactic Empire) operate on the ground level: AT-ATs, AT-STs, and the Speeder Bike. The walkers are well-armored machines with high-powered weapons, but they are slow and cumbersome. AT-ATs automatically move along a set path in Walker Assault, while AT-STs control much like a soldier but cannot enter tight spaces. Speeder Bikes have little in the way of weaponry, but they make up for it in speed and agility. They can get you where you want to go in a snap.

WALKER CONTROLS

Control	Xbox One	PlayStation 4
Move (AT-AT moves automatically)	Left Thumbstick	Left Stick
Aim	Right Thumbstick	Right Stick
Fire Primary Weapon	RT	R2
Zoom (Aim Assist)	LT	L2
Left Ability	LB	L1
Right Ability	RB	R1
Top Ability (if Available)	Y	Triangle
Sprint (AT-ST Only)	Left Thumbstick (Click)	L3
Abandon Vehicle	X	Square

AT-AT

AVAILABLE GAME MODES:	TYPE:	FACTION:
WALKER ASSAULT	FOUR-LEGGED WALKER	GALACTIC EMPIRE

AT-AT ABILITIES

Ability	Button	Description
Small Laser Cannon	Left Ability	Mounted on the sides of the head, this works best against quicker targets (like infantry).
Big Laser Cannon	Right Ability	Mounted below the head, this works best against tougher targets.
Orbital Strike	Top Ability	This artillery barrage rains destruction on a chosen location. Aim your shot until the blue reticle lines up with the desired target, and then fire.

The iconic Imperial walker is at the center of Walker Assault, a Multiplayer mode where the Rebel Alliance and the Galactic Empire fight over two of the gigantic quadrupeds. The Imperial soldiers must protect the behemoths as they walk across the battlefield, while the Rebels attempt to take them down.

Playing for the Galactic Empire, a soldier must find the AT-AT power-up in order to take control of it. It moves on rails, so there's no need to worry about directing it. Three weapons make it a menace to Rebel soldiers. A small laser cannon on each side of its head is mapped to the Left Card slot, while a pair of more powerful cannons, triggered by the Right Card button, is situated underneath the head.

The lighter upper guns are best used against quicker opponents, such as infantry forces. Save the large cannons for tougher targets like those pesky turrets. A view from above its head gives a great vantage point for the light cannons. The camera shifts below the head when the more powerful cannons are used.

An AT-AT's guns are controlled differently than other vehicles. Pressing one of the Ability buttons simply chooses an ability. Press the Fire button to use the selected weapon. The fire rate of the cannons is relatively slow, but they are powerful. Mix up your attacks to take full advantage of its arsenal.

The AT-AT is slow and cumbersome, with a limited upper range when aiming the cannons. This makes it tough to take on the quick and agile starfighters. Rely on your aerial support for that, and concentrate your gunfire on emplacements and groups of infantry.

When using an AT-AT power-up, you are limited to 60 seconds in the cockpit, so make the time count. A meter at the bottom of the HUD lets you know how much time remains.

AT-ST

AVAILABLE GAME MODES: OVERPOWER TRAINING MISSION, SUPREMACY, WALKER ASSAULT	**TYPE:** BIPEDAL WALKER	**FACTION:** GALACTIC EMPIRE	

AT-ST ABILITIES

Ability	Cool Down (Seconds)	Button	Description
Concussion Grenade Launcher	5	Left Ability	This launches three grenades and works well against groups of infantry.
Homing Missiles	10	Right Ability	This fires a projectile that homes in on a target.

An All Terrain Scout Transport is a bipedal walker equipped with a variety of armaments. A blaster cannon operates as the primary weapon, overheating when used for a long period without pause. A grenade launcher, equipped in the left slot, fires a volley of three grenades and is capable of wiping out a group of infantry. A homing missile, fired with a press of the Right Card button, can take down a starfighter as long as it has time to get a bead on the target. This makes it a versatile machine for destroying any target.

Watch the flight patterns of the starfighters, and note the best opportunities to take them down. Your homing missiles require a little time to lock on to their target. The moment a fighter appears in the distance is a great time to launch the projectile, giving it plenty of time to do its job.

The AT-ST is moved just like a soldier, even sprinting when you press in the left stick. It doesn't take long to get the hang of things. Its armor stands up to infantry gunfire very well, but watch out for anti-vehicle turrets and attacks from above. This walker can be a force to be reckoned with, but beware of complacency, as you are still vulnerable.

Available in Supremacy and Walker Assault when siding with the Galactic Empire, the walker is a great asset in most situations. However, its inability to move through small openings does limit its usefulness in certain areas. Check out the Overpower training mission to learn all of its ins and outs. These vehicles join the attacking Imperial forces on Survival missions, giving you a great opportunity to learn their weaknesses.

SPEEDER BIKE

AVAILABLE GAME MODES:	TYPE:	FACTION:
ENDOR CHASE TRAINING MISSION, SUPREMACY, WALKER ASSAULT	HOVER BIKE	GALACTIC EMPIRE, REBEL ALLIANCE

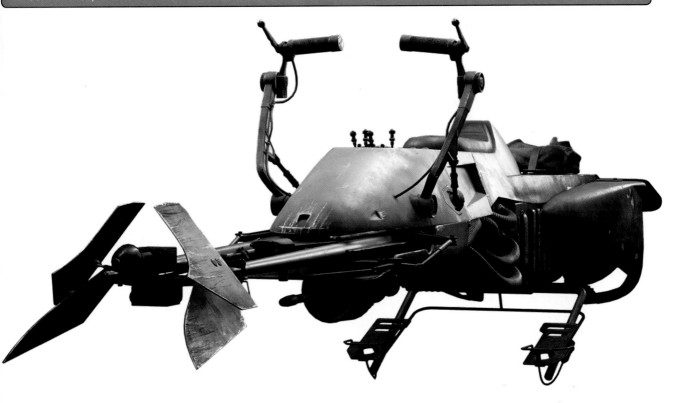

The Imperial Speeder Bike is available in Supremacy and Walker Assault, as well as the Endor Chase training mission. It is very agile and extremely fast, especially with the speed boost activated. A weak laser cannon offers a little firepower, but don't plan on taking on an entire army. Although it is an Imperial vehicle, Rebels can swipe one for their own use.

Despite it being a ground vehicle, the Hover Bike is controlled more like an aircraft. The left stick acts as the throttle, and the right stick guides it left and right. Tap into its incredible agility by strafing and changing elevation, also controlled with the two analog sticks. Use the speed boost whenever you have a clear path ahead, though a cool-down time does limit its use.

As you drive the Speeder Bike, be careful of obstacles. Its blistering speed can get you to your destination in a hurry, but one overlooked tree can take you out even quicker. Work the throttle carefully, and keep your eyes on the road ahead as you navigate denser areas.

SPEEDER BIKE CONTROLS

Control	Xbox One	PlayStation 4
Throttle Increase/Decrease	Left Thumbstick Up/Down	Left Stick Up/Down
Strafe Left/Right	Left Thumbstick Left/Right	Left Stick Left/Right
Elevation Increase/Decrease	Right Thumbstick Up/Down	Right Stick Up/Down
Aim	Right Thumbstick Left/Right	Right Stick Left/Right
Fire	RT	R2
Soft Lock (Hold)	LT	L2
Speed Boost (Nine-Second Cool Down)	LB	L1
1st/3rd Person (Hold)	Down on D-Pad	Down on D-Pad

AIR VEHICLES

Take to the skies to defend an objective, compete in a dogfight with fellow pilots, or swoop down on unsuspecting infantry. A selection of starfighters is available in Supremacy, Walker Assault, and Fighter Squadron, offering some exciting air-to-ground and air-to-air combat. The T-47 Airspeeder is not a fighter, but it can bring an AT-AT to its knees. A rear-equipped TOW-cable is the only way to defeat the Imperial behemoth, although this takes time.

The air vehicles all have three evasive maneuvers, allowing for quick 90-degree or 180-degree turns. Take advantage of these moves to mix up your movements. The more unpredictable you can be, the better off you are in a dogfight.

AIR VEHICLE CONTROLS

Control	Xbox One	PlayStation 4
Energy Distribution (Throttle)	Left Thumbstick	Left Stick
Aim	Right Thumbstick	Right Stick
Fire Primary Weapon	RT	R2
Soft Lock (Hold)	LT	L2
Left Ability	LB	L1
Right Ability	RB	R1
Top Ability (if Available)	Y	Triangle
Power Ability	LB + RB	L1 + R1
Evasive Maneuvers	Left/Up/Right on D-Pad	Left/Up/Right on D-Pad
1st/3rd Person (Hold)	Down on D-Pad	Down on D-Pad
Abandon Vehicle	X	Square

T-47 AIRSPEEDER/SNOWSPEEDER

AVAILABLE GAME MODES:	TYPE:	FACTION:
EINVASION TRAINING MISSION, SUPREMACY, WALKER ASSAULT	REPULSORLIFT	REBEL ALLIANCE

AIRSPEEDER/SNOWSPEEDER CONTROLS

Ability	Cool Down (Seconds)	Button	Description
Speed Boost	15	Left Ability	This maxes out speed for a few seconds, which is great for rapidly closing in on an AT-AT.
Sensor Jammer (10 Seconds)	15	Right Ability	This jams nearby scanners for 10 seconds, making you invisible on their radar.
TOW-Cable	N/A	Power Ability	Fired from the rear, this can take down an AT-AT by wrapping itself around the walker's legs.

The Snowspeeder is not the fastest of the air vehicles. However, its ion afterburner does give a nice speed boost when needed, even though it can only be used once every 15 seconds. A sensor jammer keeps the ship off the radar for 10 seconds, great for swooping in on a vulnerable AT-AT. The only weapon equipped on the vehicles is the primary blaster cannon. This leaves it with little attacking prowess, but a rear TOW-cable does offer the ability to take down an AT-AT.

The speeder's pace is set with the throttle, indicated by the yellow meter at the bottom of the HUD. Simply set it to the desired speed, and leave it alone. The ship's evasive maneuvers are unlike the fighters. Pressing left or right causes the ship to bank in those directions, making very tight 180-degree turns. When you push up, the ship rapidly ascends to a higher altitude before settling back down.

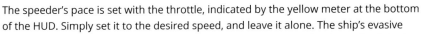

DESTROY AN AT-AT WITH THE TOW-CABLE

Fly the Airspeeder near an AT-AT, and activate the TOW-cable when prompted. Note that the walker must be vulnerable in Walker Assault. This brings up a vertical bar with an Airspeeder icon inside. Press up and down on the right stick to keep the icon inside the bar. As long as the icon remains white, you are good. It turns red when you are in danger of losing the TOW-cable's hold, although you do have a little time to recover before it is completely lost.

Four dots appear to the left, which turn blue whenever you successfully complete a lap. Each time one changes color, the vertical bar shrinks until your icon barely fits inside. Make very light adjustments to the stick to keep it in the middle. After the fourth dot, you receive confirmation of your success, and the walker is taken down. Be ready to quickly pull back to avoid flying into the ground.

Taking damage can break the cable and cause you to fail the procedure. At the very least, it can knock you off course, sending you into danger. Quickly bring the icon back into the safe range. Note that weapon fire from any walker can cause this effect.

Also, watch out when a walker is located close to a wall or cliff. This makes it extremely tough to fly around it without losing contact.

A-WING

AVAILABLE GAME MODES:	TYPE:	FACTION:
FIGHTER SQUADRON, SUPREMACY, WALKER ASSAULT	STARFIGHTER	REBEL ALLIANCE

A-WING CONTROLS

Ability	Cool Down (Seconds)	Button	Description
Shield	15	Left Ability	This temporary shield gives you a little time to get out of trouble.
Concussion Missiles	20	Right Ability	This is an explosive projectile. Lock on to your target before firing.

The RZ-1 A-wing interceptor is the Rebel alternative to the X-wing and is available in Supremacy and Walker Assault by picking up the appropriate power-up. You can also select it in Fighter Squadron when fighting for the Rebel Alliance. A well-rounded fighter, the A-wing gives you both good defense and solid offensive capabilities.

Sublight engines provide decent speed to the starfighter, while a temporary shield can be activated with the Left Card ability. Lock on to an enemy, and rip it to shreds with a direct hit of a concussion missile. TIEs can be tough to target with their squirrely movements—remain patient and wait for your opportunity.

STARFIGHTERS' ENERGY DISTRIBUTION

For all starfighters and hero ships, the speed is adjusted with the throttle, but unlike the Airspeeder, it also acts as an energy distribution system. A meter just above the fighter's health indicates the power setting. Push up, and energy is shifted to your engines, speeding you up. Push down, and power is sent to your weapon systems, slowing you down while making the fighter's primary weapon more effective.

X-WING

AVAILABLE GAME MODES:	TYPE:	FACTION:
BEGGAR'S CANYON TRAINING MISSION, FIGHTER SQUADRON, SUPREMACY, WALKER ASSAULT	STARFIGHTER	REBEL ALLIANCE

X-WING CONTROLS

Ability	Cool Down (Seconds)	Button	Description
Shield	15	Left Ability	A temporary shield gives you a little time to get out of trouble.
Proton Torpedoes	20	Right Ability	This is a powerful projectile. Lock on to your target before firing.

The T-65 X-wing is more powerful than its Imperial equivalents, though it lacks the agility and quickness of the TIEs. Very similar to the A-wing, the fighter is equipped with a temporary shield and Proton Torpedoes. It is this projectile that sets it apart from its Rebel counterpart. The ordnance does an incredible job of homing in on its target, with enough power to take down a starfighter.

Work the laser cannons in bursts to avoid overheating as you dogfight with the Imperial fighters. It may be necessary to fire ahead of your target to damage it—a message appears in the middle of your HUD when you are successful. The shield ability does not last long, but it can absorb an otherwise deadly shot, giving you a chance to flee to safer skies. Do not forget about the ship's evasive maneuvers, as they can also be a life saver.

Remember to use the energy distribution system to your advantage. As you close in on your next target, shift energy to the engines before powering up the laser cannons and lighting your opponent up. Add power back to the engines to stay behind a fleeing fighter, giving them no time to repair. Watch a TIE fighter's flight pattern. They must wait 15 seconds after using the speed boost before it comes back online. Timing your attacks can be the difference that gives your side the victory.

TIE FIGHTER

AVAILABLE GAME MODES:	TYPE:	FACTION:
FIGHTER SQUADRON, SUPREMACY, WALKER ASSAULT	STARFIGHTER	GALACTIC EMPIRE

TIE FIGHTER CONTROLS

Ability	Cool Down (Seconds)	Button	Description
Speed Boost	15	Left Ability	This gives a short burst of speed from ion engines.
Ion Cannon	20	Right Ability	This powerful ion weapon is very effective against vehicles.

The TIE fighter is the standard starfighter for the Galactic Empire. Their odd design has been the subject of many debates, but you cannot argue their effectiveness in a Fighter Squadron dogfight. Capable of very quick movements as well as a speed boost ability, the aircraft excels at evading cannon fire. It may lack the toughness of its rivals, but it compensates for this in its sheer speed.

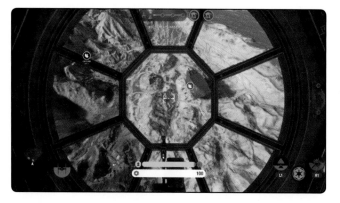

The ion cannon is extremely effective against vehicles and turrets. Lock on a target and launch the projectile to almost guarantee a kill. Take notice of when the Rebel fighters use their shields, as they are at their most vulnerable for the next 15 seconds.

Just like the Rebel starfighters, the TIEs also use an energy distribution system. Move the power to the engines for faster speeds and to the cannon for better primary weapon performance.

TIE fighters also make an appearance in Survival on Sullust. To take them down, use the provided turbolasers or equip the Ion Torpedo Star Card.

TIE INTERCEPTOR

AVAILABLE GAME MODES:	TYPE:	FACTION:
FIGHTER SQUADRON, SUPREMACY, WALKER ASSAULT	STARFIGHTER	GALACTIC EMPIRE

TIE INTERCEPTOR CONTROLS

Ability	Cool Down (Seconds)	Button	Description
Speed Boost	15	Left Ability	This gives a short burst of speed from ion engines.
Ion Cannon	20	Right Ability	This powerful ion weapon is very effective against vehicles.

Besides the wing shape, the TIE interceptor is identical to the fighter. It is similarly equipped with a speed boost, allowing you to close distances or escape in a hurry. An ion cannon locks on to Rebel targets before delivering a high-damaging shot. Use its great maneuverability and evasive moves to shake Rebel pursuers and get behind your next target.

Just like the others, the interceptor uses an energy distribution system to power its engines and cannon. Make adjustments to the throttle to best utilize it. The TIE's primary weapon is fairly underpowered, so it is sometimes necessary to shift power that way to take an opponent down.

HERO SHIPS

Controlled in the same manner as the normal starfighters, hero ships are only available in Fighter Squadron mode by collecting a special hero vehicle pick-up. They are both very well-armored and are equipped with a third ability. Just like the starfighters, these powerful aircraft also possess an energy distribution system.

Be aware that once you collect the pick-up, you become the primary target for most players on the opposing faction. Make them pay with your superior firepower and defense.

MILLENNIUM FALCON

AVAILABLE GAME MODES:	TYPE:	FACTION:
FIGHTER SQUADRON	HERO SHIP	REBEL ALLIANCE

MILLENNIUM FALCON CONTROLS

Ability	Cool Down (Seconds)	Button	Description
Shield	15	Left Ability	A temporary shield gives you a little time to escape a hairy situation.
Concussion Missiles	5	Right Ability	This is a powerful rocket. Lock on to a target, and deploy the explosive.
Speed Boost	15	Top Ability	This maxes out speed for a short period, which is great for closing in on a target or getting away.

The heavily modified YT-1300 freighter is only available in Fighter Squadron by flying an X-wing or A-wing through a hero vehicle pick-up. This instantly switches you to the Falcon. This well-armored vessel has three abilities: a shield, missiles, and a speed boost.

The hero ship already has higher armor than the normal fighters. Activate the shield ability to boost your defense for a short period, allowing you to escape trouble. The concussion missiles are high-powered rockets. Lock on to your target for an easier shot. The modified sublight engines allow the aircraft to get a significant speed boost, though it does take a little longer to get this hunk of junk going.

When you're being targeted, try to lose your pursuer with the same evasive maneuvers as the regular Rebel starfighters. Pressing left or right performs a barrel roll, while pressing up causes a 180-degree turn.

SLAVE I

AVAILABLE GAME MODES:	TYPE:	FACTION:
FIGHTER SQUADRON	HERO SHIP	GALACTIC EMPIRE

SLAVE 1 CONTROLS

Ability	Cool Down (Seconds)	Button	Description
Proton Torpedoes	5	Left Ability	This is a powerful projectile. Lock on to your target before firing.
Ion Cannon	20	Right Ability	This powerful ion weapon is very effective against vehicles.
Sensor Jammer (10 Seconds)	15	Top Ability	This jams nearby scanners for 10 seconds, making you invisible on their radar.

Slave 1 is Galactic Empire's hero ship, piloted by the bounty hunter Boba Fett. Exclusive to Fighter Squadron mode, you must collect a hero vehicle pick-up to take control of this spacecraft. This oddly shaped spacecraft is extremely agile and carries a powerful arsenal. Take yourself off the radar with sensor jammer, move in on your target, and light it up with your array of weapons.

With its Proton Torpedoes and ion cannon, Slave 1 has the unique ability to lock on to successive fighters, taking down multiple targets in a small timespan. Its firepower also allows it to directly battle the Rebel's hero ship, the Millennium Falcon, though Han Solo's freighter isn't going down too easily.

The usual evasive maneuvers are available for Slave 1. Combine that with its tight turns, and it can be difficult to target.

TURRETS

Various turrets have been set up around the environment. Either faction can employ the E-Web blaster (widely used throughout the maps), along with the ATGAR-14, DF-9, and turbolaser, which are limited to specific locations. Also, keep in mind that the turrets are destructible. Ion weapons, such as an Ion Grenade, are extremely effective against them. Watch your flank when operating one of the open turrets, as you are vulnerable to attack.

TURRET CONTROLS

Control	Xbox One	PlayStation 4
Aim	Right Thumbstick	Right Stick
Operate/Exit Turret	X	Square
Fire	RT	R2
Zoom	LT	L2

E-WEB

AVAILABLE GAME MODES:	TYPE:
ANY MODE WITH INFANTRY	STATIONARY BLASTER

E-Web turrets are located all throughout the four planets, offering decent firepower against groups of soldiers. Available to either faction, using the stationary blaster opens you up to rear and side attacks. Unless you are confident that your flanks are protected, do not spend too much time on the gun.

ATGAR-14

AVAILABLE GAME MODES:	TYPE:
SUPREMACY, WALKER ASSAULT	LIGHT ANTI-VEHICLE TURRET

This light anti-vehicle turret is effective against other turrets, while also capable of damaging vehicles. It is not enclosed, so you are vulnerable to attacks during operation. The fixed emplacement rotates 360 degrees with very limited up and down movement, though it can hit a low-flying aircraft. It is slow to shoot its powerful bolts, so aim ahead of any moving target (it is best used against stationary targets). A slow rate of fire means that you must make every shot count.

DF-9 TURRET

AVAILABLE GAME MODES:	TYPE:
SUPREMACY, WALKER ASSAULT	ANTI-INFANTRY TURRET

Found exclusively on Hoth, this fully enclosed, anti-infantry turret is great for defending objectives. Be careful in Walker Assault, as these gun emplacements are weak against their mighty firepower. The gun rotates a full 360 degrees, with limited up and down movement. It overheats after several shots, allowing you to take out a group of infantry if necessary. While it is unable to hurt other turrets and vehicles, it deals a little damage to the weakened underbelly of an AT-AT.

TURBOLASER

AVAILABLE GAME MODES:	TYPE:
SURVIVAL ON SULLUST	HEAVY ANTI-VEHICLE TURRET

Found exclusively at the Imperial base on Sullust, this anti-vehicle turret is extremely deadly against the AT-STs and TIE fighters that attack in Survival mode. Step inside the big cannon, and use its powerful laser to knock the fighters out of the sky. Fire ahead of the flying vehicles to take them down. Waiting until they fly straight out or toward your locations makes shooting them down much easier.

The high-powered laser cannon does overheat, so watch the meter just below the reticle. While it can take quite a bit of abuse, it can also be destroyed. Take control of one, and its health bar displays in place of your own.

BATTLEFRONT DATABASE

Beyond the stars, credits, and Multiplayer ranks that you earn as you play the game, awards are given as you complete tasks and reach milestones. These allow you to show off your accomplishments in Star Wars Battlefront. You can view a diorama full of 3D models, which you unlock by reaching certain goals. You earn these Trophies or Achievements by completing various actions.

DIORAMA FIGURINES

To view a scene full of character and vehicle figurines, select Diorama from the Collect menu. Figurines are spread across four islands, representing the four planets in the game. You unlock the 3D models by hitting specific milestones in Multiplayer and Missions modes. Categorized by how they are earned, the following tables list all of the figurines, along with how they are unlocked and the island on which they are found.

STORMTROOPER
0 / 10

L1 ●●●●●●●●●●●●●●●●●●●● R1

Achieve rank 10.

✕ SELECT   ● LEAVE DIORAMA

RANK AND SCORE

Collect points via in-game scoring events, accolades, and challenges to increase your rank. After you play many hours of Multiplayer, Rank 50 and 1,000,000 points are reached, and these models are unlocked.

Figurine	Unlock Description	Planet
Stormtrooper	Achieve Rank 10.	Tatooine
Princess Leia	Achieve Rank 50.	Hoth
Han Solo	Earn 1,000,000 score in Multiplayer.	Tatooine

GAME MODES

You unlock the following models by playing a whole lot of Multiplayer games. You must win 10 matches in all nine game modes, as well as play another 20 games of Walker Assault.

Figurine	Unlock Description	Planet
T-47 Airspeeder	Win 10 matches of each Multiplayer game mode.	Hoth
AT-AT	Play 30 matches of Walker Assault.	Hoth

MISSIONS

ou unlock four figurines through the Missions modes. In fact, ou must complete everything possible in the single player/ o-op side to get them. Refer to the Missions chapter for ollectible locations and full details on how to get all 75 stars.

Figurine	Unlock Description	Planet
Endor Rebel with Smart Rocket	Complete all Battle missions on Master difficulty while playing against AI.	Endor
AT-ST	Beat all Survival missions on Master difficulty.	Endor
Luke Skywalker	Find all collectibles (Missions).	Endor
Emperor Palpatine	Collect every star on every mission.	Sullust

KILLS

here are six figurines devoted to killing in *Star Wars* Battlefront. You can earn these in any mode of Multiplayer or Missions.

Figurine	Unlock Description	Planet
TIE Fighter	Destroy 150 vehicles.	Sullust
Magmatrooper	Get a total of 1,500 kills as an Imperial soldier.	Sullust
Tatooine Rebel	Get a total of 1,500 kills as a Rebel soldier.	Tatooine
Scout Trooper	Perform 250 headshot kills.	Endor
Millennium Falcon	Score 100 kills with either the Millennium Falcon or Slave I.	Tatooine
Darth Vader	Defeat 250 soldiers while playing as a hero.	Endor

GENERAL

ou unlock the following models by using a variety of items in Multiplayer and Missions modes. Equip a Trait in your Multiplayer oadout, and then score kill streaks to level it up. This level is reset at the end of each round. You must reach Level 3 with all five Traits o get the shadowtrooper. There are 13 Asset Star Cards, and each gives you a weapon. Get at least one kill with each card to get the oba Fett figurine.

Figurine	Unlock Description	Planet
X-Wing	Pick up and use 200 power-ups.	Tatooine
Shadowtrooper	Reach Level 3 at least once on every Trait.	Hoth
Boba Fett	Use all Star Cards and get a kill with every weapon.	Tatooine
Slave I	Ride in vehicles for a total of 10 hours.	Sullust

BASE COMMAND

ownload the *Star Wars* Battlefront Companion app and play the ase Command game. Get a three-star rating on the first siege in he Rebel campaign to unlock this figurine.

Figurine	Unlock Description	Planet
Twi'lek Rebel	In Base Command, achieve a three-star rating on the first siege in the Rebel campaign.	Sullust

TROPHIES AND ACHIEVEMENTS

Excluding the Platinum Trophy, there are 43 Trophies/Achievements in *Star Wars Battlefront*. Most are earned as you play through the different modes and kill enemies, though there are some that are not as straightforward. These rewards are split into categories below, with further explanation where necessary.

MULTIPLAYER COMBAT

The first 11 Achievements/Trophies are obtained in Multiplayer and are fairly straightforward. Traits reset after each round, so you must reach Level 3 within this time. When you're playing with a partner, you are allowed to select his or her Star Card Hand if desired; do this 10 times. Successfully complete 10 cooling flushes with overheated blasters in Multiplayer to get Never tell me the odds! You acquire the other Achievements/Trophies by playing each mode and by winning and killing in specific ways.

Icon	Name	Description	Trophy	Gamer Points
	A New Hope	Play every Multiplayer game mode.	Silver	40
	In a galaxy far, far away...	Win one match in each Multiplayer game mode.	Silver	40
	Never tell me the odds!	Successfully perform Cooling Flush 10 times (Multiplayer).	Bronze	15
	I suggest a new strategy	Use a partner's Star Card Hand 10 times (Multiplayer).	Bronze	15
	Shoot first	Be the first in a round to earn a kill (Multiplayer).	Silver	40
	Great shot, kid!	Kill an opponent who is using a Jump Pack (Multiplayer).	Bronze	15
	A cunning warrior	Reach level 3 once with any Trait (Multiplayer).	Silver	40
	Don't underestimate the Force	Earn a total of 100 kills while playing as a hero (Multiplayer).	Silver	40
	Crush them with one swift stroke...	Trample 25 soldiers with an AT-ST (Multiplayer).	Bronze	15
	Don't get cocky	Defeat both the Millennium Falcon and the Slave I.	Bronze	15
	A tremor in the Force	Play once as all of the different heroes (Multiplayer).	Bronze	15
	Precision shot	Get 10 headshots with the Cycler rifle (Multiplayer)	Bronze	15

MULTIPLAYER GAME MODES

You receive the following nine awards for completing specific tasks in each of the Multiplayer game modes. Refer to the Game Modes chapter for details about how each mode works.

Icon	Name	Description	Trophy	Gamer Points
	That got him!	Use a TOW-cable to destroy an enemy AT-AT in Walker Assault.	Silver	40
	Hold the line!	Kill 10 enemies while attacking or defending a control point in Supremacy.	Bronze	15
	Stay on Target	Kill 10 enemies in a round of Fighter Squadron.	Bronze	15
	What's the cargo?	Kill 10 enemies carrying the cargo in Cargo.	Bronze	15
	Playing the objective	Have the most kills in a round of Blast.	Bronze	15
	The Force is strong with this one	Earn 10 kills in a round as any hero on Hero Hunt.	Bronze	15
	I've been waiting for you	Kill 10 enemies trying to claim your team's pod in Drop Zone.	Bronze	15
	"Gonk? Gonk!"	Capture three droids in a match of Droid Run.	Bronze	15
	The power of the Force	Defeat a hero while playing as any hero on Heroes Vs. Villains.	Bronze	15

MULTIPLAYER PROGRESSION

Six Achievements/Trophies are based on game progression. Leveling up your rank, completing challenges, and earning diorama figurines, credits, and accomplishments are all required to collect all these awards.

Icon	Name	Description	Trophy	Gamer Points
	Judge me by my size, do you?	Reach Rank 25.	Bronze	15
	When 900 years old you reach...	Reach Rank 50.	Gold	55
	Tell Jabba that I've got his money	Earn a total of 25,000 credits (Multiplayer).	Silver	40
	Distinguished	Earn 100 accomplishments.	Silver	40
	Determined	Complete 25 challenges.	Silver	40
	Collector	Earn any diorama figurine in the game.	Bronze	15

MISSION

These 15 accomplishments are all received in the Missions mode. A few require some effort to complete, but they are all straightforward. Refer to the Missions chapter of this guide for full details and tips for earning each one.

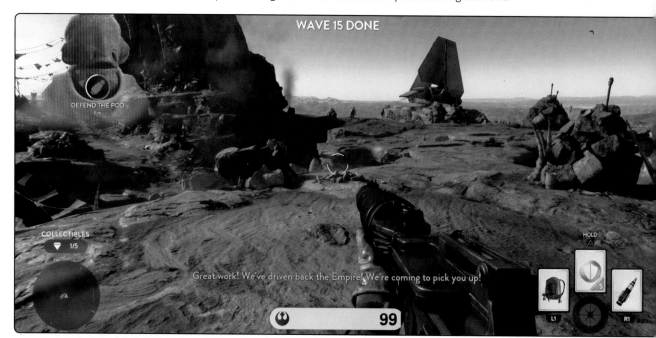

Icon	Name	Description	Trophy	Gamer Points
	Do... or do not. There is no try	Complete the tutorial.	Bronze	15
	New Recruit	Complete any mission.	Bronze	15
	Together we can rule the galaxy	Complete any mission with a friend.	Bronze	15
	All right, I'll give it a try	Earn a star on all training missions.	Bronze	15
	Impressive. Most impressive.	Earn a total of five stars from Battle missions.	Bronze	15
	Off to a good start	Win any Battle mission on Normal difficulty against the AI.	Bronze	15
	Survivor	Earn a total of five stars from Survival missions.	Bronze	15
	On the ball	Complete any Survival mission on Master difficulty within 35 minutes.	Bronze	15
	Ackbar's Elite	Complete any Survival mission on Master difficulty without dying.	Silver	40
	Scrap collector	Earn any collectible star.	Silver	40
	Your journey has only started	Complete all missions.	Bronze	15
	Master	Earn all mission stars on Master difficulty.	Gold	55
	Safety ain't the point of a joyride	Take no damage in the Endor Chase mission.	Bronze	15
	Best star-pilot in the galaxy	Destroy 10 TIE fighters within two minutes on the Beggar's Canyon mission.	Bronze	15

BATTLE BEYOND

wo accolades fit into the Battle Beyond aspect of the game. Often based on how one side is doing in a match, background interactions
dd atmosphere to a game. You'll see Ewoks fleeing from danger in the Ewok village on Endor and Y-wings attacking vulnerable AT-ATs
Walker Assault. You can earn "Not bad for a little furball" in the Forest of Endor in Survival mode. Simply hang around underneath
e Ewok village long enough, and one will hit you in the head with a rock. For Walker Defender, numerous ion weapons can take down
strafing Y-wing when you're playing for the Galactic Empire in Walker Assault. Man a Vehicle Turret or an Imperial walker (or equip the
n Torpedo Star Card), and shoot one down.

Icon	Name	Description	Trophy	Gamer Points
	Not bad for a little furball	Get hit in the head by a rock from an Ewok on Endor.	Bronze	15
	Walker Defender	Destroy a Y-wing in Walker Assault.	Bronze	15

PLAYSTATION 4 PLATINUM TROPHY

Icon	Name	Description	Trophy	Gamer Points
	Platinum (PS4 only)	Collect all other trophies.	Platinum	N/A

STAR WARS
BATTLEFRONT
EA

WRITTEN BY DAN HERRERA AND MICHAEL OWEN

DK/Prima Games, a division of Penguin Random House LLC
6081 East 82nd Street, Suite #400
Indianapolis, IN 46250

SE ISBN: 978-07440-1666-6
CE ISBN: 978-07440-1667-3

Printing Code: The rightmost double-digit number is the year of the book's printing; the rightmost single-digit number is the number of the book's printing. For example, 15-1 shows that the first printing of the book occurred in 2015.

18 17 16 15   4 3 2 1

Printed in the USA.

Credits

PROJECT MANAGER
Jesse Anderson

SENIOR DEVELOPMENT EDITOR
Chris Hausermann

BOOK DESIGNER
Jeff Weissenberger

PRODUCTION DESIGNER
Wil Cruz

PRODUCTION
Angela Graef

COPY EDITOR
Angie Mateski

MAP ILLUSTRATION
Loren Gilliland

Prima Games Staff

VP & PUBLISHER
Mike Degler

EDITORIAL MANAGER
Tim Fitzpatrick

DESIGN AND LAYOUT MANAGER
Tracy Wehmeyer

LICENSING
Christian Sumner
Paul Giacomotto

MARKETING
Katie Hemlock

DIGITAL PUBLISHING
Julie Asbury
Tim Cox
Shaida Boroumand

OPERATIONS MANAGER
Stacey Beheler

Special Thanks

Glenn Stotz

Ray Almeda

Ryan Gagerman

Paul Keslin

Viktoria Anselm

Rob Runesson

Johannes Söderqvist

Viktor Blanke

Madina Chionidi

Dennis Brännvall

William Cooper

Tommy Rydling

Christian Johannesen

Leif Westerholm